Lecture Notes
in Business Information Processing   188

Series Editors

Wil van der Aalst
  Eindhoven Technical University, The Netherlands
John Mylopoulos
  University of Trento, Italy
Michael Rosemann
  Queensland University of Technology, Brisbane, Qld, Australia
Michael J. Shaw
  University of Illinois, Urbana-Champaign, IL, USA
Clemens Szyperski
  Microsoft Research, Redmond, WA, USA

Martin Hepp
Yigal Hoffner (Eds.)

E-Commerce and Web Technologies

15th International Conference, EC-Web 2014
Munich, Germany, September 1-4, 2014
Proceedings

Volume Editors

Martin Hepp
Universität der Bundeswehr München
E-Business and Web Science Research Group
Neubiberg, Germany
E-mail: martin.hepp@unibw.de

Yigal Hoffner
Shenkar College of Engineering and Design
Department of Software Engineering
Ramat Gan, Israel
E-mail: yigal.hoffner@shenkar.ac.il

ISSN 1865-1348 e-ISSN 1865-1356
ISBN 978-3-319-10490-4 e-ISBN 978-3-319-10491-1
DOI 10.1007/978-3-319-10491-1
Springer Cham Heidelberg New York Dordrecht London

Library of Congress Control Number: 2014946232

© Springer International Publishing Switzerland 2014
This work is subject to copyright. All rights are reserved by the Publisher, whether the whole or part of the material is concerned, specifically the rights of translation, reprinting, reuse of illustrations, recitation, broadcasting, reproduction on microfilms or in any other physical way, and transmission or information storage and retrieval, electronic adaptation, computer software, or by similar or dissimilar methodology now known or hereafter developed. Exempted from this legal reservation are brief excerpts in connection with reviews or scholarly analysis or material supplied specifically for the purpose of being entered and executed on a computer system, for exclusive use by the purchaser of the work. Duplication of this publication or parts thereof is permitted only under the provisions of the Copyright Law of the Publisher's location, in ist current version, and permission for use must always be obtained from Springer. Permissions for use may be obtained through RightsLink at the Copyright Clearance Center. Violations are liable to prosecution under the respective Copyright Law.
The use of general descriptive names, registered names, trademarks, service marks, etc. in this publication does not imply, even in the absence of a specific statement, that such names are exempt from the relevant protective laws and regulations and therefore free for general use.
While the advice and information in this book are believed to be true and accurate at the date of publication, neither the authors nor the editors nor the publisher can accept any legal responsibility for any errors or omissions that may be made. The publisher makes no warranty, express or implied, with respect to the material contained herein.

Typesetting: Camera-ready by author, data conversion by Scientific Publishing Services, Chennai, India

Printed on acid-free paper

Springer is part of Springer Science+Business Media (www.springer.com)

Preface

The International Conference on Electronic Commerce and Web Technologies (EC-Web) is an established series of academic events for presenting and discussing contributions to the theory of e-business research as a field, innovative technological approaches, empirical research, user studies, and the analysis of economic effects.

This volume contains the accepted papers from the technical program of EC-Web 2014. Now in its 15th year, we aimed at providing a forum for researchers who are working on advancing the field of Web-based e-business, with a particular focus on at least one the following seven areas:

Track 1: E-Business Architectures
Track 2: Data, Information, and Knowledge Management for E-Business
Track 3: Semantic Web and Linked Open Data for E-Business
Track 4: Search, Matchmaking, Recommender and Comparison Systems
Track 5: Payment and Non-monetary Compensations
Track 6: Social Interaction in E-Business
Track 7: Economics, Management and Law

In our opinion, e-business research is undergoing a fundamental evolution, which is exciting and challenging at the same time: On one hand, micro-economic theory and other strands of economics research are gaining importance. A very visible indicator of this trend is that the established ACM Conference on Electronic Commerce series has just updated its name and focus to "ACM Conference on Economics and Computation."[1] On the other hand, meaningful research on e-business topics requires more and more a deep understanding of the technical details of the architecture of the World Wide Web. If we want to advance the support of economic activities in the World Wide Web, we have to look into the very details of how this distributed computing environment at unprecedented scale is organized. It is a pity that the two most essential documents about the philosophy and mechanics[2,3] of the World Wide Web are not mandatory reading in most computer information systems courses. It should also be more widely known that the members of the IETF Working Group HTTPbis[4], in particular Roy Fielding and Julian Reschke as editors, have done tremendous work since 2007 on revising the single most relevant mechanism that has powered e-business innovations in research and practice since day one: The Hypertext Transfer Protocol, HTTP.

---

[1] http://www.sigecom.org/ec14/
[2] http://www.w3.org/TR/webarch/
[3] http://www.ietf.org/rfc/rfc2616.txt
[4] http://trac.tools.ietf.org/wg/httpbis/trac/wiki

Our call for papers encouraged submissions in this spirit of e-business research. All in all, we received 46 submissions, of which we accepted 11 as full papers (24 %), and 8 additionally as short papers (17 %), i.e., the total acceptance rate was 41 %. The review process was organized in a two-staged fashion. First, each paper was reviewed by between two and five Program Committee members. Then, we discussed each single submission in a track chair meeting. Papers with involvement of track chairs were handled in a separate procedure by the general chairs.

Topic-wise, the two strongest fields were Track 3 (Semantic Web and Linked Open Data for E-Business) and Track 4 (Search, Matchmaking, Recommender and Comparison Systems).

EC-Web 2014 would not have been possible without the hard work of many people. We would like to thank the track chairs Naveen C. Amblee, Sören Auer, Iván Cantador, Tommaso Di Noia, Sang-goo Lee, Dirk Neumann, Geert Poels, Axel Polleres, Manu Sporny, Michael Uschold, and Erik Wilde. They helped distribute the call for papers in relevant communities and put a lot of effort into the final selection of papers. Jürgen Umbrich served as a poster and demo chair, for which submissions are solicited at the time of writing this introduction. We also would like to thank all members of the Program Committee who prepared excellent reviews. Of course, all authors who submitted to the conference deserve a big thanks, too.

EC-Web 2014 was only possible because of the decades-long effort of the DEXA Association, which organizes the DEXA conference series, of which EC-Web is a long-time component. Many academics feel exhausted after chairing a conference once. DEXA is now in its 25th year, and it is thanks to the DEXA members that this venue has been available for such a long period of time. A special thanks goes to Gabriela Wagner, who greatly supported us with many administrative tasks for the conference, and for which we owe her a big thank you.

Finally, we would like to thank Springer for their professional support and guidance during the preparation of the proceedings, and Amin Anjomshoaa for great support with the ConfDriver conference management system.

July 2014
Martin Hepp
Yigal Hoffner

Conference Organization

General Chairs

Martin Hepp   Universität der Bundeswehr München, Germany

Yigal Hoffner   Shenkar College of Engineering and Design, Israel

Poster and Demo Chair

Jürgen Umbrich   Vienna University of Economics and Business, Austria

Track Chairs

Track 1: E-Business Architectures
Erik Wilde   Siemens, USA
Sang-goo Lee   Seoul National University, South Korea

Track 2: Data, Information and Knowledge Management for E-Business
Geert Poels   Universiteit Gent, Belgium
Michael Uschold   Semantic Arts, Inc., USA

Track 3: Semantic Web and Linked Open Data for E-Business
Sören Auer   Universität Bonn und Fraunhofer IAIS, Germany
Axel Polleres   Vienna University of Economics and Business, Austria

Track 4: Search, Matchmaking, Recommender and Comparison Systems
Tommaso Di Noia   Polytechnic University of Bari, Italy
Iván Cantador   Universidad Autónoma de Madrid, Spain

Track 5: Payment and Non-monetary Compensations
Manu Sporny   Digital Bazaar, Inc., USA

Track 6: Social Interaction in E-Business

Naveen C. Amblee — Indian Institute of Management Kozhikode, India

Track 7: Economics, Management and Law

Dirk Neumann — University of Freiburg, Germany

Program Committee

Witold Abramowicz	Poznan University of Economics, Poland
Antonia Albani	University of St. Gallen, Switzerland
Naveen C. Amblee	Indian Institute of Management Kozhikode, India
Sören Auer	University of Leipzig, Germany
Nicola Barbieri	Yahoo, Spain
Alejandro Bellogín	Universidad Autonoma de Madrid, Spain
Dan Brickley	Google, USA
Robin Burke	DePaul University, USA
Ivan Cantador	Universidad Autonoma de Madrid, Spain
Kuo-Ming Chao	University of Coventry, UK
Jen-Yao Chung	IBM, USA
Paolo Cremonesi	Politecnico di Milano, Italy
Roberta Cuel	University of Trento, Italy
Edward Curry	National University of Ireland Galway, Ireland
Alfredo Cuzzocrea	ICAR-CNR and University of Calabria, Italy
Florian Daniel	University of Trento, Italy
Marco de Gemmis	University of Bari Aldo Moro, Italy
Mike Dean	Raytheon BBN Technologies, USA
Tommaso Di Noia	Polytechnic University of Bari, Italy
Asuman Dogac	Middle East Technical University, Turkey
Dieter Fensel	University of Innsbruck, Austria
Agata Filipowska	Poznan University of Economics, Poland
Frederik Gailly	Ghent University, Belgium
Mouzhi Ge	Free University of Bozen-Bolzano, Italy
Jens Gulden	Universität Duisburg-Essen, Germany
Michael Gruninger	University of Toronto, Canada
Siegfried Handschuh	Digital Enterprise Research Institute (DERI), Ireland
Conor Hayes	Insight Centre for Data Analytics, Galway, Ireland
Birgit Hofreiter	Vienna University of Technology, Austria
Christian Huemer	Vienna University of Technology, Austria
Dietmar Jannach	University of Dortmund, Germany
Alexandros Karatzoglou	Telefonica Research, Spain

Juhnyoung Lee	IBM, USA
Sang-goo Lee	Seoul National University, South Korea
Jörg Leukel	Universität Hohenheim, Germany
Charles McCathie Nevile	Yandex, Russian Federation
Jan Mendling	Vienna University of Economics and Busines, Austria
Jay Myers	Best Buy Inc., USA
Dirk Neumann	University of Freiburg, Germany
Selmin Nurcan	Université Paris 1 Panthéon - Sorbonne, France
Boris Otto	TU Dortmund, Germany
Adrian Paschke	Freie Universität Berlin, Germany
Carlos Pedrinaci	The Open University, UK
Dimitris Plexousakis	University of Crete, Greece
Geert Poels	Ghent University, Belgium
Axel Polleres	Vienna University of Economics and Business, Austria
Key Pousttchi	University of Augsburg, Germany
Francesco Ricci	Free University of Bozen-Bolzano, Italy
Dumitru Roman	SINTEF, Norway
Ana Garcia-Serrano	National Distance Education University, Spain
François-Paul Servant	Renault, France
Monika Solanki	Aston University, UK
Günther Specht	University of Innsbruck, Austria
Manu Sporny	Digital Bazaar, Inc., USA
Viswanath Srikanth	IBM, USA
Mari Carmen Suárez-Figueroa	Universidad Politécnica de Madrid, Spain
Vojtech Svatek	University of Economics Prague, Czech Republic
Chun Hua Tian	IBM, China
Robert Tolksdorf	Freie Universität Berlin, Germany
Jürgen Umbrich	Vienna University of Economics and Business, Austria
Michael Uschold	Semantic Arts, Inc., USA
Gottfried Vossen	University of Münster, Germany
Hannes Werthner	Vienna University of Technology, Austria
Erik Wilde	UC Berkeley, USA
Axel Winkelmann	University of Würzburg, Germany

Table of Contents

Data, Information, and Knowledge Management for E-Business

Implementing the WiPo Architecture 1
    Florian Stahl, Adrian Godde, Bastian Hagedorn, Bastian Köpcke, Martin Rehberger, and Gottfried Vossen

Effective Web Crawling for Chinese Addresses and Associated Information 13
    Hsiu-Min Chuang, Chia-Hui Chang, and Ting-Yao Kao

Information Need in Cloud Service Procurement – An Exploratory Case Study (Short Paper) 26
    Jan Wollersheim, Matthias Pfaff, and Helmut Krcmar

Semantic Web and Linked Open Data for E-Business

Exploiting Freebase to Obtain GoodRelations-Based Product Ontologies 34
    Marek Dudáš, Ondřej Zamazal, Jindřich Mynarz, and Vojtěch Svátek

Modelling and Linking Transformations in EPCIS Governing Supply Chain Business Processes 46
    Monika Solanki and Christopher Brewster

Validator and Preview for the JobPosting Data Model of Schema.org (Short Paper) 58
    Jindřich Mynarz

Automotive Ranges as eCommerce Data (Short Paper) 64
    François-Paul Servant, Edouard Chevalier, and François Jurain

Linked Data-Based Conceptual Modelling for Recommendation: A FCA-Based Approach (Short Paper) 71
    Angel Castellanos, Ana García-Serrano, and Juan Cigarrán

Search, Matchmaking, Recommender and Comparison Systems

Usability Assessment of a Context-Aware and Personality-Based Mobile Recommender System 77
    Matthias Braunhofer, Mehdi Elahi, and Francesco Ricci

A Linked Data Recommender System Using a Neighborhood-Based
Graph Kernel 89
   Vito Claudio Ostuni, Tommaso Di Noia, Roberto Mirizzi, and
   Eugenio Di Sciascio

Resource Recommendation in Social Annotation Systems Based on
User Partitioning 101
   Jonathan Gemmell, Bamshad Mobasher, and Robin Burke

Active Learning in Collaborative Filtering Recommender Systems 113
   Mehdi Elahi, Francesco Ricci, and Neil Rubens

Personality-Aware Collaborative Filtering: An Empirical Study in
Multiple Domains with Facebook Data 125
   Ignacio Fernández-Tobías and Iván Cantador

Modelling User Preferences from Implicit Preference Indicators via
Compensational Aggregations (Short Paper) 138
   Ladislav Peska and Peter Vojtas

Using Dependency Bigrams and Discourse Connectives for Predicting
the Helpfulness of Online Reviews (Short Paper) 146
   Matthias Mertz, Nikolaos Korfiatis, and Roberto V. Zicari

Economics, Management, and Law

Customer Load Strategies for Demand Response in Bilateral
Contracting of Electricity 153
   Fernando Lopes and Hugo Algarvio

An Inductive Approach to Reconceptualizing and Theorizing about
Digital Services (Short Paper) 165
   Mary Tate and Elfi Furtmueller

How to Create an E-Advertising Adaptation Strategy:
The AEADS Approach (Short Paper) 171
   Alaa A. Qaffas and Alexandra I. Cristea

Social Interaction in E-Business

Modelling User Behaviour in Online Q&A Communities for Customer
Support 179
   Erik Aumayr and Conor Hayes

Author Index 193

Implementing the WiPo Architecture

Florian Stahl[1], Adrian Godde[2], Bastian Hagedorn[2], Bastian Köpcke[2], Martin Rehberger[2], and Gottfried Vossen[1,2,3]

[1] WWU Münster, ERCIS, Germany
Florian.Stahl@ercis.de
[2] WWU Münster, Dept. of CS, Germany
{a.godde,b.hagedorn,basti.k,m.rehberger}@wwu.de
[3] University of Waikato Management School, New Zealand
vossen@waikato.ac.nz

Abstract. Information available online has exploded over the last 20 years, which has led to the phenomenon of information overload. This phenomenon describes the fact that it becomes increasingly harder to find relevant information in the sheer amount of information available, basically, the proverbial needle in a haystack. We have previously proposed a solution to this problem in the form of the WiPo framework that does not answer queries solely based on a pre-assembled index, but based on a subject-specific database that is sourced from the Internet, curated by domain experts, and dynamically generated based on vast user input; in addition, it allows a user to take the results offline ("Web in your Pocket"). In this paper, we describe our prototypical implementation thereof: An information platform that delivers high quality information to users, achieved by means of curation. Additionally, we elaborate on use cases, namely movie tourism and search and rescue as well as present some early evaluation results gathered in an interview study.

Keywords: Web in Your Pocket, Information Provisioning, High Quality Information, Curation, Architecture.

1 Introduction

Undoubtedly, information available online has exploded over the last 20 years. While this has the advantage that information is nowadays available which previously was not, it becomes increasingly harder for organisations as well as for individuals to find data that is really relevant to them. This phenomenon – known as information overload – is not new, however, no satisfying solution has been found so far.

As outlined in [14], early approaches of coping with the plenitude of information on the Web included directories and search engines of different kinds. Out of these, algorithmic search engines that automatically compile huge indices are most successful. Nevertheless, as we argued in [4] there are still cases where more specific information – generally niche information – is needed that cannot be provided by current search technologies.

Based on this observation, we have proposed a solution to this problem by presenting a framework that does not answer queries solely based on a pre-assembled index, but based on a subject-specific database that is sourced from the Internet, curated by domain experts, and dynamically generated based on vast user input [4]. In this way, completeness, accuracy, quality, and freshness of data can be achieved. On top of this, the result can even be taken offline, i.e., made available through a mobile device when no Internet connection is possible, which has driven home the name "Web in your Pocket" (WiPo).

Curation in our understanding refers to the long-term selection, cleansing, enrichment, preservation and retention of data and to provide access to them in a variety of forms. The concept is known, for example, from museums and has gained recognition in the library sciences where it focuses on preserving data gained through scientific experiments for later usage [1,9]. As an institution the Digital Curation Centre (DCC[1]) peruse curation in Great Britain as described for instance in [7].

Having argued how WiPo can help solving the problem of information overload in [5], it was a logical next step to implement a prototype as a proof of concept and as a vehicle for practical experiments, which we present in this paper. In essence, we have developed a topic centric information platform which provides highly user-specific results, depending on pre-set profiles and user preferences. The provided information is mined from the Internet and curated through an easy to use Web interface by human experts.

We have adopted it to the tourism case described in [4] as a working sample. More precisely, we have developed a platform that supports tourists who wish to visit locations where films have been shot, during their holidays.

In this paper, the basic ideas of WiPo will be recapitulated in Section 2 and related work outlined in Section 3. Then, Section 4 describes the implemented prototype in some detail. Penultimately, we discuss actual and potential use cases (tourism and Search and Rescue, respectively) as well as present early findings. The paper will be concluded in Section 6 by summarising key aspects as well as by outlining future work. We would like to point out that this work is largely based on a technical report [12]. However, this paper is more concise in regard to the WiPo concept and the actual implementation. Furthermore, we have added information regarding use cases and some preliminary results from an interview study conducted in early 2014.

2 The WiPo Concept

The WiPo concept was originally described in [4] and is briefly recapitulated here. WiPo is a process-based approach to information gathering, Web search, and data curation as shown in Figure 1, where thin arrows indicate a relationship between two items and block arrows represent the flow of data within the process.

---

[1] http://www.dcc.ac.uk/

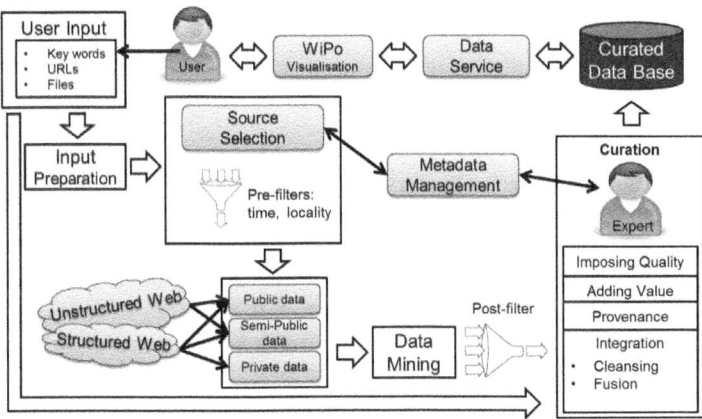

Fig. 1. Original WiPo Process

To start with, the concept provides for querying the curated database directly (top of Figure 1). However, the process of gathering data is somewhat more complex and can be detailed as follows. First, users supply keywords, a list of relevant links and potentially also (text) documents they already have. Secondly, any given URL will be crawled and fed into a classifier. Furthermore, input preparation will convert provided documents to a standard file format (e. g., XML) so that generic classifiers can be applied. The results are fed into the curation process, too. By doing that, the essence is extracted from URLs and provided documents in the form of topics or additional keywords. These mined keywords as well as the user-supplied keywords are then used to choose appropriate sources from a list of all available sources (which might also be extended based on user supplied URLs). In addition to that, relevant additional dimensions such as time or location are determined to generate a list of data sources. Pre-filters might be applied, i. e., the crawl might be limited to only frequently updated sites.

A major aspect of WiPo is the curation component, which is intended to assure high quality of the output. In order to achieve this, we suppose that an expert will verify and modify the results of Web crawls (data mining results, potentially post-filtered for relevance) prior to their delivery to the user. This expert can in some cases also be an algorithm or an externally provisioned service. The curation result will be documented in an indexed repository that also comprises meta-data for future updates and enhancements. Thus, WiPo differs from other approaches to information gathering from the Web in that it does not try to solve everything automatically but relies on human involvement.

The first prototypical implementation has some minor restrictions. First, it does not yet consider documents supplied by users as well as private Web sources. Pre-filters and post-filters are currently employed when querying the curated database (as part of the ranking) rather than before and after the actual crawl. The tasks we initially envisioned the pre- and post-filter for are currently conducted by curators.

3 Related Work

To our knowledge, there are only a few other approaches combining curation and Web Information Retrieval. As outlined in [4], Sanderson et al. [11] suggested to apply a procedure where predefined queries are send to pre-registered services on a nightly basis. Relevant information is harvested and temporarily stored. The retrieved information is then audited by data curators who decide upon its relevance. A similar harvest and curate approach was suggested by Lee et al. [6] who outline ideas to enhance their ContextMiner[2]. However, neither of these is able to make information available offline on a mobile device.

Data Tamer [15] is similar to our approach in that it is also developed as a system to curate data partially manually. However, it operates more on a database level, particularly on problems of schema integration and entity consolidation, while our approach is more high-level and deals mostly with (textual) information rather than pure data. That said, we use the terms data and information mostly as synonyms throughout this paper and in our previous works.

4 Architecture

The WiPo architecture (extensively described in [12] and depicted in Figure 2) follows the client server principle, where the client is currently implemented as a browser-based Web GUI (1,3). However, the client could also be an arbitrary application (2) as long as it supports sending request over HTTP.

The WiPo-Server has a unique system architecture with a rather complex infrastructure, based on Linux, implemented and tested on Fedora 19. It consists of a number of modules which can be accessed through the REST-based Web interface(4) which is assisted by user management (5). The core component of WiPo is the curated database (11) around which all other functionality has been developed. Namely these are: data collection – including scheduler, crawler, data extraction, and the meta database – (9); the candidate database (10); curation (7); as well as search (6); and indexing functionality (8).

4.1 Interfaces

The *graphical user interface* (GUI, Figure 2:1-3) is the entry point for both searchers and curators and serves as a means to dynamically interact with the underlying infrastructure of WiPo. On the browser side the standard tool set of HTML and JavaScript was used simplified through libraries and frameworks such as jQuery, and bootstrap[3]. This was in particular helpful for the complex

---
[2] http://contextminer.org/
[3] See http://www.jquery.com and http://getbootstrap.com/, respectively.

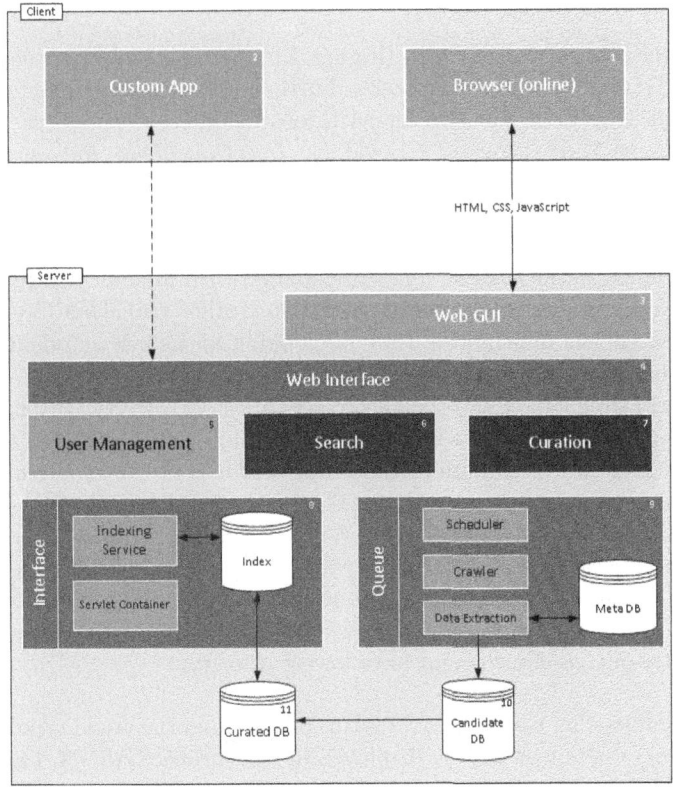

Fig. 2. WiPo Module Overview (numbers are explained in the text)

task of curation. To allow for the GUI and the actual core system of WiPo to reside on different machines – as heavy load on the back-end can be expected for full crawls – a PHP-Proxy was implemented to ensure compliance with the same origin policy enforced by JavaScript. The proxy provides two main functionalities, first, signing in users and secondly, forwarding request to the interface (4). An example of the curator GUI is presented in Figure 3 in Section 4.3.

The *Web interface* (Figure 2:4) can be seen as glue between clients and the WiPo core system. It is this component of the system that allows arbitrary software clients – as long as they can make use of the common http protocol – to use it and enables for instance app development. Its main task is to delegate requests from clients to the according internal WiPo module. In this context, *user management* (Figure 2:5) is an auxiliary module.

With respect to technology, the Web interface has been implemented as Java Servlets using Tomcat as servlet container and the Jersey framework[4] for implementing RESTful Web services in Java. Between Web interface and Web GUI, data is exchanged using the JavaScript Object Notation (JSON).

---

[4] See http://tomcat.apache.org/ and https://jersey.java.net/, respectively.

4.2 Data Collection

To obtain data from the Internet (Figure 2:9), we use an expert-supplied list of seed URLs and Nutch[5] as a crawler. Further, we have implemented a scheduler daemon that feeds the crawler with jobs of different priorities. We differentiate between three types of CrawlJobs: *UserCrawlJobs*, *ReCrawlJobs*, and *DataCrawlJobs*, which are all managed in a priority queue.

UserCrawlJobs are created when users add URLs to their search and these URLs are unknown to the system. They are created with highest priority, meaning that *UserCrawlJobs* are executed before any other *CrawlJob* to ensure that users receive the information they are looking for as fast as possible.
ReCrawlJobs are used to update outdated URLs in the WiPo meta database (last crawl time longer ago than a pre-set threshold). Every outdated URL is used as a seed for the crawler and the CrawlJob is added to the scheduler's priority queue with medium priority. *ReCrawlJobs* are automatically created on regular basis (in our experimental setting once a week).
DataCrawlJobs are used to enrich the WiPo database with new information. It is the only job with a crawl depth greater than 1, meaning that outgoing links from a seed URL are crawled, too, thus extending the body of knowledge. Similar to *ReCrawlJobs*, *DataCrawlJobs* are also created at given intervals (currently once a month) and have lowest priority.

Despite influencing the priority in terms of crawling, the crawl type also determines where a document will be displayed in the curator GUI (cf. Figure 3). In this way curators can attend to user requests first, handle re-crawls with lower priority, and if time allows, curate new documents. After successful downloads, first meta data, i.e., fetch time, last modified time, etc. are extracted. Then content extraction starts for which we use Boilerpipe[6]. Finally, the extracted content is checked for validity and is stored in the candidate database.

4.3 Curation

The curation module (Figure 2:7) connects the curator interface (and thus the curator through the curator GUI, see Figure 3) and the curated databases (Figure 2:11) as well as the candidate database (Figure 2:10). Once data has been collected by the crawler it is stored in the candidate database. These candidate documents are then reviewed by curators and transformed into curated documents. The curation module presents entries from the candidate database to curators who check them to ensure that they meet the necessary quality requirements. Also, curators can combine a number of candidates to a single curated document or extend an already existing curated document with contents from a candidate. This is the case for all types of content, i.e., texts, pictures, and

---

[5] https://Nutch.apache.org/
[6] http://code.google.com/p/boilerpipe/

videos. Furthermore, for textual content curators may recognise meaningful paragraphs and extract only these into a curated document. In addition curators can reference other curated documents that are relevant in the context and add tags that describe the document. This illustrates well the possibility of curators to combine content from several sources.

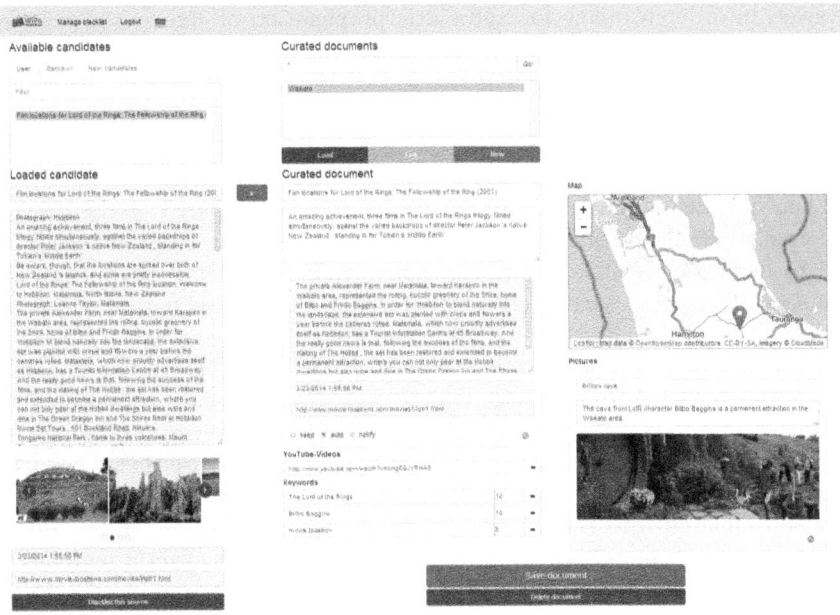

Fig. 3. Screenshot of the Curation Interface

Subsequently, the entries are moved into the curated database. Both the candidate as well as the curated database are implemented using mongoDB[7]. Even though mongoDB is schemaless, candidates and curated documents each follow a rough structure, however, the schemaless-ness allows maximum flexibility for individual documents in particular with regard to the number and types of sections in a curated document.

Particularly important parts of a curated document are segments (selections made by curators), which are identified by so-called tokens. In order to automatically identify them after re-crawling a source, the tokens must be as unique as possible and at the same time effectively processable. We chose a length of 100 characters, which makes it highly unlikely that the token does not have a unique string representation while it still allows for fairly quick processing. If there aren't enough chars, in front of or behind the chosen text segment, the tokens are shortened accordingly.

---

[7] https://www.mongodb.org/

4.4 The Update Cycle

Generally, it is important to reduce the curators' workload as much as possible, as curation is a time consuming task and human resources are expensive and limited. Whenever new content has been collected, it has to be analysed by a curator because (as of today and with the aspiration of very high quality) only humans have the ability to reliably determine the quality of an extracted text. However, in order to allow for automatic propagation of changes on a source, curators have the option to choose what happens, when the source of a curated document changes. The options are *keep*, i.e., the text remains in the curated database as is, even if the underlying source changes, *notify*, i.e., the curator will see the document again, once it has changed and can decide what to do then, and *auto*, i.e., the changes will be propagated unchecked.

When documents have been re-crawled, they are compared to the previous version of it by means of hash comparison. Only if a source has changed, it is tried to determine if any part of the source that has been used in a curated document differs from what is currently stored in the curated database. In order to do so, it is tried to find the tokens in the re-crawled document. If any of the tokens cannot be found, an automated update is not possible and the document is marked as *conflicted* and handed to the curator for review. Additionally, it is possible that a token is not unique. This means that every occurance of a begin-end token pair in the text must be identified. In the case that a begin-end token pair occurs multiple times, the text segments between the found tokens must be compared with the old text segment which is supposed to be updated. The result of the comparison can be a) one text segment exactly matches the old one and nothing needs to be changed or b) none of the found text segments exactly matches the old one. In the latter case, it has to be decided which one matches the old segment the most. Supposing that the extracted information only corresponds to the original curated data if both have a certain degree of similarity, we compute the similarity using the Dice Coefficient [2]. If no segment has a similarity of a satisfying degree, the new document is marked as *conflicted* and handed to the curator for review.

However, if a text segment (of satisfying similarity) has been found and the curator has authorized automated updating, the entry in the curated database is updated. But if the curator prohibited automated updates, the updated source is pushed into the candidate database and has to be reviewed by the curator. Changes only to the position but not the text of a segment are propagated to the meta database.

4.5 The Search Module

The search module (Figure 2:6) grants users access to curated documents, thus, representing a central element for interacting with the system. It receives user input from the Web interface and processes the queries to ensure that they fulfil the requirements of the underlying indexing service (Figure 2:8) which allows for most sophisticated searches. Also, URLs provided by the user are sent to the scheduler (Figure 2:9) to create *UserCrawlJobs*. This first step is called *pre-filtering*.

To simplify the processing of user queries, the input has been restricted by a specific syntax that currently allows only words and logical operators as well as blocks thereof but no nesting. Once queries are transformed, the *search index* (a Solr[8]-instance) retrieves relevant documents from the curated database. For this purpose the index is synchronised with the curated database using the MongoConnector[9]-daemon.

The documents found by the indexing service are compared to the users' interests and their former ratings to assure the best possible result set for each query. This is referred to as *post-filtering*. The current procedure is as follows: At first, documents that were previously excluded by the user (i.e., received a rating of 0) are removed from the indexing service's results. Next, similar to basic recommender systems (as described for instance in [10]), we calculate the cosine distance between user profiles (interests specified through tags) and document profiles (document tags specified by curators). At this point it is worth noting that both interest tags as well as document tags are suggested to users and curators, respectively, based on a common pool of tags to avoid problems with synonyms. Based on this last step, the results are re-ordered.

Ordering the results by rating takes place after that, since an explicit rating is more relevant than an implicit rating through user's interests. This approach ensures that a document, which received a high rating before, is displayed before a document with a lower rating even if the user's interests might coincide more with the inferior rated document. The last step is loading linked documents for all documents in the result set. Thus users get more information than their mere query would have discovered. Once the document stack is compiled it is returned to the Web interface. From this view users can persist articles that are of interest to them by sending them to their mobile devices[10].

5 Use Cases and Evaluation

Our prototypical implementation is realised as a platform on which information about filming locations can be found. This is discussed in more detail in Section 5.1. Then, we present an evaluation whether WiPo could be used in the context of Search and Rescue (SAR) in Section 5.2. Both use cases are placed in New Zealand (NZ) as mobile Internet coverage can be weak in some areas, making it an ideal country for WiPo.

5.1 Movie Tourism

On our platform, information on where movies have been filmed is presented in a way that incorporates information about the movie itself (sourced for instance

---

[8] https://lucene.apache.org/Solr/
[9] http://blog.mongodb.org/post/29127828146/introducing-mongo-connector
[10] We use Evernote as a means but any "read-it-later" tool with an API could be incorporated.

from Wikipedia), general tourism information for the area (sourced from local tourism and accommodation Web sites), and film trailers, snippets, and images (sourced from Youtube and Flickr). Most importantly, we provide a means to make this information available offline, so that tourists do have them at hand, when they are for example in a NZ region such as Matamata where parts of *Lord of the Rings* were shot but no Internet is available. This is in contrast to existing Web sites such as http://www.movie-locations.com/ which provides information regarding filming locations already but do so in a rather un-integrated way.

As of today, on our platform documents can be created featuring filming locations,e. g., the Hobbiton movie set, containing information regarding, opening hours and entrance fees as well as what to particularly look for. This information is enriched with images and video footage as well as general tourism information for the region. Tourists (users) looking for high quality information about filming locations and related tourism information in New Zealand (NZ) can hence use the platform to plan their holidays. Given the generally poor mobile Internet coverage in rural NZ areas, they can persist the information for offline usage. Results are tailored to their needs by matching their interests (e. g., guided tours or mountainous regions) against the tags of locations (e. g. guide tours for Hobbiton).

5.2 Search and Rescue

In a recent interview study with NZ LandSAR, we have evaluated the usefulness of WiPo in a search and rescue (SAR) environment. Here we report preliminary results of this study an extended report of which is currently in preparation [3]. For this study, we interviewed a number of key personnel within a single, regional NZ LandSAR organisation. The interviews, which took between 45 and 90 minutes, involved – besides other topics – a short live demonstration of the prototype and a discussion of the potential WiPo offers for SAR.

Through our interview partners, we identified two major strengths in WiPo that can aid SAR. First, WiPo can be useful with regard to pre-planning. This means that all information available for a certain region, or type of search (child, tourist etc.) can be gathered before an actual search. This includes static information such as maps but also dynamic information such as weather forecasts and tidal information. This can easily be achieved owing to the automated update capabilities of WiPo which make sure that the information within the WiPo system is always current. WiPo could serve as a knowledge repository for information that has been gathered in debriefing sessions so that this information – which currently mainly resides in people's heads and a non-indexed file structure – can be automatically made available for future events.

The second strength concerns making information available in the field. The WiPo search functionality can help searchers find information they specifically need and synchronise the results with their mobile devices. In particular in an urban search where Internet is available this is not a problem but also in areas where no connections are available they can pre-load the information on their way to the operating site while there still is a connection. Implementing a dedicated client, it would also be possible to realise search in such a way that it makes use of any connective it detects. Along this line is also the prospect of search managers being able to push information to the teams in the field (for instance when updated information becomes available).

Challenges we learned of include the technology adoption of Land SAR members, which is currently not too high, and would thus require training efforts, as well as potential costs associated with the tool.

6 Conclusions and Future Work

In this paper, we have presented a first implementation of the WiPo approach, as a proof of concept of a platform for providing high quality information tailored towards a user's needs. The current prototype enables Web crawling and comprehensive curation through an easy to use Web interface as well as offline availability of selected data. Also, it allows the integration of different types of content such as text, images, and video.

On the technical level, we plan to develop a dedicated mobile client to allow for true off-line usage. Furthermore, as of now curators are the bottleneck of the system. This is why we plan to unburden them by introducing better algorithmic support. This explicitly includes semantic Web technologies and content analysis.

Next will be a wider evaluation of WiPo in specific application domains. To this end, we have conducted a number of interviews with SAR people from which it can be concluded that WiPo is capable of realising improvements to the manner by which information is used by NZ LandSAR. However, some modifications to the prototypical system will be required prior to a rollout. For instance, adjustments to the curation GUI would need to be made in or to structure curator inputs, which currently are rather unlimited to allow for maximum freedom. Besides that, there is a need for other sorts of inputs such as advanced geo-data and timeline information. Overall, there appears little doubt that WiPo offers some real and concrete opportunities for SAR.

Besides this, we envision curation to be crowdsourced – maybe even through crowdsourcing marketplaces such as Mechanical Turk[11] –, and to integrate the search into users' social networks. Both ideas imply significant organisational and development efforts, while at the same time they can make the WiPo approach even more valuable. Last, in previous work [8,13] we investigated pricing models that are being used on data marketplaces. While data markets are usually trading raw data, as opposed to high-quality information in WiPo, both provide customers with valuable insights. That said, we would like to explore which pricing models can be used for WiPo in different scenarios. For instance, the assumption could be made – and has to be tested – that WiPo for SAR could be run as a service with a subscription price, while WiPo for tourists would have to generate revenue indirectly through advertising because tourists are used to getting information for free.

---

[11] https://www.mturk.com/

Acknowledgments. We gratefully acknowledge the students who implemented the prototype, which are besides co-authors Adrian Godde, Bastian Hagedorn, Bastian Köpcke, and Martin Rehberger: Rene Elsbernd, Jens Gutsfeld, Tony Hauptmann, Lars Klein, Marius Umlauf, Jonathan Schott-Vaupel, Philipp Sommer, and Alexander Voß.

References

1. Choudhury, G.S.: Case Study in Data Curation at Johns Hopkins University. Library Trends, 211–220 (2008)
2. Dice, L.R.: Measures of the Amount of Ecologic Association Between Species. Ecology 26(3), 297–302 (1945)
3. Dillon, S., Rastrick, K., Stahl, F., Vossen, G.: WiPo for SAR: Taking the Web in your Pocket when doing Search and Rescue. In preparations
4. Dillon, S., Stahl, F., Vossen, G.: Towards the Web in Your Pocket: Curated Data as a Service. In: Nguyen, N.T., Trawiński, B., Katarzyniak, R., Jo, G.-S. (eds.) Adv. Methods for Comput. Collective Intelligence. SCI, vol. 457, pp. 25–34. Springer, Heidelberg (2013)
5. Dillon, S., Stahl, F., Vossen, G., Rastrick, K.: A Contemporary Approach to Coping with Modern Information Overload. Communications of the ICISA: An International Journal 14(1), 1–24 (2013)
6. Lee, C.A., Marciano, R., Hou, C.-Y.: From harvesting to cultivating. In: Proceedings of the 9th Conference on Digital Libraries, p. 423 (2009)
7. Lord, P., Macdonald, A., Lyon, L., David, G.: From Data Deluge to Data Curation. In: Proceedings of the UK e-Science All Hands Meeting (2004)
8. Muschalle, A., Stahl, F., Löser, A., Vossen, G.: Pricing Approaches for Data Markets. In: Castellanos, M., Dayal, U., Rundensteiner, E.A. (eds.) BIRTE 2012. LNBIP, vol. 154, pp. 129–144. Springer, Heidelberg (2013)
9. Palmer, C.L., Allard, S., Marlino, M.: Data curation education in research centers. In: Proceedings of the 2011 iConference, pp. 738–740 (2011)
10. Rajaraman, A., Ullman, J.D.: Mining of Massive Datasets. Cambridge University Press (2011)
11. Sanderson, R., Harrison, J., Llewellyn, C.: A curated harvesting approach to establishing a multi-protocol online subject portal: Opening information horizons. In: 6th ACM/IEEE-CS Joint Conference on Digital Libraries (2006)
12. Stahl, F., Godde, A., Hagedorn, B., Köpcke, B., Rehberger, M., Vossen, G.: Implementing the wipo architecture. Technical Report 20, ERCIS — European Research Center for Information Systems, Münster (2014)
13. Stahl, F., Löser, A., Vossen, G.: Preismodelle für Datenmarktpläze. Informatik-Spektrum 37(1) (2014)
14. Stahl, F., Vossen, G.: From Unreliable Web Search to Information Provisioning based on Curated Data. EMISA Forum 32(2), 6–20 (2012)
15. Stonebraker, M., Bruckner, D., Ilyas, I.F., Beskales, G., Cherniack, M., Zdonik, S.B., Pagan, A., Xu, S.: Data Curation at Scale: The Data Tamer System. In: CIDR (2013), http://www.cidrdb.org

Effective Web Crawling for Chinese Addresses and Associated Information

Hsiu-Min Chuang, Chia-Hui Chang, and Ting-Yao Kao

Dept. of Computer Science and Information Engineering, National Central University
Chungli, Taoyuan, Taiwan
{showmin1205,kao800208}@gmail.com,
chia@csie.ncu.edu.tw

Abstract. With the advance of wireless networks, location-based services have become very important as people often need to query for addresses of unfamiliar locations through Web and then locate the position on the map. Existing geographic information systems based on crowd-sourcing are insufficient and have a slow update progress. However, it can actually be complemented by automatically extracting addresses of location entities and associated information from general pages. Thus, effectively crawling webpages with addresses is a practical challenge for enriching the location entity database. This research is devoted to automatic address and associated information extraction to provide information retrieval on maps, i.e. integrating the process of location entity query on Web and positioning on maps. We build a geographic information system of location entities by crawling the Web via three strategies for Chinese addresses. One point two seven (1.27) million distinct Chinese addresses are crawled using 1.08 million HTTP requests, leading to a return-of-investment of 1.169.

Keywords: Crawling strategies, Chinese postal address extraction, Associated information extraction, Geographic information retrieval.

1 Introduction

With the popularity of mobile devices and wireless networks, location-based services have gained a lot of attentions. Among many location-based services, locating the position of location entities is the key element that is constantly used in our daily life. For instance, tourists may need to locate hotels or restaurants nearby; drivers may need to find a parking lot or gas station. Although the Web contains a wealth of geographic information, most postal address information and map services are not well combined. A common task is to copy individual address from a Web page and paste it to other Web site with map service. According to Sanderson and Kohler [17], as much as 20 percent of Web queries have a geographic relation, with 15 percent directly mentioning a specific place. Thus, a necessity here is to combine address information with map service.

However, the descriptions for stores from the existing geographic location databases, such as Google Maps and Yahoo! Maps, are built based on crowd-sourcing and have a slow update progress. Such manual annotations are not necessarily needed because the Web pages already contain location-related information [1]. The insufficiency of current location database can actually be complemented by automatically crawling the Web for location entities' addresses and extracting their associated information. Thus, how to effectively identify these pages from a large scale of WWW documents and automatically build a database of location entities to support information search on maps is the challenge we will face in this paper.

To collect Web pages containing location entities, we proposed three strategies from various aspects including (1) surface-Web (or shallow) crawling with initial seed URLs, (2) deep Web crawling of yellow-page websites that are supported by a location entity database via URL analysis, and (3) keyword-based queries based on search engines. For the first strategy on surface Web crawling, the initial seed URLs and priority of URLs are crucial factors for efficient and exhausted crawling of the Web. Similarly, queries for the search engine will also be important. As for deep crawling of yellow-page websites such as Yelp[1] and TripAdvisor[2] usually provide multiple location entities with addresses in one page and is more cost-effective. Finally, the third strategy makes use of search engines by submitting queries that contain cue words such as "address", "street", "road", or city names, etc. We compare the performance of three crawling strategies and combine them to speed up the crawling process. The amount (1.27 million) of distinct Chinese addresses is collected.

In addition to the crawling of Web pages for address-bearing pages, associated information for each location entity supports search on maps and are indispensable. Moreover, we compare the performance of our geographical location entity information system (GLEIS) with the commercial app "What's The Number[3]" and an online editable map "Wikimapia.org" to demonstrate its practicality in geographic information retrieval.

The rest of the paper is organized as follows. Section 2 describes related work on crawling technologies, address extraction, associated information extraction and geographic information retrieval. Section 3 introduces the system architecture for crawling, associated information extraction and the retrieval model. This section focuses on three crawling strategies for Chinese address extraction and illustrates the method for associated information extraction. The experiment is explained and analyzed in Section 4. Finally, we conclude this paper in section 5.

2 Related Work

This paper is related to three research topics including: crawling strategies, addresses and associated information extraction, and geographic information retrieval. The details will be described below.

---

[1] http://www.yelp.com
[2] http://www.tripadvisor.com
[3] http://whatsthenumberapp.com/

2.1 Crawling

There are several kinds of Web crawlers designed for data acquisition. Shkapenyuk and Suel [18] categorized different strategies based on the crawling domain and purpose.

1) Breadth-First Search Crawler: Bread-first search (BFS) is the most common strategy to construct a search engine or a large repository. BFS crawlers usually start out at a small set of pages and explore other pages by linking in a breadth first fashion. According to Najork and Wiener [14], breadth-first crawling strategies discover high-quality pages early because more important webpages with many links are found early.

2) Recrawling Pages for Updates: As Web is a constantly changing environment, maintaining an up-to-date search index with limited crawling bandwidth is important. Therefore, Cho and Garcia-Molina [7] studied incremental crawlers for the "freshness" of search engines.

3) Focused Crawling: Contrary to general-purpose search engines, the goal of focused crawler is to selectively seek pages that are relevant to a pre-defined set of topics. Many approaches have been proposed based on URL analysis and machine learning techniques. Chakrabarti et al. [5] designed a robust crawler by training a classifier and distiller to explore the high-quality collections of Web documents.

4) Crawling the Deep Web: Deep Web refers to pages that are generated dynamically from databases by summiting appropriate queries. Since such Web pages contain search results of consolidated information, they are usually of high value for integration. He et al. [9] gave a survey of the six aspects to accessing deep web contents, while Olston and Najork [15] proposed the challenges of Web crawling, including scale, content selection and social obligation and illustrated the crawling ordering models for batch and incremental crawling strategies.

2.2 Address and Associated Information Extraction

Information extraction (IE) is the task of automatically extracting structured information from unstructured text documents, which is designed to test how much machine can understand the messages written in natural language and automate mundane tasks. Address extraction, which is a specific kind of IE, extracts complete addresses and has many social and economic applications [7, 17].

In addition to postal address extraction, associated information of an address refers to description of the location entity that is indispensable for (geographical) information retrieval. Chang and Li [6] defined the task for Web pages with multiple addresses. Using the extracted addresses as a hint to locate associated information for each address, they grow a string pattern of HTML tags from each address landmark as long as each information block is not overlapped. However, such tag patterns can be fragmented due to optional fields and nested data.

2.3 Geographic Information Retrieval

To provide search for points of interest (POIs), geographic information retrieval (GIR) systems need to build index and rank location entities after crawling and geoparsing from unstructured documents of the Web. State-of-the-art search engines like Google and Yahoo began their map service in 2005 and 2002, respectively. In addition to geoparsing, some map services also acquire POIs by crowdsourcing from online users. For example, Wikimapia is an open-content collaborative mapping project launched in 2006. Ahlers and Boll [1] proposed a location-based search engine that automatically derived spatial context from unstructured Web resources in 2007. They adopted focused crawler by heuristically crawl Web pages with spatial relation and proposed a directory-driven geoparser to extract addresses in Germany. As the volume of POIs affects the GIR service, their recent researches [2, 3] focus on location entity extraction from deep Web such as yellow pages and Wikipedia for more information. While current concern is the enrichment of the database, location entity disambiguation is also a challenge.

3 System Architecture

To build our GIR system, we proposed an architecture based on postal address extraction as shown in Fig. 1. First, we crawl Web pages containing postal addresses using three different crawling strategies. Next, a machine-learning based method is applied for postal address extraction based on [13]. To find associated information for multiple extracted addresses from the page that contains these addresses, we apply a heuristic of mutually exclusive maximum subtree (MEMS) to extract associated information for each address. Finally, an index is built from the associated information to support users' search requests as shown in Fig. 2.

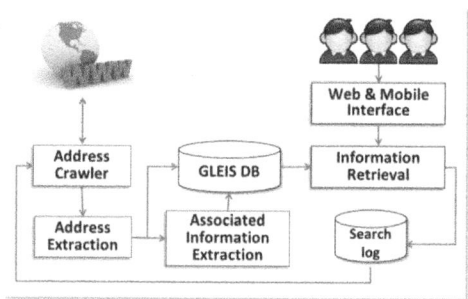

Fig. 1. The overview of the process of GLEIS

3.1 Crawling Strategies

(1) Baseline Crawler

The baseline crawler adopts a BFS approach which starts from a set of initial seeds including Yahoo portal, some organization websites and Top 5 Google search results using address characters as queries. The crawler then downloads and parses these pages for new URLs extraction. Fig. 3 shows the process of the baseline crawler. For each downloaded Webpage from WWW, the crawler parses new URLs into the URL queue. In this shallow crawling, the priority of all URLs in URL queue is the same. Thus, the number of the extended URLs growth exponentially with the number of URLs in a page.

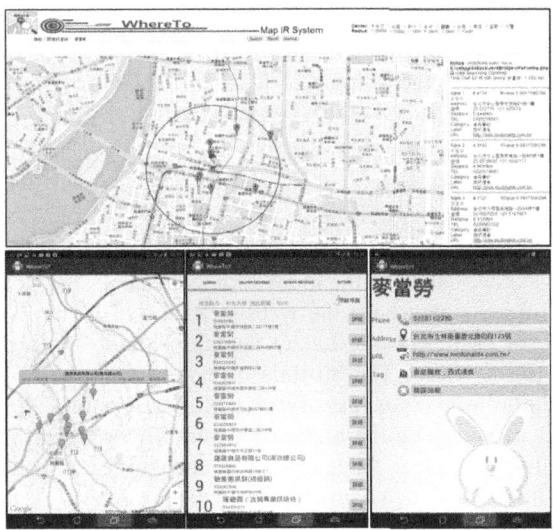

Fig. 2. The interface of GLEIS. The top figure is geo-map Web site for desktop browser; the bottom figure is the app interface for android. Users can use a keyword and set the search range to find out the appropriate entity list. The associated information includes TEL, address, URL, and simple description.

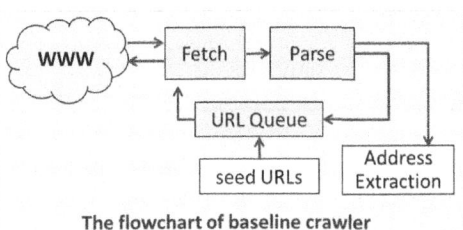

Fig. 3. The process of the baseline crawler

(2) Yellow Page Crawler

Yellow pages usually provide consolidated business entities with entity names, addresses, phone numbers and some description about the products they provide. Such websites often contain systematic URLs that can be generalized by assigning appropriate parameters to obtain these location entities. The question is how to obtain yellow-page websites for unfamiliar categories such as "yelp" for restaurants, "tripAdvisor" for hotels. In this paper, we focus on how to find yellow-page websites using two heuristic approaches.

a) Using "Yellow-page" as Query: The first intuition to find yellow-page websites is to use special words such as "yellow page" (黃頁), "quick search" (特搜), or "network" (網) to query search engines for candidate websites. We can also combine these keywords with location types such as "restaurant" or "travel". As shown in Table 1, some deep Web sites are found by manual filtering. Unfortunately, this method does not provide an estimate for the volume of location entities indexed by each yellow-page website. Therefore, we proposed the second heuristic as follows.

b) Using Store Names as Query: Suppose we know some location entities for particular domain, for example, "Fridays" and "Alinea" for restaurants, and "COSTCO" and "supervalu" for supermarkets, we can use these entity names as queries to find yellow-page websites from the union of the search results (denoted by W). For each website, we calculate the number of store names indexed by the website, i.e. the number of queries that have the website as one of its top K search result to estimate the scale of each website. Let Q denotes the set of store names used as queries to obtain top K URLs. The hit ratio of a website, x, is the number of store names that have the website, x, as one of its top K search result divided by |Q|. Table 2 shows the top 5 website with the highest hit ratio for restaurant and supermarket, respectively. Finally, we select "iPeen" as the deep website since Wikipedia and Facebook require more sophisticate procedures to extract data.

Table 1. Yellow-page websites selected using queries "yellow pages" (黃頁), "restaurant & quick search" (餐廳&特搜) and "travel&network" (旅遊&網)

Query No.	yellow page (黃頁)	restaurant & quick search (餐廳&特搜)	travel & network (旅遊&網)
1	iyp.com	gs04.url.tw	okgo.tw
2	web66.com	walkerland.com	emmm.tw
3	yp.518.com	ysm.emarketing.yahoo.com	travel.network.com
4	directory.com	ustv.com	easytravel.com
5	trade.1111.com	tw.openrice.com	tw.tranews.com

Table 2. Top 5 yellow page websites for "restaurant" and "supermarket" domains exclude blog and news websites. The reason of excluding blog and news websites is that the free-text style is not suitable to adopt yellow-page crawling strategy and is hard to extract data records.

List No.	Website Domain Name for restaurant	hit ratio	Website Domain Name for supermarket	hit ratio
1	iPeen.com	100%	Wikipedia.org	90%
2	104.com.tw	80%	Facebook	90%
3	518.com.tw	80%	104.com.tw	90%
4	TripAdvisor.com	80%	iPeen.com	80%
5	wowprime.com	80%	1111.com.tw	80%

(3) Query-Based Crawler

In this scenario, we use Google search engine to return top N results with M queries formed by address patterns and keywords such as restaurant and hotel. The address patterns are composed of 26 city names in Taiwan and the address-bearing characters like "*(路or街or段or巷or弄)*號". At the beginning, location type keywords are assigned by category words such as restaurant, hotel, bank, post office, parking lot and gas station. The obvious difference of the crawling process with the baseline crawler is without crawling outward new URLs from these downloaded pages as shown in Fig. 4. One observation is that the performance of the baseline crawler is very low and therefore we consider the search result of the query as a seed URL and crawl top K links in the search result only, not outward links. As shown in Fig. 5, with increasing the crawling depth, the more repeated webpages of the query-based crawler. Here, we set $N=500$ as the fixed depth for initial crawling.

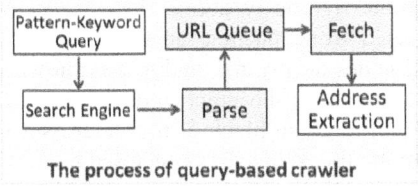

Fig. 4. The process of query-based crawler

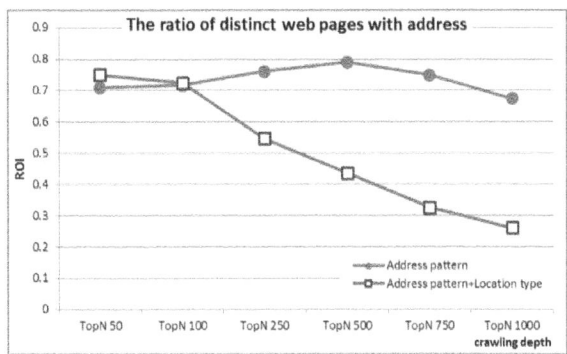

Fig. 5. The ratio of distinct web pages with address. The result is reasonable because we find many store addresses are recommended or reposted in different web pages such as blogs and business directories.

3.2 Associated Information Extraction

Our job is to find associated information for the each extracted address from the pages that contain the addresses. For a web page which contains a single address, the whole page can be used as a description for this web page. Thus, the task here focuses on associated information extraction from web pages that contain multiple addresses. One observation is that many web pages with multiple postal addresses often have associated information arranged regularly forming address blocks. Since the rendering is controlled by HTML tags, they should present some regularity.

We focus on the boundary detection using DOM tree path instead of detailed record patterns from HTML tag string. Document object model (DOM) is a standard representation of HTML documents. Every element, label, and text in HTML is denoted by some nodes in the DOM tree. To focus on the boundary of the associated information, the following three assumptions are made in this study.

1) Associated information for an address forms a continuous block encompassing the address.

2) The information blocks associated with each address are mutually exclusive.

3) We assume that the information block of an address is contained in a single sub-tree in the DOM tree such that each information block expands the region as long as they are mutually exclusive.

These three assumptions rigorously define the concept of record boundary for addresses that are extracted from machine generated pages. For example, suppose there are four numbered nodes n_8, n_{15}, n_{23}, and n_{25}, as shown in Fig. 6. According to the above mentioned assumptions, the numbered nodes n_6, n_{11}, n_{22}, and n_{24} will be taken as the root for the information block of four addresses respectively since these information blocks are mutually exclusive (as enclosed by the dotted line in Fig. 6).

Suppose the input page is first transformed into a DOM tree T and a set of N postal addresses, which are located in the terminal nodes of the DOM tree T, is given. If an address is scattered in multiple nodes, these nodes would be combined into one terminal node. The path p_i of each address/terminal node t_i is an array list of nodes from root to t_i in order, i.e. $p_i[k]$ is denoted the k-th node of p_i from root as shown in Table 3.

An ancestor node $a_i = p_i[k]$ is called the farthest distinguishable ancestor (FDA) of its node t_i if it is the farthest node from t_i and is distinct from all ancestor nodes of other addresses. In other words, $p_i[k-1]$ is an ancestor of some address nodes t_j; $j_6 = i$. For example, the farthest distinct ancestors for the four address nodes are exactly node n_6, n_{11}, n_{22}, and n_{24}, the associated information block the process aims to discover (see Table 3).

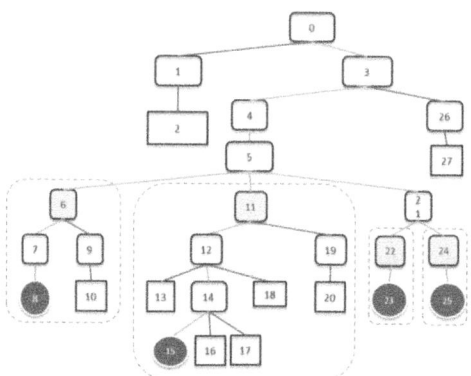

Fig. 6. The associated information block for four addresses

Table 3. Example for FDA algorithm

Address node	Path P	FDA
$t_1 = n_8$	$p_1 = /0/3/4/5/6/7/8$	$a_1 = n_6$
$t_2 = n_{15}$	$p_2 = /0/3/4/5/11/12/14/15$	$a_2 = n_{11}$
$t_3 = n_{23}$	$p_3 = /0/3/4/5/21/22/23$	$a_3 = n_{22}$
$t_4 = n_{25}$	$p_4 = /0/3/4/5/21/24/25$	$a_4 = n_{24}$

3.3 Ranking Algorithms

The geographic information retrieval system ranks the associated information of the addresses according to users' query. Let D be the Web pages collection of the associated information. We adopt the query likelihood model [8] to estimate $P(Q|D)$ probability for query Q. Using Bayes rules, we calculate by:

$$P(D|Q) = P(Q|D)P(D) \qquad (1)$$

We ignore the normalizing constant $P(Q)$. $P(Q|D)$ is the query likelihood given the Web pages collection. The unigram language model for the document is calculated:

$$P(Q|D) = \prod_{i=1}^{n} P(q_i|D) \qquad (2)$$

where q_i is query words to compose the query. The estimation for the probability is by:

$$P(q_i|D) = \frac{f_{q_i,D}}{|D|} \qquad (3)$$

where $f_{qi,D}$ is the number of times word q_i occurs in document D and $|D|$ is the number of words in D. It estimates the maximum likelihood $f_{qi,D}$.

4 Experiments

4.1 Experiment Design and Evaluation Measure

To demonstrate the effectiveness of the three Web crawling strategies, we evaluate our approaches based on the number of addresses crawled and the number of HTTP requests made. The first measure we define is the address-bearing ratio (ABR) which measures the percentages of pages that contain address entities:

$$\text{ABR} = \text{\# of pages containing addresses} / \text{\# of visited Web pages} \qquad (4)$$

Because some pages may contain multiple address entities, a more precise measure is the return on investment (ROI) which is defined as the number of distinct addresses divided by the number of visited web pages:

$$\text{ROI} = \text{\# of distinct addresses} / \text{\# of visited Web pages} \qquad (5)$$

In the second experiment, the performance of associated information extraction is evaluated via geographic information retrieval. We adopt the ap@k which summarizes the ranking by averaging the precision values from the rank positions where a relevant document was retrieved:

$$\text{ap@k} = \frac{1}{c}\sum_{i=1}^{c} precision_i \qquad (6)$$

where $precision_i$ is the precision at rank i and c is the number of relevant entities from top k search results [8]. We use ap@k for evaluating the task of finding as many relevant documents as possible while still reflecting the intuition that the top-ranked documents are the most important.

4.2 Results and Discussion

Fig. 7 shows the address-bearing ration at different stages of the crawling process. From the trend of these curves, the query-based crawler and yellow-page crawler are much better than the baseline crawler. The ABR for yellow-page crawler is increasing for the initial stage because of the necessity to visit directory pages. Query-based crawler has varying performances at different stages due to the popularity of various cities.

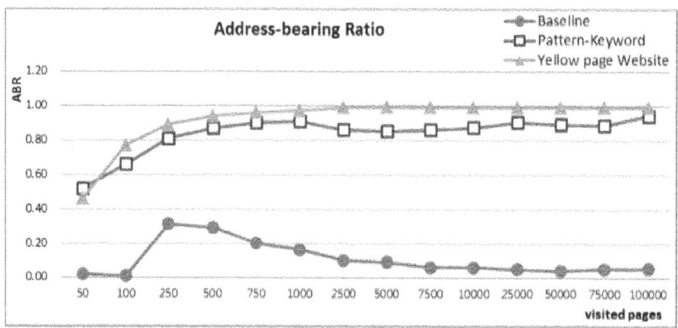

Fig. 7. Address-bearing ratio versus the number of visited webpages for three crawling strategies

Table 4 shows the amount of addresses extracted by three crawling strategies: the baseline crawler, query-based crawler and yellow-page website crawler. In terms of address-bearing ratio (ABR), the query-based crawler has similar performance with the yellow-page crawler (94.1% and 99.9%), which is much better than that of the baseline crawler (0.4%). In average, there are 0.581 addresses per page for the query-based crawler, which is also higher than 0.318 for the baseline crawler. If we consider only distinct addresses, the difference in performance is more obvious. As we can see, the ROI for the query-based crawler (0.547) and yellow-page crawler (6.950) is much higher than the ROI for the baseline crawler (only 0.001). Overall, the yellow-page crawler has the best performance in terms of ABR and ROI.

Table 4. The extracted addresses of three crawler strategies

Items		Baseline	Query-Based Crawler	Yellow Page Crawler
# Visited Webpages	(a)	132,628,290	982,767	105,727
# Webpage with Address	(b)	508,038	925,135	105,693
# Extracted Address	(c)	1,034,402	2,364,853	944,864
# Distinct Address	(d)	161,807	537,351	734,752
Adress-Bearing Ratio	(e) = (b) / (a)	0.004	0.941	0.999
Avg. addresses per page	(f) = (d) / (b)	0.318	0.581	6.952
Return-On-Investment	(g) = (d) / (a)	0.001	0.547	6.950

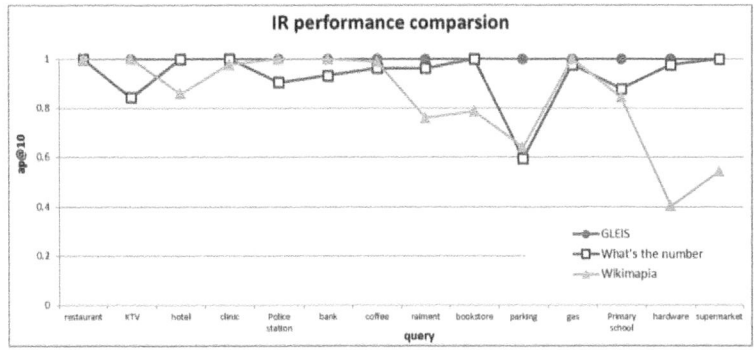

Fig. 8. The performance of three geographic information retrieval systems for 14 common POI queries

Because the amount of all store addresses in Taiwan is hard to obtain precisely, the ratio of extracted addresses in a small sample is used to estimate the population of total addresses. To estimate the ratio of current extracted addresses in Taiwan, we randomly sample 100 addresses from Web using three different keyword queries including "store addresses" (店家地址), "address list" (地址清單) and "recommended stores & address" (推薦店家&地址) to verify the ratio of extracted entities in Taiwan. From the 1,272,283 distinct addresses, 74, 70 and 78 addresses are found respectively. Thus, we can say the crawled addresses are less than 74% of the address entities in Taiwan.

The second experiment is used to evaluate the enrichment of the associated information and the performance of the geographic information retrieval. We choose the famous commercial app "What's The Number" and an online map "Wikimapia.org" for comparison. "What's The Number" is an IR-orient location-based search engine service that supply TEL and address of location entities for many countries, while Wikimapia.org is an open-content collaborative project which allow users to mark any geographic entities on the map.

We tried fourteen queries around Taipei at coordinate (25.047921, 121.517082), and measured ap@10 for top 10 search results for three systems (without scale limits). As shown in Fig. 8, it shows our ap@10 is higher than "What's the number" because the some irrelevant entities affect the ranking order and reduce the ap@10. In contrast, the ranking order is more correct. Fig. 9 compares the amount of entities retrieved by three systems. Our GLEIS system has better performance in restaurant, bank, raiment and supermarket.

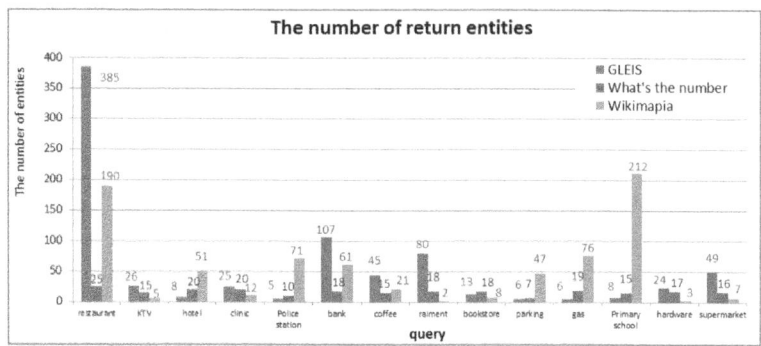

Fig. 9. The number of entities retrieved by three geographic information retrieval systems for 14 common POI queries

5 Conclusions and Future Work

In recent years, location-based services have received increasing attention from many aspects. However, existing location databases are based on crowd-sourcing and have a slow updating progress. The insufficiency of current location database can actually be improved by automatically extracting location entities' addresses and their associated information from general Web pages.

In this study, we proposed three strategies for address-bearing pages crawling and applied the idea of mutually exclusive maximum subtree (MEMS) for associated information segmentation from Web pages with multiple addresses (location entities). Based on a million of distinct addresses crawled, we implemented an information retrieval service based on query likelihood model (QLM). The experiments showed the effectiveness of the Web crawlers and the performance of information retrieval. It demonstrated the possibility of associated information extraction for geographical information retrieval.

There are many research issues for constructing a geo database. For example, adaptive crawling for new entity updates and verification of the crawled location entities are all very important. Meanwhile, the extraction of the associated information by entity name recognition is also a promising approach for enhancing description of the location entities.

References

1. Ahlers, D., Boll, S.: Location-based Web Search. In: The Geospatial Web, pp. 55–66. Springer (2007)
2. Ahlers, D.: Business entity retrieval and data provision for yellow pages by local search. In: Integrating IR Technologies for Professional Search, ECIR (2013)
3. Ahlers, D.: Lo mejor de dos idiomas – cross-lingual linkage of geotagged wikipedia articles. In: Serdyukov, P., Braslavski, P., Kuznetsov, S.O., Kamps, J., Rüger, S., Agichtein, E., Segalovich, I., Yilmaz, E. (eds.) ECIR 2013. LNCS, vol. 7814, pp. 668–671. Springer, Heidelberg (2013)

4. Buttler, D., Liu, L., Pu, C.: A Fully Automated Object Extraction System for the World Wide Web. In: ICDCS, pp. 361–370 (2001)
5. Chakrabarti, S., Van den Berg, M., Dom, B.: Focused crawling: a new approach to topic-specific Web resource discovery. In: WWW (1999)
6. Chang, C.-H., Li, S.-Y.: MapMarker: Extraction of Postal Addresses and Associated Information for General Web Pages. In: WI, pp. 105–111 (2010)
7. Cho, J., Garcia-Molina, H.: The Evolution of the Web and Implications for an Incremental Crawler. In: VLDB 2000 Proceedings of the 26th International Conference on Very Large Data Bases, pp. 200–209 (2000)
8. Croft, W.B., Metzler, D., Strohman, T.: Search Engines, information retrieval in pracitce. Pearson (2010)
9. He, B., Patel, K., Zhang, Z., Chang, K.C.C.: Accessing the deep web: A survey. Communications of the ACM 50(5), 95–101 (2007)
10. Kayed, M., Chang, C.-H.: FiVaTech: Page-Level Web Data Extraction from Template Pages. IEEE Trans. Knowledge Data Engineering 22(2), 249–263 (2010)
11. Laender, A.H.F., Ribeiro-Neto, B.A., da Silva, A.S., Teixeira, J.S.: A Brief Survey of Web Data Extraction Tools. SIGMOD Record 31(2), 84–93 (2002)
12. Liu, B., Grossman, R.L., Zhai, Y.: Mining Data Records in Web Pages. In: SIGKDD, pp. 601–606 (2003)
13. McCallum, A.: Efficiently inducing features of conditional random fields. In: UAI, pp. 403–410 (2003)
14. Najork, M., Wiener, J.L.: Breadth-first crawling yields high-quality pages. In: Proceedings of the 10th International Conference on World Wide Web, pp. 114–118 (2001)
15. Olston, C., Najork, M.: Web Crawling. Foundations and Trends in Information Retrieval 4(3), 175–246 (2010)
16. Ourioupina, O.: Extracting geographical knowledge from the Internet. In: ICDMAM, pp. 108–113 (2002)
17. Sanderson, M., Kohler, J.: Analyzing Geographic Queries. In: Workshop on Geographic Information Retrieval (SIGIR), Sheffield, UK (2004)
18. Shkapenyuk, V., Suel, T.: Design and Implementation of a High-Performance Distributed Web Crawler. In: Proceedings of the 18th International Conference on Data Engineering, San Jose, CA, USA, February 26-March 1 (2002)

Information Need in Cloud Service Procurement – An Exploratory Case Study

Jan Wollersheim[1], Matthias Pfaff[1], and Helmut Krcmar[2]

[1] Fortiss GmbH, München, Germany
{wollersheim,pfaff}@fortiss.org
[2] Technische Universität München, München, Germany
krcmar@in.tum.de

Abstract. Cloud computing enables the on-demand self-service procurement of standardized IT services over the internet. However, to efficiently use electronic markets and platforms for exchanging cloud services, a common understanding of the service to be exchanged is required between the organizations providing and the organizations in need of the service. Currently, only a few rather specific criteria catalogues are available to address this need, only focusing on certain types or specific aspects of cloud services. It remains unclear upon which general characteristics organizations require information when procuring cloud services. To identify this broad set of information, we conducted 16 interviews with small-to-large organizations. Combining the responses with literature-based findings, we identified a set of 39 items that form the essential set of characteristics required by an organization when procuring cloud services. This set provides a starting point for the development of a domain-specific vocabulary, service descriptions, and supports the decision-making process of procuring organizations.

Keywords: Cloud Service, Service Description, Case Study.

Traditionally, IT outsourcing providers try to engage in long-term relationships with their clients, providing them with customized IT services. Clients rely on the expertise and detailed solution descriptions offered by potential service providers to specify their individual service demand. Typically, an initial Request for Information (RFI) is sent out to providers describing an approximate demand while asking for a detailed solution specification. The client expects the service provider to present bite-sized information. Subsequently, the client may use this information as a blueprint for a more detailed demand specification, distributed among multiple vendors in a second step of the procurement process. In contrast to those iteratively and individually specified services, cloud computing services are rather standardized offerings. Cloud services, by definition, are designed to be purchased, integrated and used with minimal provider interaction [1], rendering individual requests, such as RFIs, inapplicable [2]. The industrialized IT-delivery model of cloud services is defined as "enabling ubiquitous, convenient, on-demand network access to a shared pool of configurable computing resources that can be rapidly provisioned and released with minimal management effort or service provider interaction" [3]. Consequently, in the cloud computing market, prospective service customers must independently gather all relevant information regarding an offered service [4]. In turn, procuring organizations need to specify their service demand, and providers need to specify their service offerings, in every detail, to enable any matching of supply and demand. However, customers struggle to specify their demand, and providers struggle to identify the essential elements of cloud service descriptions - those service characteristics for which almost every customer will ask. First catalogues of cloud service characteristics emerged in academia and corporate practice, investigating specific aspects, but the following still remains unclear:

What is the essential set of service characteristics that describes the information needed by organizations when procuring cloud services?

To answer this research question, we first review the academic and practitioner-oriented literature, followed by an empirical analysis of requirements of small to large organizations towards cloud service descriptions, addressing the gaps identified in current literature.

1 Related Work

Academic research investigating the set of information important to organizations when in the process of procuring cloud services is scarce and addresses different foci [5]. Repschläger et al. [6] and Binz et al. [7] focus on rather specific, technical aspects such as the design and functionality of the interface used to manage and port software packages from one service provider to another. In corporate practice, first sets of such criteria focus on aspects such as security [8,9] or specific service functionalities [10]. As cloud services may be traded on electronic markets, ontologies provide a way to describe this type of IT service [11]. For example, the GoodRelations Ontology [12] could be of use to describe specific aspects, such as provider and payment details. To address and structure the full range of information demands of organizations, the quality models defined by the international standard "Systems and software Quality Requirements and Evaluation" (SQuaRE - ISO/IEC 25010) [13] can be used. This standard sets forth the following:

1. "A quality in use model composed of five characteristics [...] that relate to the outcome of interaction when a product is used in a particular context of use." [13]
2. "A product quality model composed of eight characteristics [...] that relate to static properties of software and dynamic properties of the computer system." [13]

The norm SQuaRE provides a list of quality characteristics that are important when determining quality needs throughout the procurement. Moreover, it provides a list of characteristics when measuring the quality of the service received throughout operations [13]. As the quality the customer will receive during service operations is rather unknown at the time of procurement, proxy values might be of use. As suggested by

Grönroos [14], characteristics of a provider's image could be used in this sense as a filter or proxy for unknown quality characteristics. Furthermore, as SQuaRE is designed for IT services, in general, some of the more cloud-specific aspects outlined in the research by Repschläger et al. [15] or Hoberg et al. [5] are not addressed in such detail. However, to enable a more efficient procurement process of cloud services for small and mid-sized organizations, sets of service properties are required that focus on the most important criteria while omitting security specifics or technical interfaces, which become more important in certain procurement settings only. Adding up all characteristics, vocabularies, ontologies, etc., means a high number of items to be considered when procuring. This high number of items would undermine one of the cloud service advantages - the ability to focus on the needs of agile organizations [16].

2 Research Approach

To answer the previously formulated research questions and to identify the essential set of information that small- and medium-sized companies need during the procurement process, the remainder of this paper has been organized as follows. We first introduce a case study we performed to gather the needed empirical data. Before analyzing the requirements of organizations with respect to cloud service descriptions, an overview of the research approach is provided. Subsequently, we present and discuss our empirical research results. Finally, we present the essential set of information organizations require when procuring cloud services. This set is derived from explorative group interviews with representatives of small-, medium- and large-sized organizations that have at least limited experience in procuring cloud services.

To gather the needed insights into this contemporary and complex sourcing model within a real-life context, we chose an exploratory case study approach [cf. 17] following the guidelines of Paré [18]. In general, the unit of analysis is the process executed by an organization when specifying a cloud service demand. Specifically, we aim at the identification of the particular set of characteristics an organization uses to characterize its cloud service demand. Within each organization investigated, the list of requirements, agreed upon by the procurement team, forms the cornerstone for all following processes within the procuring organization. At the same time, the list of requirements represents the essential set of information this organization requests when in search for cloud services, e.g., on electronic service markets. To gather insights on procurement processes in corporate practice, while accounting for extraneous variations regarding the set of information identified, we selected interview participants that met the following criteria: (i) represented a large-, medium or small-sized (ii) private sector organization that (iii) successfully executed a procurement process for at least one cloud service. As proposed by [cf. 19], we included organizations of varying sizes. Moreover, the focus on private sector organizations is driven by specific restrictions applying exclusively to public sector organizations (e.g., the Federal Information Security Management Act of 2002; Title 44 United States Code § 3541, et seq.). We identified 4 interview partners who were involved in the procurement of cloud services at large organizations, and 12 who were involved in the procurement at medium- or small-sized organizations. In addition to the interviews, additional feedback was collected by follow-up emails. For greater richness of detail and to increase the validity of our findings, each interview was attended by at least two researchers - one leading the interview and discussion and the second researcher taking notes and asking follow-up questions. In total, we completed three semi-structured group interviews with representatives of large organizations and two interviews with representatives of small- and medium-sized organizations. Table 1 provides an overview of our interview partners, the type of organization to which their answers refer and the position of the interviewee within the organization.

Table 1. Overview of interviewees

ID	Type of Company	Position of Interview Participant within Organization	
1	Large	Middle Management	Procurement
2	Large	Senior Corporate Counsel	Legal
3	Large	External	Consultant
4	Large	External	Senior Consultant
5	Medium	Team Lead	IT Department
6	Medium	Team Lead	IT Department
7	Small	Executive	Business Department
8	Medium	Founder	CEO
9	Small	External	Consultant
10	Medium	Team Lead	IT Department
11	Small	Staff	IT Department
12	Small	Founder	CEO
13	Small	External	Consultant
14	Medium	Team Lead	Business Department
15	Small	Staff	IT Department
16	Small	Founder	CEO

All four interviewees involved in cloud service procurement at large organizations were interviewed in 3 group-interview sessions, each lasting between 60 and 120 minutes. The 12 remaining interviewees were questioned in 2 sessions, each lasting 120 minutes. To provide a focused discussion on a specific and structured purpose, we chose group interviews as our interview technique as proposed in [20,21]. Moreover, this technique allowed us to collect the information an organization perceives when procuring cloud services. To structure the interviews and discussions, an interview guideline was used. First, the interview participants described themselves and briefly described their general experience with the procurement of cloud services. Next, the participants were asked to recall the set of information they used in their previous cloud sourcing activities and to report on single characteristics and lists of characteristics they used. Subsequently, lists of characteristics were presented based on the academic and practitioner-oriented literature review and the initial feedback from the group. Moreover, collected data were enriched with contextual information derived from the group discussions. Based on the responses and suggestions throughout the discussion, a catalogue of service properties representing the information need was collected at the end of each session. In a subsequent interview-session, this list of characteristics collected was presented to the participants for respondent validation [17], followed by a renewed discussion of the characteristics included and excluded. Based on notes taken in this subsequent discussion, a refined set of characteristics was collected and supplemented with a short summary of the researchers [18].

3   Information Needs of Cloud Service Buyers

Table 2a and 2b display the set of information gathered, structured according to the dimensions used in SQuaRE - ISO/IEC 25010 [13] and expanded by the image dimension being a proxy for unknown quality-in-use characteristics [14]. The SQuaRE dimensions cover functional suitability, performance, compatibility, usability, reliability, security, maintainability and portability. Functional suitability addresses a service's functional completeness, correctness and appropriateness [13]. Performance addresses a service's time behavior and capacity. Compatibility addresses the degree to which a service can exchange information with other products or services. A service's usability addresses aspects such as the learnability and operability of the service. Reliability addresses a service's maturity. Security addresses aspects such as confidentiality and data integrity. Maintainability addresses the degree of effectiveness and efficiency with which a product or system can be modified by the intended maintainers. Portability addresses the replace-ability of the service.

Table 2a. Information need when procuring a cloud service

Dimension	Information need
Func. suitability	Type of functionality the service is offering (IaaS & PaaS or SaaS)
Func. suitability	Support obligations (scope and response-times)
Func. suitability	Internationality of support
Func. suitability	Communication channels for customer queries
Performance	Guaranteed availability of service
Performance	Guaranteed throughput of service (parallel users supported)
Performance	Network bandwidth and redundancy
Performance	Initial provisioning time (hours until initial service use possible)
Performance	Elasticity supported (provisioning time (hours) after scaling-request)
Compatibility	Supported interfaces to application services
Compatibility	Supported interfaces to other platform- or infrastructure services
Compatibility	Supported Interfaces (interoperability to 3rd party applications).
Usability	Amount of factors determining a service's fee (cost transparency)
Usability	Possibilities to configure using options and rules
Usability	Supported techniques to authenticate users
Usability	Offered tutorials, demos and trainings for users and administrators
Reliability	Liability and compensation for SLA-violation
Reliability	Naming of (sub-)contractors involved

Table 2b. Information need when procuring a cloud service

Dimension	Information need
Security	Guaranteed data separation (Multi-tenancy)
Security	Security measures - Organization and Staff
Security	Security measures – Infrastructure and Technical
Security	Possibilities to audit provider/sub-contractors
Security	Degree of protection sufficient to process personal data (§9 BDSG)
Maintainability	Minimum contract duration and extensions
Maintainability	Self Service Possibilities to scale up/down
Maintainability	Backup and Recovery Possibilities
Maintainability	Update-Management Possibilities
Maintainability	SLA-Monitoring Possibilities
Maintainability	Handling of emergencies - Response times
Maintainability	Response times upon customer requests
Portability	Possibilities to export data stored with the service
Portability	Full data deletion upon contract termination
Image	Name and address of provider
Image	Stability of provider (years since foundation)
Image	Place of service provision (place where data are processed & stored)
Image	Duration provider offers a service (months)
Image	Reference customer(s), incl. phone numbers
Image	Service assessments by experts or customers

4 Conclusion

The diverse positions and departmental backgrounds of our interviewees within their organizations show that stakeholders of multiple departments engage in the procurement of cloud services. The interviewees reported that some of the departments involved emphasize distinct information needs and try to push specific lists of characteristics, either self-initiated or derived, from lists set up by associations of professionals or consultants. Summed up, the interviewees agreed upon the listed criteria shown in Table 2a/b as being a comprehensive set to be used at the start of the procurement process. Depending upon individual needs within the organization procuring cloud services, the importance of specific criteria might vary. This needs to be reflected when weighting criteria to personal needs in common decision support methods that help to solve multi-criteria decision problems, such as the analytic hierarchy process (AHP) or utility value analysis.

The need to potentially add more criteria during the procurement process was emphasized by those interviewees representing large organizations. All of the large organizations structure and classify their data and data sources existing within the organization according to a predefined set of protection classes. This protection class, in turn, defines the security measures to which a service storing or processing these data must comply (see [22] for the detailed approach). In addition to information needed to analyze and assess a service's characteristics, organizations require information on the quality they can expect when using the service. The interviewees would like to know whether they can expect a service to always be up and running and to be provided by a supportive and professional organization. Information provided by other organizations or the duration of a service that is already being offered are some of the proxy values organizations use to gather information on the quality they can expect. Furthermore, all of the interviewees state that the agile cloud market and its quickly emerging and vanishing service offers require agile and lean procurement processes, especially as the frequency of procurement and termination increases. However, the interviewees reported unclear formulated and incomplete service descriptions. This lack of clarity, in turn, requires manual requests for further information throughout the service procurement process. Reducing the current mismatch of information provided by service vendors and the set of information demanded by service-using organizations might not only enable automated searches for required services, it might be one of the next steps towards an agile and lean cloud service procurement.

Even if organizations need to comply with certain rules and regulations that require extending this set, the 39 items identified form the underlying basis. We, thereby, contribute to the sparse empirical research on cloud service procurement. Our findings form a starting point for further research and can be used by service providers to be able to develop meaningful and comprehensive service descriptions for prospective customers. Furthermore, this paper highlights the need for further research in service description languages and ontologies in the domain of cloud services. Thus, the outlined findings provide a conceptualizing overview of service properties to be covered by ontologies and vocabulary for the domain of cloud services.

Acknowledgements. The information in this document was developed in the context of the project Value4Cloud, which is funded by the German Federal Ministry for Economics and Technology (FKZ: 01MD11043A). The responsibility for the content of this publication lies with the authors.

References

1. Mell, P., Grance, T.: The NIST Definition of Cloud Computing. Communications of the ACM 53(6), 50 (2010)
2. Wollersheim, J., Krcmar, H.: Purchasing processes for cloud services - An exploratory study of process influencing factors. In: Giannakis, M., Johnsen, T., Miemczyk, J., Kamann, D.-J., Bernardin, E. (eds.) 22nd Annual IPSERA Conference, Nantes, France, pp. 1285–1295 (2013)
3. NIST: The NIST Definition of Cloud Computing - Recommendations of the National Institute of Standards and Technology - Special Publication 800-145 (2011)
4. Wollersheim, J., Hoberg, P., Krcmar, H.: Procurement of Cloud Services: Seven Principles to Success. In: Wästlund, E., Edvardsson, B., Gustafsson, A., Bitner, M.J., Verma, R. (eds.) 13th International Research Symposium on Service Excellence in Management (QUIS), Karlstad, Sweden, pp. 423–431 (2013)

5. Hoberg, P., Wollersheim, J., Krcmar, H.: The Business Perspective on Cloud Computing - A Literature Review of Research on Cloud Computing. Paper Presented at the 18th Americas Conference on Information Systems (AMCIS), Seattle, USA (2012)
6. Repschlaeger, J., Zarnekow, R., Wind, S., Turowski, K.: Cloud Requirements Framework: Requirements and Evaluation Criteria to Adopt Cloud Solutions. Paper presented at the 20th European Conference on Information Systems (ECIS), Barcelona, Spain (2012)
7. Binz, T., Breiter, G., Leyman, F., Spatzier, T.: Portable Cloud Services Using TOSCA. IEEE Internet Computing 16(3), 80–85 (2012)
8. BSI: Eckpunktepapier - Sicherheitsempfehlungen für Cloud Computing Anbieter - Mindestanforderungen in der Informationssicherheit. Bundesamtes für Sicherheit in der Informationstechnik - BSI, Bonn, Germany (2012)
9. CSA: Security Guidance for Critical Areas of Focus in Cloud Computing V2.1. Cloud Security Alliance - CSA, Seattle, USA (2009)
10. Youseff, L., Butrico, M., Da Silva, D.: Toward a Unified Ontology of Cloud Computing. Paper Presented at the Grid Computing Environments Workshop, Austin, Texas, USA (2008)
11. Pfaff, M., Krcmar, H.: Semantic Integration of Semi-Structured Distributed Data in the Domain of IT Benchmarking. Paper Presented at the 16th International Conference on Enterprise Information Systems (ICEIS), Lisbon, Portugal (2014)
12. Hepp, M.: GoodRelations - The Web Vocabulary for E-Commerce, http://wiki.goodrelations-vocabulary.org/Main_Page
13. ISO/IEC 25010: Systems and software engineering - Systems and software Quality Requirements and Evaluation (SQuaRE), ISO, Geneva, Switzerland (2011)
14. Grönroos, C.: Service Management and Marketing: Customer Management in Service Competition, 3rd edn. John Wiley & Sons, Chichester (2007)
15. Repschlaeger, J., Wind, S., Zarnekow, R., Turowski, K.: Decision Model for Selecting a Cloud Provider: A Study of Service Model Decision Priorities. Paper Presented at the 19th Americas Conference on Information Systems (AMCIS), Chicago, USA (2013)
16. Willcocks, L., Venters, W., Whitley, E.A.: Moving to the Cloud Corporation - How to face the challenges and harness the potential of cloud computing. Palgrave Macmillan, Basingstoke (2014)
17. Yin, R.K.: Case Study Research: Design and Methods, 4th edn. Sage, Thousand Oaks (2009)
18. Paré, G.: Investigating Information Systems with Positivist Case Study Research. Communications of the Association for Information Systems 13, 233–264 (2004)
19. European Commission: The new SME definition, http://ec.europa.eu/enterprise/policies/sme/files/sme_definition/sme_user_guide_en.pdf
20. Morgan, D.L.: The focus group guidebook. Sage, Thousand Oaks (1998)
21. Frey, J.H., Fontana, A.: The group interview in social research. The Social Science Journal 28(2), 175–187 (1991)
22. BSI: IT-Grundschutz-Kataloge. Bundesamt für Sicherheit in der Informationstechnik - BSI, Bonn, Germany (2011)

Exploiting Freebase to Obtain GoodRelations-Based Product Ontologies

Marek Dudáš, Ondřej Zamazal, Jindřich Mynarz, and Vojtěch Svátek

University of Economics, Prague
{xdudm12,ondrej.zamazal,jindrich.mynarz,svatek}@vse.cz

Abstract. Application of semantic web technologies in e-commerce depends on the availability of product ontologies. However, such ontologies are not yet available for many industries and developing them from scratch is costly. We present a method of reusing parts of the Freebase schema by transforming it into a GoodRelations-based product ontology, using our Pattern-based Ontology Transformation Framework. We demonstrate our method on a part of the Freebase Medicine schema, which we transformed into a product ontology covering prescription drugs.

Keywords: ontology development, ontology transformation, non-ontological resources, GoodRelations, product ontology, Freebase.

1 Introduction

It can be expected that a better level of automation in e-commerce can be achieved by annotating product and service data with RDF. Appropriate ontologies or vocabularies, typically expressed in the standard OWL language,[1] are needed for that. GoodRelations (GR) [1] is an ontology covering the relationships between a possible seller, buyer and the product/service offered.[2] GR is supposed to serve as a basis for specific product ontologies that can be created as its vertical extensions.[3] One of the advantages of this approach is that the core structure of a product ontology does not have to be developed from scratch. Another, probably more important, advantage is that if several product ontologies covering different products share the GR basis they can be integrated into an application much easier than if each was created using different modeling style. A software tool working with data annotated with GR-based product ontologies can benefit from the unified modeling style: their code can be simpler when the developers can rely on the fact that all ontologies have the same basic structure (this is explained in more detail in Section 2.1). As the GR itself is already quite widely adopted [2], GR-based product ontologies and data annotated with them

---
[1] http://www.w3.org/TR/owl2-overview/
[2] There is also Schema.org, which has now GR basically integrated as its e-commerce core.
[3] In this paper we call such ontologies "GR-based".

can also be expected to have a better chance of adoption or exploitation than proprietary product ontologies and data. The problem is that such ontologies are not yet available for many industries; it seems that their only reliable sources are currently the 'specific industries' section of the GR cookbook[4] and the ontology collection developed in the OPDM project.[5] Developing a new product ontology from scratch might be very time consuming. Transforming shallow non-ontological models into OWL only saves a fraction of the effort, even if leveraging a specialized framework such as that from [3]. Yet, there are already knowledge models that are both thematically suitable and exhibit a relatively rich structure, and thus are worth considering for this purpose. However, since they do not comply with all Semantic Web best practices, never mind assuring compatibility with pivotal vocabularies such as GoodRelations, a certain kind of transformation is still needed. An outstanding example of this resource is the Freebase schema [4]. In this paper we argue that it is possible to obtain a GR-based product ontology from a part of Freebase with the help of our pattern-based ontology transformation framework [5]; this task can be viewed as a solution of *import-based extrinsic incoherence* ('adapting legacy ontologies to a canonical modeling style') as mentioned in [6]. Specifically, we demonstrate how a part of the Freebase Medicine schema can be transformed into a GR-based prescription drug ontology (the domain was chosen because drugs are usually well-documented in public contracts). The resulting ontology was evaluated by experimental usage in another project, involving matchmaking of public contracts with suppliers [7], where we hope to improve the matchmaking by exploiting product ontologies.

Section 2 contains a summary of principles of GR-based product ontologies and the employed transformation framework. In Section 3 we explain how the transformation has been performed. Section 4 describes the evaluation of the ontology. Section 5 surveys related research, and Section 6 concludes the paper.

2 Exploited Technologies and Resources

2.1 GoodRelations-Based Product Ontologies

Available guidelines for the design of a GR-based product ontology[6] prescribe, among other things, the following:

- all product classes should be subclasses of the *gr:ProductOrService* class
- object properties for specifying product parameters should be subproperties of either *gr:quantitative-* or *gr:qualitativeProductOrServiceProperty*
- subproperties of *gr:quantitativeProductOrServiceProperty* should have range specified to gr:QuantitativeValueFloat or gr:QuantitativeValueInteger
- data properties should be subproperties of *gr:datatypeProductOrService Property* and used only if there is a good reason; even properties with numerical range should be modeled as object properties.

---

[4] http://wiki.goodrelations-vocabulary.org/Cookbook
[5] http://purl.org/opdm
[6] http://wiki.goodrelations-vocabulary.org/Documentation/Extensions

The task of turning a generic ontology covering a product and its properties into a GR-based product ontology is thus mainly in identifying relevant classes and properties, making them subclasses and subproperties of appropriate GR entities, and modifying their range so that the rules such as the above-mentioned are fulfilled.

Such alignment of a product ontology with GR allows for example an easy design of an automatic GUI generator. GUI elements for entering property values can be created automatically according to the parent property: a selection of possible values for subproperties of *gr:qualitativeProductOrServiceProperty*, a number field for subproperties of *gr:quantitativeProductOrServiceProperty*. The latter can also be accompanied with a field for measurement units as there is already a property for specifying those integrated in GR. GR also allows to assign an interval instead of an exact value to a quantitative property. We are developing such GUI generator for an application that will allow entering product specification data to a public contract, but a similar GUI generation principles could be used for e.g. a product search application. In the matchmaking scenario, the property structure can be exploited in comparing product specifications. E.g. different values of a qualitative property indicates different products while a slight difference between two quantitative values might mean that the two products are interchangeable.

2.2 Transformation Framework

The involved transformation framework can be viewed as a more sophisticated variant of using SPARQL updates. It is based on transformation patterns (expressed in XML[7]) consisting of three parts: source ontology pattern, target ontology pattern and pattern transformation. The source pattern describes a fragment that is to be found in the ontology and transformed into the fragment described by the target pattern. The pattern transformation describes how the two fragments are connected. Based on this information the transformation framework computes and applies the necessary ontology updates: axioms and entities are either added or removed. Unlike SPARQL update, however, the transformation can be user-assisted. After the first phase of the transformation, the occurrences (instances) of the source pattern are displayed to the user and it is possible to select only a subset of the instances that are then transformed while the unselected rest are kept intact. We employed this mechanism to select classes representing GR product classes and qualitative classes based on manual analysis of the schema, as we currently do not have an automated way of determining which classes in the ontology have such a meaning.

The framework is available as a Java library.[8] To make its application easier, we developed a graphical user interface, called GUIPOT.

---

[7] The schema for the files is available at http://nb.vse.cz/~svabo/patomat/tp/tp-schema.xsd
[8] http://owl.vse.cz:8080/releases.html

2.3 GUIPOT

GUIPOT is a plugin for Protégé 4.[9] It allows the user to load a transformation pattern and display a list of pattern instances detected in the given ontology. If one or more instances from the list are selected, they are highlighted in a classical Protégé hierarchy view and also visualized in a node-link view on the left part of the plugin window (Figure 1). The visualization can be switched to four different levels of detail. The default one uses OntoGraf[10] and displays classes as nodes with properties as links between them (according to domain/range relationships). A more detailed view where properties and complex relationships between classes (e.g. complementOf) are displayed as separate nodes is implemented using SOVA[11] visualization plugin. SOVA is also used for less detailed overviews of class hierarchy where the class nodes are laid out with spring layout or tree layout algorithms. The detailed views show fragments of the ontology involved in the selected pattern instances. The overviews show the whole ontology with entities involved in the selected pattern instances highlighted.

When the user is satisfied with the selection, s/he just clicks the "Apply Transformation" button. The right part of the window shows the ontology after transformation, with affected entities indicated by red arrows and highlighted or focused in the visualization (analogically to the visualization of selected pattern instances). The transformed ontology can then be loaded into Protégé with a single click and then either edited manually or transformed with another pattern.

3 Transforming the Freebase Schema

3.1 Overview of the Process

The translation of Freebase Schema into RDF is already solved, since Google offers a Freebase RDF dump.[12] To obtain a GR-based product ontology from the dump, we have to select relevant classes and properties and align their modelling style with that indicated in Section 2.1. This can be done in a semi-automated way using the transformation framework in GUIPOT.

Simple pre-processing was needed before the Freebase schema could be loaded as an ontology into Protégé. As the dump is too big (>200GB), we filtered the relevant part of the file using the Linux grep command (exploiting the naming conventions of Freebase – all entities related to one topic have the same prefix in their name). Furthermore, we had to retype the instances of *rdf:Property* to *owl:ObjectProperty* (since all Freebase properties are, syntactically, conceived as object properties, possibly valued by a custom class of, e.g., 'all integers'), using a simple SPARQL update query.

---

[9] http://owl.vse.cz:8080/GUIPOT/
[10] http://protegewiki.stanford.edu/wiki/OntoGraf
[11] http://protegewiki.stanford.edu/wiki/SOVA
[12] https://developers.google.com/freebase/data

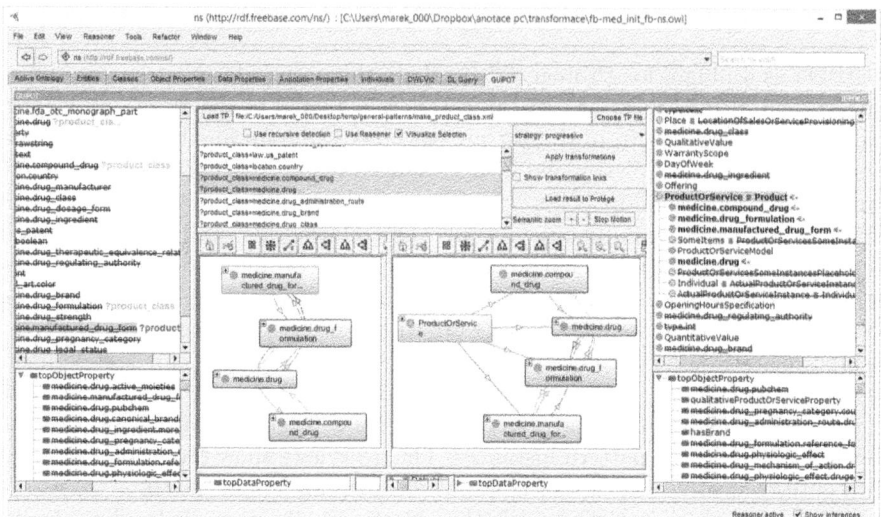

Fig. 1. A screenshot of GUIPOT where the transformation pattern for making selected classes subclasses of gr:ProductOrService is being applied: the left part shows selected instances of the pattern, the right part shows the transformed ontology

We designed 14 transformation patterns[13] for aligning the modelling style of an ontology obtained from Freebase. When they are applied sequentially, they transform the preprocessed (as described above) ontology obtained from Freebase into a GR-based product ontology. The patterns are designed to be reusable on other parts of Freebase schema than the one described in this paper: they should allow the transformation of virtually any Freebase schema part related to a selected product into a GR-based product ontology in a few hours (including the initial schema analysis and the above described preprocessing).

The whole transformation process is shown in Fig. 2. The resulting Drug ontology (DON) has 27 classes, 34 object properties, 17 data properties and 6 individuals, altogether 84 entities described with 715 axioms.

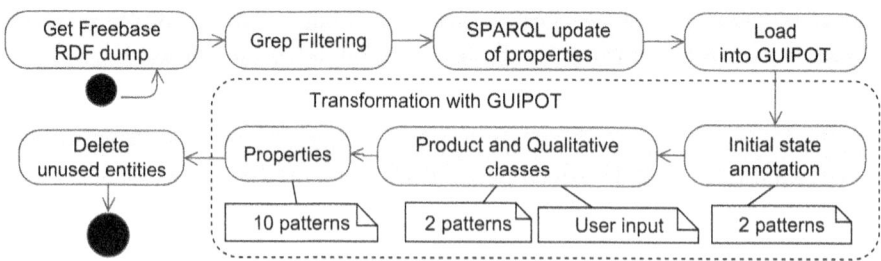

Fig. 2. Diagram of the transformation process

---

[13] All patterns, the transformed ontology and details about the evaluation can be found at http://pages.vse.cz/~xdudm12/ecweb2014/ (or http://bit.ly/1eEP3yL).

3.2 The Transformation Patterns

The first two patterns are 'helper' patterns used to annotate the initial state of the ontology. The annotation is removed from the entities as they are transformed, which allows leaving them out of further transformations and also to delete entities that have not been touched by any transformation at the end of the process; they are not supposed to be part of the product ontology as they have not been selected by any transformation.

The next two patterns require user assistance. A list of all classes is presented to the user and s/he decides which of them are to be transformed into subclasses of *gr:ProductOrService* and *gr:QualitativeValue*.

The application of the fifth pattern leads to transformation of qualitative properties to subproperties of gr:qualitativeProductOrServiceProperty.

The sixth pattern is used to transform qualitative properties in a similar way as the previous pattern. The difference is that in this case, properties with range of a subclass of gr:ProductOrService are transformed. Only two of them are selected, the rest of them represent inverse properties (e.g. "drugs with this formulation" linking a formulation to a drug when there is already a property linking a drug to a formulation) and are not included into the final product ontology to keep it lightweight.

The remaining patterns are designed to transform properties according to their range. They do not require any selection of the pattern instances: all detected instances are transformed. The range is changed from the custom Freebase class (like *type.int* or *type.text*) to either an appropriate GR class (e.g. *gr:QuantitativeValueInteger*) or a datatype. In the latter case, the object property is transformed into a datatype property.

Three of these patterns are more complex and thus are discussed in more detail. Pattern no. 7 finds properties whose range is a class that is a domain for two other properties with ranges of Freebase classes *type.text* and *type.float* where the text property is used to specify units of the value specified by the float property. The same situation is already modeled in GoodRelations and the additional two properties are unnecessary. The former property is transformed into a subproperty of *gr:quantitativeProductOrServiceProperty* with range of *gr:QuantitativeValueFloat* and the other two properties can be removed at the end of the transformation process. Pattern no. 8 transforms properties with range of *type.boolean* into instances of a newly created class *Feature* (subclass of *gr:QualitativeValue*). A property *hasFeature* is created with range set to *Feature*. (Follows modeling style used in Vehicle Sales Ontology[14] – a model example of a GR-based product ontology.) Pattern no. 10 is designed for properties with range of *type.enumeration*: they are made subproperties of *gr:qualitativeProductOrServiceProperty* and their range is changed to a newly created subclass of *gr:QualitativeValue*. A new datatype property is also created with that class as a domain. The intention is to make the values of the property dereferencable. A summary of all transformation patterns is shown in Table 1.

---

[14] http://purl.org/vso

Table 1. Simplified overview describing what entities are transformed by each pattern identified by its number, the last column specifies whether the user has to select the transformed entities manually. Abbreviations are used: 'float' object property means object property with range of type.float (a Freebase class), gr:qualit...Property means gr:qualitativeProductOrServiceProperty etc.

#	Transformed entities	Transformed into	U
1	classes	original state annotation	
2	object properties	original state annotation	
3	selected classes	subclasses of gr:ProductOrService	x
4	selected classes	subclasses of gr:QualitativeValue	x
5	object properties with range of gr:QualitativeClass subclass	subproperties of gr:qualit...Property	
6	object properties with range of gr:ProductOrService subclass	subproperties of gr:qualit...Property	x
7	'float' object properties with unit specification	subproperties of gr:quan...Property with range of gr:QuantitativeValueFloat	
8	'boolean' object properties	instances of class Feature	
9	'datetime' object properties	datatype subproperties of gr:data...Property	
10	'enumeration' object properties	subproperties of gr:qualit...Property	
11	'float' object properties	subproperties of gr:quan...Property with range of gr:QuantitativeValueFloat	
12	'int' object properties	subproperties of gr:quan...Property with range of gr:QuantitativeValueInteger	
13	'rawstring' object properties	datatype subproperties of gr:data...Property	
14	'text' object properties	datatype subproperties of gr:data...Property	

3.3 Example of a Transformation Pattern – Pattern No. 5 in More Detail

The *axioms* part of the source ontology pattern (Figure 3) describes the axioms which the entities and placeholders from *entity_declarations* must fulfill. After the pattern is loaded, the ontology is searched for combinations of entities that when used to instantiate the placeholders hold the axioms. The placeholder ?m represents the qualitative object properties we are looking for. The first two axioms ensures that these properties have the range of a subclass of *gr:QualitativeValue*. Here we exploit the fact that we have already transformed relevant classes into subclasses of *gr:QualitativeValue* with the previous transformation pattern. The third axiom ensures that only the properties that were not yet transformed are taken into account.

The *pattern transformation* (<pt>) part of the target ontology pattern (Figure 4) defines the connection between the source and target ontology pattern. The placeholders are instantiated with the selected instances of the source ontology pattern. Axioms defined in the target ontology pattern (<op2>) are added into the ontology. The most important is the first axiom which makes

```
<entity_declarations>
    <placeholder type="ObjectProperty">?m</placeholder>
    <placeholder type="Class">?range_class</placeholder>
    <entity type="Class">&gr;QualitativeValue</entity>
    <entity type="AnnotationProperty">&owl;deprecated</entity>
</entity_declarations>
<axioms>
    <axiom>ObjectProperty: ?m Range: ?range_class</axiom>
    <axiom>Class: ?range_class SubClassOf: QualitativeValue</axiom>
    <axiom>ObjectProperty: ?m Annotations: deprecated true</axiom>
</axioms>
```

Fig. 3. Source ontology pattern part of the pattern for transformation of qualitative properties

```
<op2>
    <entity_declarations>
        <placeholder type="ObjectProperty">?OP2_m</placeholder>
        <placeholder type="Class">?OP2_range_class</placeholder>
        <entity type="ObjectProperty">
            &gr;qualitativeProductOrServiceProperty</entity>
        <entity type="Class">&gr;QualitativeValue</entity>
        <entity type="AnnotationProperty">&owl;deprecated</entity>
    </entity_declarations>
    <axioms>
        <axiom>ObjectProperty: ?OP2_m SubPropertyOf:
            qualitativeProductOrServiceProperty</axiom>
        <axiom>Class: ?OP2_range_class SubClassOf:
            QualitativeValue</axiom>
        <axiom>ObjectProperty: ?OP2_m Range:
            ?OP2_range_class</axiom>
        <axiom>ObjectProperty: ?OP2_m Annotations:
            deprecated false</axiom>
    </axioms>
</op2>
<pt>
    <eq op1="?m" op2="?OP2_m"/>
    <eq op1="?range_class" op2="?OP2_range_class" />
</pt>
```

Fig. 4. Target ontology pattern (op2) and pattern transformation part (pt) of the pattern for transformation of qualitative properties

the qualitative properties found using the source ontology pattern subproperties of *gr:qualitativeProductOrServiceProperty*. The second and third axioms are there only to keep the range class intact: the standard behaviour of the transformation framework is to remove axioms defined in the source ontology pattern from the ontology. The fourth axiom disables the deprecated annotation on the transformed object property.

3.4 Use Case Lessons Learned for the Transformation Framework

Keeping the Description of the Entity During Its Transformation. When the type of the entity is not changed during its transformation, its annotations (labels, comments etc.) and other axioms describing it are kept intact. In case of *heterogeneous* transformation, when the entity is transformed into an entity of different type, e.g. in case of the pattern no. 8 where an object property is transformed into an instance, all annotations and other axioms related to that entity and not specified in the transformation pattern are removed from the ontology. That might be unpleasant – e.g. the label of a property may be still valid even though the property is transformed into an instance. The only current solution is to explicitly define all annotations and axioms that are to be kept into the transformation pattern. This is not a big issue in case of this Freebase schema transformation as most of the entities that are transformed into different types do not have any annotations. A possible future improvement of the transformation framework related to this issue is to automatically add annotations that would link the new (transformed) entity to the original one.

Instances. So far, we have been focusing on the transformation of the schema (i.e. TBox). The transformation does not deal with existing Freebase instances (i.e. ABox), even though it would obviously be useful to transform the data along with the schema so that the Freebase instances might be reused together with the schema. Adding such functionality to the transformation framework should not be technically difficult and we are currently considering it.

Namespaces. The transformation patterns do not change the prefix of transformed entities - their URI is kept intact. As the transformed entity is obviously not the same as the original entity, its URI should be different. This can be solved easily with Protégé where the namespace of all entities can be changed by one command.

4 Evaluation

4.1 Evaluation by Usage

As the main motivation and purpose of the ontology is its use in our matchmaking project, we made a preliminary evaluation of its coverage by using it experimentally. We manually annotated[15] 10 public contracts (selected as having extensive documentation) focusing on specifications of demanded and offered drugs included in publicly available plain-text documentation of the contracts. Some contracts included more than one drug and each contract had several contenders – 79 instances of *gr:Offering* were created. Only 4 classes and 3 properties from DON were used in the annotation, i.e. approx. 8% of DON was needed to annotate the drugs as described in the documentation. One property was identified as missing and had to be added to DON. Hence, we can say that 8 concepts were needed to annotate the product data (the 4 classes, 3 properties from DON and the one added property) of which 7 were covered by the ontology as extracted from FB, i.e. the ontology covered 87.5% of the specific domain.

4.2 Evaluation by a Group of Test Users

While the previous evaluation was done by the authors of this paper (i.e. expert users), we decided to also test the user-friendliness of DON to lay users in the domain of drug supply public contracts (as the above mentioned 8% exploitation of concepts from DON might indicate it is too complex for our use case). 15 students with basic knowledge of OWL were given a brief (one hour) introduction to GR, DON and Ontowiki and a written manual describing its usage. Then they were asked to annotate one instance of a *gr:Offering* including a drug specified in some public contract (the selection was up to the students) using the same classes and properties as above. 3 students made no apparent mistakes; 4 others only made one mistake in unit specification (they were asked to use UN/CEFACT codes as GR documentation recommends) and were also considered as successful; i.e. about 47% of the students were able to use DON correctly. Furthermore, the mistakes were mostly in the usage of GR; only two errors were in incorrect usage of DON. Each student spent more than an hour creating the annotation, which was mainly caused by technical difficulties with Ontowiki (for this reason, precise time measurement did not make sense). Similar annotations done by an expert user after solving most of the difficulties took about 5–10 minutes each.

4.3 Evaluation against a Similar Ontology

We also measured similarity to a reference ontology by counting precision and recall measures based on [8]. We took part of the RDF representation of Schema.org describing the Drug concept as the reference ontology. To abstract from structural differences between Schema.org and DON, we limited the comparison to properties having as their domain the Schema.org Drug class and properties having as their domain one of the classes representing a drug in DON. The equivalence of the properties was evaluated according to the similarity of their meaning, as defined in their descriptions and comments. Recall was computed as the proportion of properties from the drug part of Schema.org (DSchema) that have an equivalent in DON:

---

[15] Using Ontowiki: http://aksw.org/Projects/OntoWiki.html

$$\frac{(DSchema \cap DON)}{DSchema} = 14/38 \approx 37\%$$

Precision is analogical – the proportion of DON properties that have an equivalent in the drug part of Schema.org :

$$\frac{(DON \cap DSchema)}{DON} = 22/37 \approx 59\%$$

The comparison suggests that basic properties are covered in both schemas. However, the relatively high values might be influenced by the involvement of Google in both Schema.org and Freebase.

5 Related Research

[3] presents guidelines and a pattern-based framework for re-engineering non-ontological resources (NOR), such as classification schemas, into OWL ontologies. The framework is very versatile and might have been even applicable to Freebase proprietary data format if its OWL representation wasn't already available. Our OWL-to-OWL transformation framework might still be useful for the refinement of an ontology produced by the NOR-to-OWL transformation.

A similar project targeted directly on product ontologies is PCS2OWL [9] – a framework for transformation of non-ontological product classifications such as eCl@ss[16] into GR-based product ontologies. Although such classifications sometimes include product properties descriptions and PCS2OWL should allow to transform even those, it focuses mainly on transformation of the product taxonomy. Freebase schema contains richer description of product properties (e.g. including their range) but there is virtually no information about the product class hierarchy. We thus believe that our approach could be combined with PCS2OWL, e.g. by enriching the class taxonomy created with PCS2OWL by properties extracted from Freebase.

A method for transformation of existing knowledge sources into conceptual data models is proposed in [10]. Although it focuses on rather opposite direction of the transformation and shows an example of transformation of an OWL ontology into a Power Designer conceptual model, it also mentions Freebase as a possible resource.

6 Conclusion and Future Work

We have shown that a GR-based product ontology can be obtained from Freebase by extracting a relevant portion of the Freebase RDF dump (using simple text-based filtering with grep) and transforming its modelling style using the pattern-based ontology transformation framework. The preliminary evaluation

---

[16] http://www.eclass.de

suggests that the resulting ontology is not perfect and might need minor manual refinement. However, the usage of the ontology in our specific use case has so far been successful, the ontology seems to be quite easy to use and its similarity to part of Schema.org suggests it covers most of the important concepts from its domain. We plan to do more thorough testing in the future including transformation of more product ontologies and running matchmaking algorithms (from [7]) over the data. We have already extracted mobile phone and digital camera product ontologies from Freebase but these ontologies are yet to be evaluated.

Acknowledgements. This research is supported by VŠE IGA project F4/34/2014 (IG407024) and EU ICT FP7 under No. 257943 (LOD2 project). Ondřej Zamazal has been supported by the CSF grant No. 14-14076P.

References

1. Hepp, M.: GoodRelations: An ontology for describing products and services offers on the web. In: Gangemi, A., Euzenat, J. (eds.) EKAW 2008. LNCS (LNAI), vol. 5268, pp. 329–346. Springer, Heidelberg (2008)
2. Ashraf, J., Cyganiak, R., O'Riain, S., Hadzic, M.: Open ebusiness ontology usage: Investigating community implementation of goodrelations. In: LDOW (2011)
3. Villazón-Terrazas, B., Gómez-Pérez, A.: Reusing and re-engineering non-ontological resources for building ontologies. In: Ontology Engineering in a Networked World, pp. 107–145. Springer (2012)
4. Bollacker, K., Evans, C., Paritosh, P., Sturge, T., Taylor, J.: Freebase: a collaboratively created graph database for structuring human knowledge. In: Proceedings of the 2008 ACM SIGMOD International Conference on Management of Data, pp. 1247–1250. ACM (2008)
5. Šváb-Zamazal, O., Svátek, V., Iannone, L.: Pattern-based ontology transformation service exploiting OPPL and OWL-API. In: Cimiano, P., Pinto, H.S. (eds.) EKAW 2010. LNCS, vol. 6317, pp. 105–119. Springer, Heidelberg (2010)
6. Dudáš, M., Svátek, V., Török, L., Zamazal, O., Rodriguez-Castro, B., Hepp, M.: Semi-automated structural adaptation of advanced E-commerce ontologies. In: Huemer, C., Lops, P. (eds.) EC-Web 2013. LNBIP, vol. 152, pp. 51–58. Springer, Heidelberg (2013)
7. Nečaský, M., Klímek, J., Mynarz, J., Knap, T., Svátek, V., Stárka, J.: Linked data support for filing public contracts. Computers in Industry (2014)
8. Maedche, A.: Ontology learning for the semantic Web. Kluwer Academic Publishers (2002)
9. Stolz, A., Rodriguez-Castro, B., Radinger, A., Hepp, M.: PCS2OWL: A generic approach for deriving web ontologies from product classification systems. In: Presutti, V., d'Amato, C., Gandon, F., d'Aquin, M., Staab, S., Tordai, A. (eds.) ESWC 2014. LNCS, vol. 8465, pp. 644–658. Springer, Heidelberg (2014)
10. Trinkunas, J., Vasilecas, O.: Ontology transformation: From requirements to conceptual model. Scientific Papers, University of Latvia, Computer Science and Information Technologies 751, 52–64 (2009)

Modelling and Linking Transformations in EPCIS Governing Supply Chain Business Processes

Monika Solanki and Christopher Brewster

Aston Business School
Aston University, UK
{m.solanki,c.a.brewster}@aston.ac.uk

Abstract. Supply chains comprise of complex processes spanning across multiple trading partners. The various operations involved generate large number of events that need to be integrated in order to enable internal and external traceability. Further, provenance of artifacts and agents involved in the supply chain operations is now a key traceability requirement. In this paper we propose a Semantic web/Linked data powered framework for the event based representation and analysis of supply chain activities governed by the EPCIS specification. We specifically show how a new EPCIS event type called "Transformation Event" can be semantically annotated using EEM - The EPCIS Event Model to generate linked data, that can be exploited for internal event based traceability in supply chains involving transformation of products. For integrating provenance with traceability, we propose a mapping from EEM to PROV-O. We exemplify our approach on an abstraction of the production processes that are part of the wine supply chain.

Keywords: Supply chains, EPCIS, Transformation events, ontologies, Semantic Web, Linked data.

1 Introduction and Motivation

Data integration in supply chains for the purposes of tracking, tracing and transparency is increasingly becoming an important challenge. Barcodes and more recently RFID tags have provided initial solutions to this challenge by recording the traces of product movement as specific occurrences of "events". Some examples of supply chain events include: receiving or shipping of goods, aggregating small units into large consignments, storing goods on a specific shelf in a specific store at a specific business location, transactions carried out on a specific quantity of goods and more recently production of new artifacts from existing ones via the process of transformation.

The Electronic Product Code Information Services (EPCIS)[1] and the Core Business Vocabulary[2], are event oriented specifications prescribed by GS1[3] for enabling traceability [3] in supply chains. The data associated with the business context of scanning a barcode or RFID tag is encapsulated within the abstraction of an "EPCIS event".

Recently the EPCIS specification has been revised and a new event type "Transformation Event" has been introduced. Transformation events capture information that are part of an event or a series of events in which one or more physical objects are consumed as inputs to produce one or more outputs. Transformation events are mostly likely to be recorded and utilised in a production/manufacturing scenario where internal operations need to be tracked to guarantee product safety, increase consumer confidence and improve the overall traceability of the supply chain.

Agri-food is one of the most important sectors which could benefit from enabling transformation event based internal traceability. Transformation events when recorded using self describing metadata descriptors in a format that enables sharing and linking of information, could provide valuable insights while investigating and identifying causes of food outbreaks and epidemics. Event based traceability information made available as linked data could seamlessly enable tracing back from finished goods to processing facilities, ingredients and even further back to the crop growing and cattle harvesting conditions in the farm.

In this paper we present a framework for the formal modelling and representation of transformation events in supply chain business processes. We extend EEM(EPCIS Event Model)[4] - our domain model for representing supply chain, EPCIS events on the Web of data to include transformation events As provenance is a crucial aspect of traceability, we present a mapping of key entities in EEM and its supporting vocabulary, CBVVocab[5] into entities from the PROV-O[6] ontology for provenance interchange on the Web. Finally we show how the integrated datasets can be interrogated by exploiting inferences over expressive characteristics of relationships asserted between event instances and SPARQL 1.1 features such as property chaining. Our exemplifying scenario is an abstraction of the steps involved in the production of wines within the wine supply chain.

The paper is structured as follows: Section 2 presents our motivating scenario. Section 3 provides a brief background on the conceptual model behind EEM and presents related work. Section 4 illustrates the modelling of transformation events. Section 5 presents a mapping of EEM entities to PROV-O. Section 6 presents our traceability architecture and formalisation of the queries for our motivating scenario. Section 7 presents conclusions.

---

[1] http://www.gs1.org/gsmp/kc/epcglobal/epcis
[2] http://www.gs1.org/gsmp/kc/epcglobal/cbv
[3] http://www.gs1.org/
[4] http://purl.org/eem#
[5] http://purl.org/cbv#
[6] http://www.w3.org/ns/prov-o

2 Data Integration in the Wine Supply Chain

We present a scenario from the processing stages of wines in a winery, which is an integral part of the wine supply chain. As illustrated in Figure 1, the process of transforming grapes into bottled wines involves the following main operations: *Grapes pressing*, *Musts treatment*, *Fermentation*, *Blending* and *Bottling*.

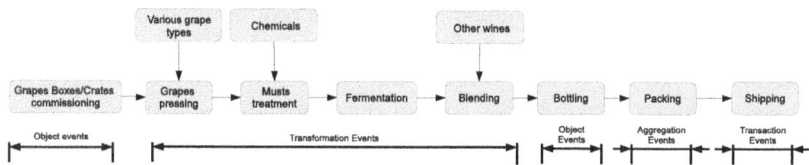

Fig. 1. EPCIS events generated during the wine processing stages

At each of these stages, event based data (timing, location and business context) recorded for the transformation events, have to be integrated with process related information such as data about the inputs and machinery used in the processing, environmental variables such as temperature and humidity, data about the tanks used for the storage of intermediate products, quantities and measurements of the inputs consumed and outputs produced. Besides linking to the data from the transformation processes, data on bottled wine also needs to be linked to the meteorological and botanical information on the grapes used in its production. Some data is entirely internal to the winery such as the temperature of a given vat at a given time, other data is external such as that provided by laboratory tests or data about the soil conditions of vineyards, not all of which may owned by a particular winery.

In order to derive traceability information, the integrated datasets need to be appropriately reasoned about and interrogated against the traceability metrics. While, there is a possibility that some information, e..g, provenance of grapes used in the production could be made available without querying the interlinked knowledge base, for realising event based traceability, the queries need to be formulated such that the information retrieved is directly associated to an EPCIS event, i.e., the fact that specific boxes/crates of grapes were actually used in the production of wines has to be derived by querying for transformation events that utilised the grapes in those boxes/crates as inputs and following the typed links to extract the information from the event instances.

Here we provide some examples of informal queries for deriving traceability information from the integrated datasets at the winery:

Q1 **Tracking Ingredients:** What were the inputs consumed during processing in the batch of wine bottles shipped on date X ?
Q2 **Tracking Provenance:** Which winery staff were present at the winery when the wine bottles were aggregated in cases with identifiers X and Y?

Q3 **Tracking External Data:** Retrieve the average values for the growth temperature for grapes used in the production of a batch of wine to be shipped to Destination D on date X.

3 Background and Related Work

An Electronic Product Code (EPC) [7] is a universal identifier that gives a unique, serialised identity to a specific physical object. As the RFID-EPC tagged object moves through the supply chain, EPCIS implementing applications deployed at key locations record data against the EPC of the object.

EEM is an OWL 2 DL ontology for modelling EPCIS events. EEM conceptualises various primitives of an EPCIS event that need to be asserted for the purposes of traceability in supply chains. A companion standard to EPCIS is the Core Business Vocabulary(CBV) standard. The CBV standard supplements the EPCIS framework by defining vocabularies and identifiers that may populate the EPCIS data model. *CBVVocab*[8] is an OWL ontology that defines entities corresponding to the identifiers in CBV. Development of both the ontologies was informed by a thorough review of the EPCIS and the CBV specifications and extensive discussions with trading partners implementing the specification. The modelling decisions [11] behind the conceptual entities in EEM highlight the EPCIS abstractions included in the ontology. The EEM ontology structure and its alignment with

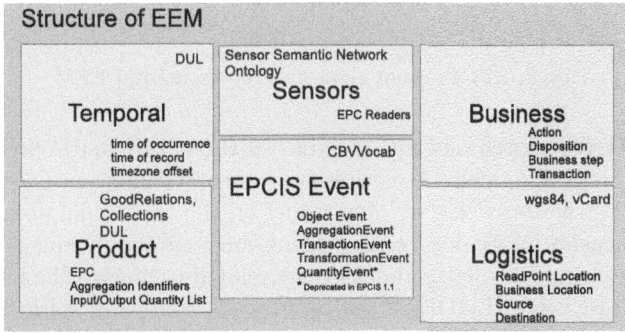

Fig. 2. Structure of EEM and its alignment with external ontologies (noted in blue coloured text)

various external ontologies is illustrated in Figure 2. The ontology is composed of modules that define various perspectives on EPCIS. The *Temporal* module captures timing properties associated with an EPCIS event. It is aligned with temporal properties in DOLCE+DnS Ultralite (DUL)[9]. Entities defining the

---

[7] http://www.gs1.org/gsmp/kc/epcglobal/tds/tds_1_6-RatifiedStd-20110922.pdf
[8] http://purl.org/cbv#
[9] http://ontologydesignpatterns.org/ont/dul/DUL.owl

EPC, aggregation of EPCs and quantity lists for transformation events are part of the *Product* module. The GoodRelations[10] ontology is exploited here for capturing concepts such as an Individual Product or a lot (collection) of items, SomeItems of a single type. Information about the business context associated with an EPCIS event is encoded using the entities and relationships defined in the *Business* module. RFID readers and sensors are defined in the *Sensor* module. The definitions here are aligned with the SSN[11] ontology.

Some of the main conceptual entities in EEM are illustrated in Figure 3. EEM defines a generic event class and four specialised event classes. EPCISEvent is the "abstract" root or super class of all events. ObjectEvent, AggregationEvent, QuantityEvent[12], TransactionEvent and TransformationEvent are specialised classes of EPCISEvent. For further details on EEM and its applications in real world scenarios, the interested reader is referred to [10, 11].

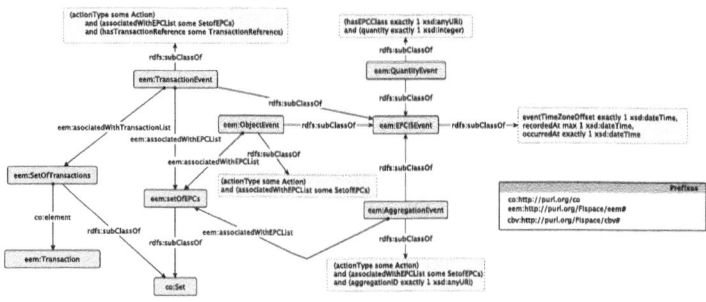

Fig. 3. EPCIS event classes as represented in EEM

Semantic Web research has widely explored the notion and representation of events as ontological models. A plethora of interpretations can be derived from and assigned to the term "Event" depending on the contextual domain and the temporal dimension of its occurrence. The Event ontology[13] emerged from the need of representing knowledge about events related to music. The Linking Open Descriptions of Events (LODE) [14] [9] ontology is similar in spirit to the EEM in that it focuses on the four factual aspects of an event. The Simple Event Model (SEM)[15], with weak semantics and requirements drawn from the domain of history and maritime security and safety is presented in [13]. In contrast to some of the general purpose event models, EEM is domain specific. For practical purposes, the data model underlying EEM, restricts the entities, relationship and attributes to a subset of the EPCIS specification, albeit a large subset.

---

[10] http://purl.org/goodrelations/v1
[11] http://purl.oclc.org/NET/ssnx/ssn
[12] Deprecated in the revised version of EPCIS
[13] http://motools.sourceforge.net/event/event.html
[14] http://linkedevents.org/ontology/
[15] http://semanticweb.cs.vu.nl/2009/11/sem/

Tracking and tracing of food products through the supply chain has become a major issue both for research and practice in the industry. Thompson et al. provide an excellent overview of the area, even if focussed on seafood, and discuss the potential of a number of technologies [12]. One of the important points is that because tracking and tracing is mandated by law, legal frameworks in one region of the world, say the EU, impact food producers all over the world because of the interlinked nature of food systems. Fritz and Schiefer provide a more recent perspective on the importance and complexity of tracking and tracing systems [4] and consider a number of technologies including RFID and what role they can play. Ruiz-Garcia et al. [8] present a software architecture for managing tracking and tracing in a web-based system. Their approach makes use of OGC standards rather than GS1 standards.

The use of RFID technology in tracking and tracing in agri-food has its origins in livestock tracking (since the 1980s). Much recent work has explored how RFID tags can be used in various agri-food sectors such as the cold chain [1], halal food [2], and perishable foods [5,6]. An analysis of the use of RFIDs and EPCIS on food tracablity is provided in [7]. However, despite the widespread interest and concern, little work has focused on utilising Semantic Web standards and linked data technologies for the representation of supply chain events and traceability in the agri-food sector.

4 Extending EEM with Transformation Events

Transformation events capture information that is part of an event or a series of events in which one or more physical objects are consumed as inputs to produce one or more outputs.

The informal semantics of transformation events as described in the revised EPCIS specification are outlined below:

- A *TransformationEvent* captures information about an event in which one or more physical or digital objects are fully or partially consumed as inputs and one or more objects are produced as outputs.
- Input and output objects are identified through their serialised EPCs and/or quantity lists that define the quantities of the objects, the EPCClass (lot or batch identifiers) and the units of measurements.
- Some transformation business processes take place over a long period of time, and so it is more appropriate to represent them as a series of associated EPCIS events.
- The revised EPCIS specification defines a special attribute called "TransformationID" that provides the association between related transformation events. It is included as a common attribute among the events that are involved in realising a collective operation.
- When a specific transformation event is associated with other transformation events, the inputs to any of those events may have contributed in some way to each of the outputs in any of those same events. In this scenario, it is not mandatory to provide inputs and outputs for all the participating events.

- However, if a transformation event is not associated with any other transformation event, then it is mandatory for the event to define either the input EPCs or the input quantity list and the output EPCs or the output quantity list.

A `TransformationEvent` is an `EPCISEvent`. Input and Outputs EPCs lists for transformation events are represented as `SetOFEPCs`, specialising from `Set`[16].

Quantity attributes for input and output objects are represented as `QuantityElement` that specialises from `item`[17]. It has an `EPCClass` identifier and specifies a quantity along with its unit of measurement. We propose the use of vocabularies such as QUDT[18] for defining quantities and units of measurement that form a `QuantityElement`.

`InputQuantityList` and `OutputQuantityList` are composed of `QuantityElement` individuals. The EPCIS specification does not impose any ordering constraints on the elements in the list. We therefore define the lists as specialising from `bag`[19] rather than a list[20].

A `TransformationEvent` may be associated with other transformation events. While TransformationID is prescribed as the relating attribute, we believe that in the context of ontologies as data models, relationships between resources are the key enablers of data integration and therefore instead of including the "TransformationID" as a literal in the definition of the event, we introduce a special predicate that enables the association between events. We define an object property `associatedWithTransformtionEvent`, characterised as symmetric and transitive, that defines the relationship between transformation events.

We incorporate the constrains on the inputs and outputs as highlighted above and assert the following definition of a `TransformationEvent`:

```
Class: TransformationEvent
SubClassOf:
((EPCISEvent
  and (associatedWithTransformationEvent only TransformationEvent)
  and ((associatedWithInputEPCList only SetofEPCs)
  or   (hasInputQuantityList only InputQuantityList))
  or ((associatedWithOutputEPCList only SetofEPCs)
  or   (hasOutputQuantityList only OutputQuantityList)))
  or (EPCISEvent
  and (((associatedWithInputEPCList some SetofEPCs)
  or   (hasInputQuantityList some InputQuantityList))
  and ((associatedWithOutputEPCList some SetofEPCs)
  or   (hasOutputQuantityList some OutputQuantityList)))))
```

---

[16] http://purl.org/co/
[17] http://purl.org/co/item#
[18] http://qudt.org/1.1/vocab/dimensionalunit
[19] http://purl.org/co/bag#
[20] http://purl.org/co/list#

5 Augmenting Event Descriptions with Provenance

Provenance in the wine supply chain is of critical importance. While many of the entities in EEM implicitly provide provenance related information about an event, mapping these entities to a dedicated provenance vocabulary such as PROV-O[21], provides an abstraction layer that facilitates retrieving information using a vocabulary specifically defined for that purpose.

Table 1 illustrates the mapping[22] between the key concepts in EEM and CBVVocab to entities in PROV-O.

Table 1. Mapping EEM and CBVVocab to PROVO-O

EEM entity	mapping	PROV-O concept
EPCISEvent	rdfs:subClassOf	Entity
EPC	rdfs:subClassOf	Entity
EPCReader	rdfs:subClassOf	Agent
Action	rdfs:subClassOf	Activity
ReadPointLocation	rdfs:subClassOf	Location
recordedByReader	rdfs:subPropertyOf	wasAttributedTo
eventOccurredAt	rdfs:subPropertyOf	generatedAtTime
hasReadPointLocation	rdfs:subPropertyOf	atLocation
CBV entity	mapping	PROV-O concept
BusinessStep	rdfs:subClassOf	Activity

Mapping Action to Activity associates it with a PROV Agent through the wasAssociatedWith relationship. This provides us with the capability to assert facts about entities involved in carrying out an Action, recorded as part of an event description. The practical implication of this mapping wrt. the scenario outlined in Section 2 is that winery staff involved in carrying out the processing of wines can be linked to the events themselves. This information could be extremely useful in investigating claims of counterfeit wines being introduced in the supply chain.

6 Linking Transformation Events

Figure 4 illustrates our framework for generating linked data from legacy data sources that are part of the information system deployed at the winery.

From RDB to RDF for Events in the Winery

We acquired data from an RFID winery pilot currently running in Spain. The datasets were originally stored in a MySQL relational database. As the original

---
[21] http://www.w3.org/ns/prov-o
[22] http://fispace.aston.ac.uk/ontologies/eem_prov.html

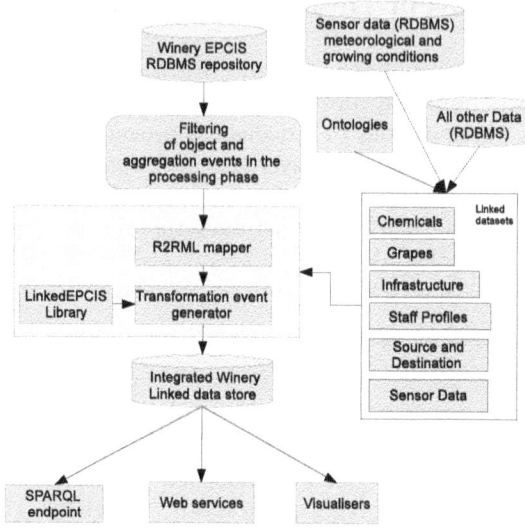

Fig. 4. Generating and interlinking transformation events

datasets were curated when transformation events were not yet a part of the EPCIS specification, the EPCIS events raised during the processing phase were recorded as aggregation events or object events.

We implemented an "Event filtering" component that filtered the events recorded during the processing phase from the database. The filtering algorithm took into consideration the time between event occurrence, the disposition type and the business step type defined for an event in order to filter it as a transformation event.

We wrote an R2RML[23] mapping script to map the relational database entries and generate linked data using the EEM and CBVVocab ontologies. The process of mapping took into consideration the integration with the other datasets and generated corresponding transformation events as linked data.

Integrating Event Data with Supporting Data

As highlighted in Section 2, in order to achieve full traceability, event data needs to be integrated with supporting data that contextualises the events. Traceability data being commercially sensitive, most trading partners are wary[24] of sharing it outside their B2B setup. Based on representative data from the pilot, we generated synthetic linked datasets for supply chain artifacts such as: grapes, the environmental parameters (sensor data) under which they were grown, equipment used in the processing stages from grape pressing to bottling, chemicals

---

[23] http://www.w3.org/TR/r2rml/
[24] Due to this constraint, we are unable to reproduce the actual real-time product, infrastructure and environmental datasets in this paper.

used in the treatment of wines, volumes of outputs produced at each stage, profiles of winery staff and final destinations for the wines.

The integrated datasets were stored in a triple store (OWLIM-SE 5.4.686) to be queried later for traceability information. The linked data generation and query applications were built using our LinkedEPCIS[25] library which provides a Java API and a reference implementation for capturing EPCIS events as linked data.

Traceability Queries

Section 2 highlighted some informal traceability queries for the winery scenario. We formalised those queries in SPARQL 1.1 and executed them against our integrated linked data store for the winery.

- **Tracking Ingredients(Q1):** The query illustrates the usage of reasoning with querying via the transitive and symmetric characteristics of the object property `associatedWithTransformationEvent` and the property path feature of SPARQL 1.1 on the property chain "item o itemContent". A single query allows us to recursively retrieve all the inputs associated with a set of transformation events.

```
PREFIX eem: <http://purl.org/eem#>
PREFIX co:  <http://purl.org/co/>
PREFIX prov: <http://www.w3.org/ns/prov#>
PREFIX ssn: <http://purl.oclc.org/NET/ssnx/ssn#>
SELECT ?input1 ?input2 WHERE{
      ?event1 a eem:TransformationEvent;
              eem:associatedWithTransformationEvent ?event2;
              eem:eventOccurredAt ?occurred;
              eem:hasInputQuantityList ?iql1;
      ?iql1   co:item/co:itemContent ?input1.
      ?event2 eem:eventOccurredAt ?occurred;
              eem:hasInputQuantityList ?iql2.
      ?iq2    co:item /co:itemContent ?input2.}
```

- **Tracking Provenance(Q2):** The query highlights the use of our mapping between the PROV-O ontology and EEM to track the provenance of the winery staff present when the wines bottles are aggregated.

```
SELECT ?staff ?x WHERE{
   ?event  a prov:Entity;
           eem:hasAggregationURI ?x;
           eem:action ?action.
   ?action prov:wasAssociatedWith ?staff.}
```

- **Tracking External Data(Q3):** The query shows end-to-end traceability where information is recursively traced back from the transaction/shipping event to the growth temperature in the location where the grapes were grown.

---

[25] https://github.com/nimonika/LinkedEPCIS

```
SELECT ?temperature WHERE{
  ?event a eem:TransactionEvent;
         eem:destination ?d;
         eem:eventOccurredAt ?x;
         eem:associatedWithEPCList ?epcTList.
  ?epcTList co:element ?epcAgg.
  ?aevent a eem:AggregationEvent;
          eem:hasAggregationURI ?epcAgg.
          eem:associatedWithEPCList ?epcList.
  ?tevent a eem:TransformationEvent.
          eem:associatedWithOutputEPCs ?epcOutList;
          eem:hasInputQuantityList ?qtyInList;
          ?qtyInList co:item/co:itemContent ?input.
  ?input a GrapeVariety;
         gr:grownAt ?loc;
  ?loc   a prov:Location.
  ?sensor a ssn:SensingDevice;
          prov:atLocation ?loc;
          ssn:madeObservation ?temp.
   ?temp  ssn:hasValue    ?tempValue.
  BIND (AVG(?tempValue) AS ?temperature)}
```

7 Conclusions

Little work has been done so far in the SW/LD community for the representation of traceability information in supply chain business processes. The representation of EPCIS events in an unambiguous and machine interpretable way is an important step towards achieving the objectives of sharing and interlinking traceability information both within organisations and among trading partners in a supply chain. In order to realise the vision, we have developed: EEM, an OWL DL ontology which incorporates the primitives required to represent EPCIS events using Semantic Web standards and linked data principles and LInkedEPCIS, a library for generating linked data based on types and typed links from EEM.

In this paper we have extended EEM with a new EPCIS event type, "TransformationEvent" that enables internal traceability, specifically in the production and manufacturing sectors, by providing the types and relationships to record the inputs consumed and outputs produced over a series of related processing stages. As provenance is a key requirement for tracking and tracing solutions, we have mapped EEM to PROV-O. Finally we have exemplified our approach for the wine supply chain where we develop an infrastructure for generating linked data from legacy sources and deriving traceability information using reasoning. Work is currently in progress on implementing a linked traceability monitor that provides relevant warnings in real time when an anomaly in the processing stages is detected, by monitoring the transformation events.

Acknowledgements. The research described in this paper has been partially supported by the EU FP7 FI PPP projects, SmartAgriFood (http://smartagrifood.eu) and FISpace http://www.fispace.eu/

The authors would like to thank Prof. Iñigo Cuiñas (Universidade de Vigo, Spain) for providing us the winery EPCIS datasets which forms the basis of this paper.

References

1. Abad, E., Palacio, F., Nuin, M., de Zárate, A.G., Juarros, A., Gómez, J., Marco, S.: RFID smart tag for traceability and cold chain monitoring of foods: Demonstration in an intercontinental fresh fish logistic chain. Journal of Food Engineering 93(4), 394–399 (2009)
2. Anir, N.A., Nizam, M.N.M.H., Masliyana, A.: The users perceptions and opportunities in Malaysia in introducing rfid system for halal food tracking. WSEAS Trans. Info. Sci. and App. 5(5), 843–852 (2008)
3. Främling, K., Parmar, S., Hinkka, V., Tätilä, J., Rodgers, D.: Assessment of EPCIS standard for interoperable tracking in the supply chain. In: Borangiu, T., Thomas, A., Trentesaux, D. (eds.) Service Orientation in Holonic and Multi Agent. SCI, vol. 472, pp. 119–134. Springer, Heidelberg (2013)
4. Fritz, M., Schiefer, G.: Tracking, tracing, and business process interests in food commodities: A multi-level decision complexity. International Journal of Production Economics 117(2), 317–329 (2009)
5. Grunow, M., Piramuthu, S.: RFID in highly perishable food supply chains remaining shelf life to supplant expiry date? International Journal of Production Economics 146(2), 717–727 (2013)
6. Piramuthu, S., Farahani, P., Grunow, M.: Rfid-generated traceability for contaminated product recall in perishable food supply networks. European Journal of Operational Research 225(2), 253–262 (2013)
7. Ringsberg, H.A., Mirzabeiki, V.: Effects on logistic operations from rfid- and epcis-enabled traceability. British Food Journal 116(1), 104–124 (2014)
8. Ruiz-Garcia, L., Steinberger, G., Rothmund, M.: A model and prototype implementation for tracking and tracing agricultural batch products along the food chain. Food Control 21(2), 112–121 (2010)
9. Shaw, R., Troncy, R., Hardman, L.: LODE: Linking Open Descriptions of Events. In: Gómez-Pérez, A., Yu, Y., Ding, Y. (eds.) ASWC 2009. LNCS, vol. 5926, pp. 153–167. Springer, Heidelberg (2009)
10. Solanki, M., Brewster, C.: Consuming Linked data in Supply Chains: Enabling data visibility via Linked Pedigrees. In: Fourth International Workshop on Consuming Linked Data (COLD 2013) at ISWC, vol. 1034. CEUR-WS.org Proceedings (2013)
11. Solanki, M., Brewster, C.: Representing Supply Chain Events on the Web of Data. In: Workshop on Detection, Representation, and Exploitation of Events in the Semantic Web (DeRiVE) at ISWC. CEUR-WS.org Proceedings (2013)
12. Thompson, M., Sylvia, G., Morrissey, M.T.: Seafood traceability in the United States: Current trends, system design, and potential applications. Comprehensive Reviews in Food Science and Food Safety 4(1), 1–7 (2005)
13. van Hage, W.R., Malais, V., Segers, R., Hollink, L., Schreiber, G.: Design and use of the Simple Event Model (SEM). Web Semantics: Science, Services and Agents on the World Wide Web 9(2), 128–136 (2011)

Validator and Preview for the JobPosting Data Model of Schema.org

Jindřich Mynarz

Department of Information and Knowledge Engineering,
University of Economics, W. Churchill Sq. 4, 130 67 Prague 3, Czech Republic
jindrich.mynarz@vse.cz

Abstract. The paper describes a tool for validating and previewing instances of Schema.org JobPosting described in structured data markup embedded in web pages. The validator and preview was developed to assist users of Schema.org to produce data of better quality. The paper discusses the implementation of the tool and design of its validation rules based on SPARQL 1.1. Results of experimental validation of a job posting corpus harvested from the Web are presented. The validation's findings indicate that publishers of Schema.org JobPosting data often misunderstand precedence rules employed by markup parsers and ignore case-sensitivity of vocabulary names.

Keywords: data validation, HTML markup, Schema.org, SPARQL 1.1.

1 Introduction

Usability of linked data vocabularies can be enhanced by tools. Tools can provide users with feedback on their use of a vocabulary. Validators, for instance, can automate a part of vocabulary conformance checking. Validation rules can be considered as an additional vocabulary level, as they can make explicit some of the assumptions of vocabulary creators and thus provide better guidance to vocabulary users. Following similar reasoning, Kontokostas et al. argue that *"vocabularies, ontologies and knowledge bases should be accompanied by a number of test-cases, which help to ensure a basic level of quality"* [2].

Validators can support vocabulary users in providing better input for harvesters of structured data. Validation rules can capture application-specific requirements for data collected by the harvesters. For example, a lot of search engines and social networks already provide validators for checking the structured data they accept.[1]

The topic of data validation is well explored, even though for RDF data there is a lack of established standards for validation. To get an overview of the current efforts in RDF validation W3C convened the RDF Validation Workshop [3] that

---

[1] For example, Google's Structured Data Testing Tool (http://www.google.com/webmasters/tools/richsnippets) or Facebook's URL debugger (https://developers.facebook.com/tools/debug).

yielded submissions mapping approaches to testing integrity constraints on RDF data, many of which were based on SPARQL and some offered validators for Schema.org data [4].

This paper describes a validator and preview for instances of Schema.org's JobPosting.[2] The main reason for developing the presented tool was twofold. While validation should serve Schema.org users to suggest where data quality can be improved, preview should show how much structured data can be recovered from given HTML markup.

The principal use case for the described tool is the DámePráci.eu project,[3] which is focused on online job market. The proposed means to achieve the aims of the project are based on leveraging structured data embedded in web pages. In order to make data integration from multiple sources feasible, the project encourages publishers of job postings to enrich their web sites with the Schema.org JobPosting markup. Moreover, to improve the Schema.org's coverage of the job market domain an extension of the core vocabulary was proposed.[4] Even though the validator and preview are based on validation rules that are specific to its application in the DámePráci.eu project, most of the employed rules are general and applicable to any web pages instantiating Schema.org JobPosting. As of late 2013, Schema.org data could be found in around 15 % of web pages contained in Google's search index [5], while a large share of these pages featured JobPosting markup,[5] which indicates that the tool may be relevant to a wider audience.

The following sections describe the JobPosting validator and preview, covering the method it is based on, its implementation, design of validation rules and experimental application on a corpus of job postings.

2   Validation Method and Its Implementation

The described tools employs rule-based approach to validation. Validation rules are expressed as SPARQL CONSTRUCT queries that check absence of erroneous graph patterns in the validated data. If the rule's pattern matches the processed data, RDF graph describing the detected violation is produced by the body of CONSTRUCT query form. Violations of validation rules are described using the SPIN RDF vocabulary.[6]

Validation rules are supplemented with a background knowledge base, which is loaded with Schema.org data model and additional named graphs with enumerations, including ISO 4217 currency codes and ISO 639-1 language codes. Access to the background knowledge base for validation rules allows them to perform schema-aware validation without the need to encode schema constrains into the rules.

---

[2] http://schema.org/JobPosting
[3] http://damepraci.eu/
[4] http://www.w3.org/wiki/WebSchemas/JobMarket
[5] Extraction of Common Crawl from November 2013 by Web Data Commons reported to have found 21 million instances of schema:JobPosting in Microdata markup only (http://webdatacommons.org/structureddata/2013-11/stats/stats.html).
[6] http://spinrdf.org/

Complementing the validation functionality, the JobPosting *preview* offers a human-readable view of the extracted data. Based on visual inspection of the preview results users may find syntactic errors in their markup that cause some marked-up data to be missing from the preview. Design of the preview uses tree layout and is heavily inspired by existing tools, such as Google's Structured Data Testing Tool.

A demo instance of the JobPosting validator and preview can be found at http://validator.damepraci.cz, while its source code is available at https://github.com/OPLZZ/job-posting-validator.

3 Validation Rules

Development of the validator's rules proceeded from an initial sample of web pages annotated with schema:JobPosting markup, so that rules applicable in practice are prioritized. The sample consisted of 15 web pages to which RDFa Lite markup was added by 10 students of New media studies at the Charles University in Prague. As the developement of validation rules was mostly driven by examples of empirical data, no relation to formal data quality metrics was intended. The rules focus on semantic errors, albeit these are frequently caused by incorrect markup syntax. Non-recoverable syntax errors are caught either by RDFa parser or SPARQL 1.1 query parser and reported to users, skipping the execution of further validation rules.

A general direction in the design of validation rules was to assume open world semantics and limit errors to contradictions. This approach differs from some of the existing validation tools that reinterpret ontology axioms *"via integrity constraint semantics, which uses a closed world assumption and a weaker form of the unique names assumption in which two individuals are considered to be different unless they are explicitly stated to be equal"* [2]. However, the chosen design intent is not a strict requirement for all validation rules, some of which adopt the closed world intepretation of the underlying JobPosting data model. In the following part, we discuss how different aspects of data quality are covered by the developed rules.

Data Completeness. The validator has only a single requirement for the content of data and that is to have at least 1 instance of the schema:JobPosting class. Other type information, including class instantiations and explicit datatypes, is treated as optional. However, the validation rules report empty literal values, as they likely indicate an ommission by the data publisher. Some data is required conditionally, depending on existence of other data. It is the case of qualifiers, such as currency associated with compensation offered for the described job posting, that are required in presence of data that needs to be qualified. For example, if compensation value is provided, currency needs to be stated as well, as compensation value is meaningless without a unit given by currency.

Distinction between Datatype and Object Properties. Validation rules detect object properties used with literal values and datatype properties given URIs or blank nodes as their object. Ignored or confused distinction between datatype and object properties may be an indication that the markup authors prefer simpler syntax of datatype properties in order to avoid expressing more complex nested objects or skip difficulties with finding objects' URIs, but it can also be a symptom of incorrect nesting of HTML elements.

Conflicting Data. Three basic cases of conflicting data are checked by the validation rules. Use of mutually-exclusive properties is reported; e.g., JobPosting must not have both `schema:location` and `schema:isRemoteWork` with the object set to `true`. Cardinality violation is reported for functional properties; e.g., more than one value of the `schema:startDate` property. Third case of conflicting data is covered by a validation rule that tests incompatible class membership inferences based on `schema:domainIncludes` and `schema:rangeIncludes` axioms. In this case, `schema:domainIncludes` and `schema:rangeIncludes` do not have any inference semantics defined, so they are reinterpreted with the inference rules of `rdfs:domain` and `rdfs:range`. For the purposes of validation, we assume incompatible class membership to be defined as membership in two or more distinct classes that are not in subclass relation; i.e. one is not stated or inferred to be `rdfs:subClassOf` of the other.

Datatype Violations. Validation of literals not conforming to their datatype, either explicitly stated or inferred, is where regular expressions are used. The validation rules report dates not conforming to regular expressions, non-existent dates (e.g., February 30), or, in cases of specific properties, dates from the future. Some of these rules rely on XPath casting errors raised when constructor functions for XML Schema built-in datatypes are provided with incorrect input. For example, SPARQL 1.1 expression BIND (xsd:duration(?invalidDuration) AS ?test) results in an error causing the ?test variable to be unbound, which can be checked with !bound() functional form. Finally, some datatype-related rules employ interval limits; e.g., number of available vacancies (`schema:availableVacancies`) must be a positive number.

Invalid Codes. Closed world assumption was adopted for validation of codes, for which code lists enumerating every valid code are available. The codes that are checked by validation rules include language codes and currency codes. Valid codes for both cases are loaded as a part of the setup of the background knowledge base.

Having described the developed validation rules, the next section continues with their experimental application on real data harvested from the Web.

4 Experimental Validation of JobPosting Corpus

We performed an experimental validation of a JobPosting corpus harvested from the Web to examine how the validator fares on existing published data.

A preliminary task to validation was to prepare a sample of web pages to include in the validated corpus.

In order to find web pages with JobPosting markup, a Google Custom Search Engine (CSE) limited to instances of Schema.org's JobPosting class was configured [1]. Using Google CSE's REST API 1332 seed URLs, corresponding to 752 distinct pay-level domains (PLDs), were obtained. A custom crawler was created to discover more web pages with JobPosting markup given the seed URLs. This web crawl yielded 42 872 web pages containing instances of Schema.org's JobPosting class marked up either in RDFa or HTML5 Microdata. These web pages were subsequently validated and the validation results were explored via search and aggregations. Four most common types of errors are listed in Table 1, which includes all types of errors found in at least 1 % of the validated web pages.

Table 1. Distribution of the most common detected errors

Error	Percentage	Most common path to error
Datatype property used as object property	48.9	`schema:title`
Empty literal value	19.1	`schema:addressRegion`
Incorrect character case in `schema:Postaladdress`	16.5	-
Object property used as datatype property	11.6	`schema:jobLocation`

An expected kind of error that appeared frequently in validation results was empty literal value of property's object. Errors of this type may be caused by using incomplete data to generate HTML from fixed templates. In our experience, they are less common in manually annotated web pages, which was the case for the previously mentioned sample of web pages annotated by students.

When it comes to rules testing the correct use of object and datatype properties, our general expectation was that users would more likely treat object properties as datatype ones rather than vice versa, in order to avoid more complex markup using nested objects or references to external data. However, the opposite is true for the examined corpus of web pages. In fact, the most frequent type of error that was found in almost half of the corpus is the use of datatype properties with URIs or blank nodes as objects. Upon manual inspection of several randomly chosen web pages containing this error, it seems that a major cause of the error is misunderstanding of precedence rules employed by markup parsers. Both RDFa[7] and Microdata[8] specifications give precedence to values of attributes, such as `href`, which are interpreted as resources identified by URIs, and overshadow text content of HTML elements. Markup creators may not be aware of this behaviour and thus inadvertently use datatype properties incorrectly, especially when marking up anchor (`<a>`) elements.

---

[7] http://www.w3.org/TR/rdfa-syntax/#h5_using-href-or-src-to-set-the-object
[8] http://www.w3.org/TR/microdata/#values

On the other hand, the use of object properties with literal values is less prominent in the validation results. The most common property exhibiting this error is `schema:jobLocation`, which is used with literal values in 6.5 % of the validated web pages. Prevalence of errors associated with this property might be a reflection of the complexity of the JobPosting data model, which requires two intermediate resources connected by `schema:jobLocation` and `schema:address` properties in order to attach postal address information to a job posting.

A prevalent error was found in incorrect character case used for `schema:PostalAddress` class written as `schema:Postaladdress`. The error was present in 16.5 % of the validated web pages and spread across 116 unique PLDs. Both RDFa and HTML5 Microdata syntaxes are case sensitive and treat `schema:PostalAddress` and `schema:Postaladdress` as distinct names due to the different character case. The wide array of domains featuring markup with this error may imply that it was spread by copying and pasting.

5 Conclusion

We argue that the presented JobPosting validator and preview can guide users to improve the quality of structured data markup in their web sites. The experimental validation of a JobPosting corpus showed that the tool is able to reveal many widespread errors in real data. The experiment's results hint that many errors violating semantic integrity constraints are in fact caused by incorrect syntax. Even though the tool was developed in specific context of DámePráci.eu project, it showed to be useful for Schema.org JobPosting data in general.

Acknowledgements. The research presented in this paper was partially supported by the project of Operational Programme Human Resources and Employment no. CZ.1.04/5.1.01/77.00440. The author would like to thank to Vojtěch Hýža for providing guidance in development with Ruby on Rails.

References

1. Bodas, N.: Create a search engine with schema.org types. In: Google Custom Search Blog, March 24 (2014), WWW: http://googlecustomsearch.blogspot.cz/2014/03/create-search-engine-with-schemaorg.html [cit. April 04, 2014] [online]
2. Kontokostas, D., Westphal, P., Auer, S., Hellmann, S., Lehmann, J., Cornelissen, R., Zaveri, A.: Test-driven evaluation of linked data quality. In: Proceedings of the 23rd International Conference on World Wide Web, pp. 747–758 (2014)
3. RDF Validation Workshop report (2013), WWW: https://www.w3.org/2012/12/rdf-val/report [cit. April 04, 2014] [online]
4. Simister, S., Brickley, D.: Simple application-specific constraints for RDF models. In: RDF Validation Workshop: Practical Assurances for Quality RDF Data (2013)
5. Zaino, J.: Where Schema.org is at: a chat with Google's R.V. Guha. In: Semanticweb.com (November 13, 2013), WWW: http://semanticweb.com/schema-org-chat-googles-r-v-guha_b40607 (cit. April 04, 2014)

Automotive Ranges as eCommerce Data

François-Paul Servant, Edouard Chevalier, and François Jurain

Renault, Dir. de l'Informatique, Service Intelligence Artificielle Appliquée
{francois-paul.servant,edouard.chevalier,francois.jurain}@renault.com

Abstract. Exposing data about customizable products is a challenging issue, because of the number of features and options customers can choose from, and because of the intricate constraints between them. The lack of a well-established way to publish such data on the web impedes the development of the e-business-related benefits that we could expect. Building on previous work at Renault, this paper shows that a few additions to Schema.org could foster the publishing of data about complex products such as new cars.

Keywords: Structured eCommerce data, Configuration, Automotive, Linked Data, Schema.org, GoodRelations.

1 Introduction

The publishing on the web of structured data about products has become mainstream, thanks to the Schema.org initiative and to the GoodRelations vocabulary. It allows better e-business performance by increasing the visibility of commercial offers. This improves in particular the accuracy of search engines: when instructed to index well identified and precisely described products, they can add them to their "knowledge graph" of known entities. This has interesting results for products such as books: search results list actual products rather than mere web pages, and include links to commercial offers with price, ratings, etc.

However, suppose you are looking for, say, a small car with a gasoline engine, a sun-roof and a navigation system, and you are concerned with the price and with CO_2 emissions; your search engine probably won't help you there.

This is hardly surprising: cars are more complicated to describe than books, and the data needed to respond to such requests is simply not online. Books are searched on the basis of a very small set of properties (title, author,...); they are well identified, e.g. through ISBN; and comparisons between commercial offers only involve completely defined products. In contrast, cars are customizable, a crucial aspect of the problem: rather than fully specified products, what you compare are sets of them, that is, partially defined products.

The description of automotive ranges raises some challenging issues. Cars indeed have many optional features, and ranges of new cars are therefore huge: more than 10^{20} different cars are for sale at Renault. Furthermore, and this is the tricky point, there are constraints between the features that invalidate many of their combinations: only one chance in 100,000 to define an existing Renault car, if you pick at random from the available features without taking the constraints into account. The definition of a range of new cars is a "Constraint Satisfaction Problem": it cannot be represented accurately as a simple tabular data-sheet that just lists some predefined properties of car models. It could be represented by means of Semantic Web languages [3], but only sophisticated automatic reasoning would make these data usable in practice, a capability that cannot be expected from simple agents. This rules out the option, when publishing data on the web.

The fact is, there is no shared, well established way to publish data about cars. Schema.org includes nothing about vehicles, and nothing about the handling of partially defined products in general, a key point when describing ranges of new cars. This impedes the publishing of such data: no how-to on one hand, nothing to expect in terms of SEO on the other hand.

It can be done, nonetheless: to facilitate the sharing of data between in-house systems and web applications, Renault publishes structured data on the web that describe its commercial range[1] (as pure RDF[2], as RDFa markup in HTML[3]). This work contributes a domain-independent solution for the description of ranges of customizable products, based on their modeling as graphs of "Partially Defined Products" (PDP), with each PDP (or Configuration) linking to those that refine it [2]. This is formalized in the "Configuration as Linked Data Ontology" ("COLD")[4], a lightweight vocabulary (3 core classes, 5 properties) available under a Creative Commons license.

This paper builds on these results to propose a lightweight extension to Schema.org to make it support PDP handling. It is structured as follows: section 2 lists related works. Section 3 summarizes the important points of our earlier paper about the configuration process as linked data [2]. In section 4, we discuss the fact that the solution, being generic, is meant to be complemented by domain-dependent vocabularies. Section 5 takes the point of view of a search engine: the published data being huge, can it be effectively indexed? Finally, section 6 proposes a minimal extension to Schema.org.

2 Related Work

The GoodRelations (GR) ontology has become a de-facto standard for the publishing of e-business data on the web, a status reinforced by its integration into Schema.org. GR allows the description of product offerings [1]. In a clean separation of concerns, it has been designed to be used in combination with additional ontologies for product types and their properties, such as the "Product Types Ontology"[5].

---

[1] http://purl.org/configurationontology/quickstart
[2] http://uk.co.rplug.renault.com/product/gen?as=ttl
[3] http://uk.co.rplug.renault.com/product/gen?embed=true
[4] http://purl.org/configurationontology
[5] http://www.productontology.org

The main subject of this paper is therefore the question of the use of PDPs in GR descriptions. This problem seems not yet solved, nor substantially addressed, considering that, e.g., the GR cookbook for "product variants"[6] is empty to date. It could be argued that GR's ProductOrServiceModel class, an abstraction used to model "prototypes" of products, along with the ability to derive descriptions of actual products from it, could be used for the purpose of describing PDPs, but it requires non-standard reasoning.

Product ontologies developed as extensions to GR, such as those from the OPDM project[7], or the "Vehicle Sales Ontology"[8] (VSO), seem to define properties only meant to be used in the descriptions of completely defined products; in spite, in the case of VSO, of its focus on a domain where product customization is an important topic.

In the precise context of our work - the description of ranges of new cars - the main contribution that we know of is Volkswagen's "Car Option Ontology"[9], an extension to VSO. The approach is different from the Configuration Ontology we advocate: they include the constraints between options in the publication, using a proprietary vocabulary. This puts the burden of the reasoning on the client, requiring it to have reasoning capabilities.

3 Configuration as Linked Data

3.1 Principles

As ranges of customizable products are too large to be enumerated, they are defined in intention. The description of a family of similar products (typically those of the same "model") is based on a "lexicon", i.e., a set of variables representing the relevant descriptive attributes: body type, type of fuel, color, etc. In a completely defined product, each of these variables is assigned only one value. Such a value is called a "specification" in ISO-10303 STEP AP 214 terminology, a term that we have retained in the definition of our ontology. Then a set of constraints restricts the possible combinations of specifications. The definition of a range of customizable products is therefore a Constraint Satisfaction Problem (CSP) - a class of problems well known to be computationally hard.

The configuration process, which helps a customer to make her choice among a range of customizable products, one step at a time, feature after feature, can be modeled as the traversal of a graph of "Partially Defined Products" (PDP), or "Configurations", each configuration linking to those that refine it. Each Configuration, that is, each step of the configuration process, is identified by the list of the features selected so far. When accessing the corresponding URI, we get the data that describe the Configuration, in particular the links that allow to select among the remaining choices.

---

[6] http://wiki.goodrelations-vocabulary.org/index.php?title=Cookbook/Variants
[7] http://www.ebusiness-unibw.org/ontologies/opdm/
[8] http://purl.org/vso
[9] http://purl.org/coo

The "Configuration as Linked Data" ontology (COLD) describes the classes and properties involved in the modeling of the configuration process as Linked Data. It is really simple, with three main classes (Configuration, Specification and ConfigurationLink), and a few properties that model the state of a specification with respect to a given configuration: is it chosen? implied? possible? etc.

Let's take an example to make things clear: a very simple range of cars, consisting of only one model ("foo:Model1"); a customer can choose the fuel type (either diesel or gasoline), and the gearbox type (automatic or manual), with one constraint: the automatic gearbox is only available with a gasoline engine (the total number of different completely defined cars is therefore 3). A configurator application identifies all partially defined configurations, and describes them with COLD. For instance, the "Model1 with a diesel engine" (remember that its gearbox is necessarily a manual one):

```
foo:Model1DieselConf cold:chosenSpec foo:Model1, foo:Diesel ;
    cold:impliedSpec foo:Manual.
```

On the "Model1 with a gasoline engine", a customer still can choose the gearbox:

```
foo:Model1GasConf cold:chosenSpec foo:Model1, foo:Gasoline;
    cold:possible [a cold:ConfigurationLink;
        cold:specToBeAdded foo:Manual;
        cold:linkedConf foo:Model1GasManualConf];
    cold:possible [a cold:ConfigurationLink;
        cold:specToBeAdded foo:Automatic;
        cold:linkedConf foo:Model1GasAutoConf].
```

We see here the linked data nature of the representation of the range: each value of the "possible" property associates a specification that can be chosen (e.g. foo:Manual) and the link to the corresponding refined configuration (foo:Model1GasManualConf).

3.2 Salient Points

- Configurations are first-class objects, identified by URIs, and are therefore easily shared between applications.
- The complexity of the range is hidden from the client. All reasoning takes place inside the service publishing the data, no reasoning capability is required from the client agent.
- Ranges can be crawled, either starting from the root of the dataset or from any configuration, and following links whose semantics is precisely defined.
- The approach is domain-independent.
- It integrates nicely with GoodRelations (in GR terms, a Configuration is a ProductOrServiceModel).

4 Domain-Dependent Thesauri

The "Configuration as Linked Data" ontology is generic: it is independent of the variables and specifications that define a product. In other words, it provides a framework that needs to be complemented with dedicated, domain-dependent vocabularies, to define the specifications. This pattern should not be a problem, thanks to Schema.org's "additionalType" property: the Product Types Ontology follows the same pattern vis-a-vis GoodRelations.

Note the shift from vocabularies aimed at describing products, with fine-grained properties such as "fuelType", to vocabularies aimed at defining instances and classes of specifications, such as "FuelType". This shift is needed to describe PDP's, because a PDP is more than a Completely Defined Product with some properties left undocumented: its description requires the ability to state more than one kind of relationship between a PDP and a given Specification. This shift, which appears to be a very natural one anyway, offers great flexibility when describing products, including completely defined ones; e. g. it allows to define hierarchies of classes of Specifications (such as Sunroof>ElectricSunroof).

Let us also note that the COLD framework allows publishers to use their own terms when describing their products. This is an important point, because:

- the whole purpose of the configuration process is to produce an order for a completely defined product; which implies its definition in the manufacturing company's terms,
- no precision is lost, in contrast to what would happen if we had to map to a different vocabulary (no vendor will downgrade the description of his own product for the sole purpose of making it comparable to others' products),
- it makes it possible to publish the data as they are in the publisher's systems, at no additional cost, still leaving open the option to enhance the published data later.

5 Indexing Configurations

COLD gives us the means to precisely describe ranges of customizable products, making it easy to crawl them, following links whose semantics is precisely defined. Our ranges are very large, though; we avoid the complexity of describing and handling a CSP through an increase in the size of the published data: this is the price of simplicity.

Therefore, the indexing of configurations by search engines can only be partial. Does it matter? The typical person searching for a car will enter a limited number of specifications: "a small car with gasoline engine, sunroof and air conditioning", for instance. Even if they vary from person to person, the set of popular features will probably be small, because not all the specifications are of equal interest: the sunroof, the navigation system, etc. are probably more important - for a customer as well as for a search engine, or a vendor - than, say, the capacity of the fuel tank; usually, people do not search for "negative specifications" (such as "without sunroof"); moreover, the popular features are a function of the car model: when indexing configurations corresponding to low-end models, air conditioning may be important; not so with high-end models, where it is always included. So, when indexing configurations corresponding to a given model, it is probably enough to only index the configurations including up to, say, 4 features chosen among 15; amounting to a quite manageable set of less than 1901 configurations to index, per car model. Thus, for any car model, search engines will be able to store and return the exact configurations matching the conjunctions of popular terms they expect to find in user queries; then, users will be just one click away from the corresponding pages in vendors' configurator web applications, a major improvement in the precision of search results.

So, search engines can make effective use of configuration data, by choosing the links they want to follow in the dataset, and by stopping when they want. Publishers of these data can also limit the links they provide in the data, or give clues to search engines; for instance, with the "no-follow" directive if the data is provided as markup within HTML.

6 Proposal for Schema.org

As COLD is very simple, it could serve as a basis for the description of customizable products in Schema.org, which currently provides no way to handle them. It can be streamlined further: some of the properties are specific to advanced configurator applications and can be left out (e.g. the "impossible" property that allows a user to choose a Specification incompatible with its previous selections, at the cost of discarding some of them). Also, as a Configuration is essentially a ProductOrServiceModel, a new type may not be needed for them.

What, then, is the bare minimum? At the core of COLD is the idea to describe products through their features ("Specifications" in COLD parlance), using a small set of general properties to make precise the kind of the relationship between the product and a given feature: is it possible, implied, etc.

The idea to describe products through their features is shared by several Schema.org extension proposals[10], and by a planned extension to GR, "ProductFeature"[11], meant to allow the publishing of arbitrary property-value pairs. Basically, they suggest the creation of a new "Feature" type ("Feature", being probably more appropriate than "Specification"), and of a "feature" property.

The exact semantics of this property needs to be precisely defined, however. It should not be used when a feature is only possible; indeed, two features may be possible on a given product while their conjunction is not; also, selecting a possible feature may increase the price. Therefore, using this property for features that are only possible results in an ambiguity regarding the description of PDPs. On the other hand, cold:chosenSpec and cold:impliedSpec can safely be made subProperties of it. Getting back to our earlier example, we may write:

---

[10] http://thematix.com/ontologies/travel/lodging/Feature.html
[11] http://wiki.goodrelations-vocabulary.org/Documentation/Product_features

```
foo:Model1DieselConf :feature foo:Model1, foo:Diesel, foo:Manual.
foo:Model1GasConf :feature foo:Model1, foo:Gasoline;
    cold:possible [a cold:ConfigurationLink;
        cold:specToBeAdded foo:Manual;
        cold:linkedConf foo:Model1GasManualConf];...
```

Consumer applications, knowing only the Schema.org extension, can now obtain the structured info they need to correctly index these configurations by their features, while those knowledgeable about COLD can grab more; namely, the links to the refined configurations and the precise semantics attached to those links; in other words, they can crawl the refined configurations in a smart way.

The "cold:possible" property and the "ConfigurationLink" class may be too complex to be accepted by Schema.org. Workarounds are possible: search engines can always follow the corresponding hypertext links in the HTML instead, and producers of data can always point search engines to the configurations they regard as interesting, using the sitemap file of their websites.

However, recent proposals[12,13] suggest Schema.org might be ready to tackle reified properties. We hope it will: that would provide the required framework to represent ConfigurationLinks, and we would then come close to a seamless integration of COLD's main functionalities.

7 Conclusion

Data about customizable products can be published effectively as Linked Data. Most, if not all, configurator applications on the web could be modified to publish data that way. It gets us accurate descriptions of complex ranges of products, which can be crawled by simple agents. The published data are huge, but they can be effectively indexed by search engines. With minimal additions to Schema.org, the description of configurable products such as cars could gain momentum, opening new opportunities.

References

1. Hepp, M.: GoodRelations: An ontology for describing products and services offers on the web. In: Gangemi, A., Euzenat, J. (eds.) EKAW 2008. LNCS (LNAI), vol. 5268, pp. 329–346. Springer, Heidelberg (2008)
2. Chevalier, E., Servant, F.-P.: Product customization as linked data. In: Simperl, E., Cimiano, P., Polleres, A., Corcho, O., Presutti, V. (eds.) ESWC 2012. LNCS, vol. 7295, pp. 603–617. Springer, Heidelberg (2012)
3. Badra, F., Servant, F.-P., Passant, A.: A Semantic Web Representation of a Product Range Specification based on Constraint Satisfaction Problem in the Automotive Industry. In: OSEMA Workshop ESWC (2011),
http://ceur-ws.org/Vol-748/paper4.pdf

---

[12] https://www.w3.org/wiki/WebSchemas/RolesPattern
[13] https://www.w3.org/wiki/WebSchemas/PropertyValuePairs

Linked Data-based Conceptual Modelling for Recommendation: A FCA-Based Approach

Angel Castellanos, Ana García-Serrano, and Juan Cigarrán

ETSI Informática
Universidad Nacional de educación a Distancia (UNED)
C/ Juan del Rosal 16, 28040 Madrid, Spain
{acastellanos,agarcia,juanci}@lsi.uned.es

Abstract. In a recommendation task it is crucial to have an accurate content-based description of the users and the items. Linked Open Data (LOD) has been demonstrated as one of the best ways of obtaining this kind of content. The main question is to know how useful the LOD information is in inferring user preferences and how to obtain it. We propose a novel approach for Content Modelling and Recommendation based on Formal Concept Analysis (FCA). The approach is based in the modelling of the user and content related information, enriched with LOD, and in a new algorithm to analyze the models and recommend new content. The framework provided by the ESWC 2014 Recommendation Challenge is used for the evaluation. The results are within the average range of other participants, but further work has to be carried out to refine the approach using LOD information.

Keywords: Linked Data, Recommender Systems, Formal Concept Analysis.

1 Introduction

Recommender Systems (RS) have traditionally followed two main approaches: Collaborative Filtering (CF) that puts together similar users and Content-Based (CB) that puts together similar items. A recommendation task has to cope with different problems [11]. One of the main problems is related to the paucity of information (e.g. cold start [12] or scarcity [2]). Linked Open Data (LOD) [3] is shown as a remarkable alternative to solve that. LOD has been consumed mainly for data enrichment in order to improve the performance of the recommender systems [10, 5]. However, given a recommendation scenario, the way in which this data can be linked with the items and users has to be defined [9, 4]. Basically, these proposals follow two methods: the use of the SPARQL language to search for specific information or to take advantage of the LOD structure to infer relationships and obtain related information. As a result of works such as the aforementioned and other initiatives, several specific datasets have been published: The DBbook database, The DBPedia mappings to MovieLens1M dataset or DBPedia Mappings to Last.fm dataset.

This paper proposes a novel approach based on Formal Concept Analysis (FCA) [7]. LOD, and more specifically DBPedia-extracted data, are used to create a semantic item description to be taken into account in the modelling step. Based on this FCA modelling, an algorithm is proposed to manage the models and recommend new contents. FCA has been applied both for CF [13] and CB approaches [8]. However, most of these works barely delve into the possibilities of FCA for modelling. This work tries to go a step further in the application of FCA for recommendation: Can the inferred semantic-based formal concepts be useful to infer user preferences? To answer this question an experimental work based on the ESWC 2014 Challenge is conducted. Our main aim is to prove whether LOD information can be useful in generating a concept-based modelling which can link with the user preferences. The hypothesis is that, if the user preferences (and the subsequent user activity) are somehow dependant with the content of the consumed items, the power of FCA to organize and model content should be useful in modelling this dependency. The proposal, the experiments conducted and the obtained results is presented below.

2 Recommendation Approach Description

The recommendation approach runs on an FCA-based content modelling. By means of FCA an offline model of the data is created. Then, the FCA-based recommendation algorithm explores the model to extract relationships containing valuable recommendations. Finally, a pruning of the raw recommendations is conducted to select only the most suitable ones.

The main construction of the FCA theory is the *formal concept* that is derived from a *formal context*. A *formal context* $\mathbb{K} := (G, M, I)$, can be seen as an incidence matrix that presents the set of *has-a* relationships (I) between objects (G) and attributes (M). Strictly, a *formal concept* is a pair (A, B), where $A \subseteq G$ is a set of objects (*extent*), and $B \subseteq M$ is a set of attributes (*intent*), such as: 1) the extent A consists of all the objects related to all the attributes in the intent B; and 2) the intent B consists of all the attributes shared by the objects in extent A.

Formal concepts can be ordered by their extents in a *subconcept-superconcept relationship* according to their *extents*: $(A, B) \leq (C, D) :\Leftrightarrow (A, B) \subseteq (C, D) \Leftrightarrow A \subseteq C$. This ordered relationship is a generalization-specialization, and it can be proven to be a lattice. Because concept lattices are ordered sets, they can be naturally displayed in terms of *Hasse diagrams*. In a *Hasse diagram*: 1) there is exactly one node for each formal concept; 2) if, for concepts $C1$ and $C2$, $C1 \subseteq C2$ holds, then $C2$ is placed above $C1$; and 3) if $C1 \subseteq C2$ but there is no other concept $C3$ so that $C1 \subseteq C3 \subseteq C2$, there is a line joining $C1$ and $C2$.

The recommendation scenario can be interpreted as a bipartite graph partitioned into users (U) and items (I). The edges in this graph, $\rho = r(u, i)$, establish the relationship of the user u with an item i weighted with a rating r. Following the FCA theory, the triple (U, I, ρ) can be interpreted as a *formal context* (or a *recommendation context*), from which a set of formal concepts (A, B) can be inferred, where A is the user set sharing the item set B. This set of *formal concepts* can be organized in a *recommendation lattice*, which can be represented according to a *Hasse Diagram*.

This user-item representation is the so-called *UserItemLattice*. The *UserItemLattice* reflects a CF recommendation scenario: users are organized according to their shared items. FCA can be also applied to the CB scenario: organizing items according to their content. In this case, the *recommendation context* includes the relationships between items and their content (LOD-based features). Consequently, the set of inferred *formal concepts* (I, C) will include the items (I) sharing a set of content (C). The *recommendation lattice* that organizes these *formal concepts* will be referred to as the *ItemContentsLattice*.

2.1 The Recommendation Approach

The proposed recommendation approach is inspired in the CF approach in [6]. Our work is a generalization to deal with multilevel recommendation and a CB approach. So, two approaches are proposed: A CF approach based on the *UserItemLattice* and a CB approach based on the *ItemContentsLattice*. The CF approach extracts the recommendations by applying to each user u the following algorithm:

```
Get object concept of u: (γu); target_concepts_list:= {γu}
for level = 0 to N
    for each target_concept ∈ target_concepts_list
        Get child concepts ([S₁,...,Sₙ]) of target_concept
        Get sibling_concepts ([B₁,...,Bₙ]), where Bₙ= child_concept of the parent_concept
        for each Sᵢ:= (U, I) ∈ [S₁,...,Sₙ] if u ∈ U == false then
            Add Sᵢ to the Reco_Candidate_FC_List
            Add Sᵢ to the new_target_concepts_list
        target_concepts_list:=new_target_concepts_list
        for each Bᵢ:=(U.I) ∈ [B₁,...Bₙ]  if u ∈ U == false then
            Add Bᵢ to the Reco_Candidate_FC_List
            Add Bᵢ to the new_target_concepts_list
        target_concepts_list += new_target_concepts_list
for each Formal Concept FC := (U, I) ∈FC:=(U,I)∈ Reco_Candidate_FC_List
    for each item i ∈ I Recommend item i
```

Fig. 1. Collaborative Filtering based Recommendation Algorithm. Being N the number of levels (above and below the target concept level) to look for recommendations, a son concept the concept linked in the level below and a parent concept the concept linked in the level above.

The CB algorithm is also based on the lattice structure to conduct the recommendations, although its functioning is slightly different. Given a user to be recommended and its item set (i.e. the items consumed by them), the recommendations are offered by apply the following algorithm:

```
for each item i ∈ UserItemSet
    Get object concept of i (γi); target_concepts_list:= {γi}
    for level = 0 to N
        for each target_concept ∈ target_concept_list∈
            Get child concepts ([S₁,...,Sₙ]) of target_concept
            Get sibling concepts ([B₁,...,Bₙ]) where Bᵢ= child concept of the parent concept
```

```
        for each Sᵢ:=(I,C) ∈ [S₁,...,Sₙ]
            if i ∈ Sᵢ == false then
                Add Sᵢ to the Reco_Candidate_FC_List;
                Add Sᵢ to the new_target_concepts_list
        target_concepts_list:= new_target_concepts_list
        for each Bᵢ:=(I,C) ∈ [B₁,...,Bₙ] if i ∈ Bᵢ== false then
                Add Bᵢ to the Reco_Candidate_FC_List
                Add Bᵢ to the new_target_concepts_list
            target_concepts_list += new_target_concepts_list
        target_concepts_list:= {yi}
    for each Formal Concept FC:=(U,I)∈Reco_Candidate_FC_List
        for each item i ∈ Ii ∈ I Recommend item i
```

Fig. 2. Content Based Recommendation Algorithm. Being N the number of levels (above and below the target concept level) to look for recommendations, a son concept the concept linked in the level below and a parent concept the concept linked in the level above of a given one.

3 Performed Experiments

The test bed proposed is the *ESWC 2014 Recommendation Challenge* [1], a challenge for the application of LOD to the recommendation task. The organizers provided the participants with the DBbook dataset that did not include any item content. To enrich the annotation we took advantage of the DBPedia endpoints to download the information related to them. Nevertheless, the information in DBPedia as regards each item is extensive and related to different aspects. After reviewing all of this information, we selected only those data we considered more related to the interest of a given user to a given item (abstract, literaryGenre, country, language, name and subject). Restricting the enrichment process to only DBPedia data does not take advantage of the full power of the LOD Cloud. However, this issue is out of the scope of the aim of this work: to show the advantages of a conceptual data modelling applied to a semantic driven representation, no matter what this representation could be.

The recommendation approach to perform a ***Recommendation in the Wild*** is based on predicting the ratings of a group of fixed items so the CB approach appears to be more suitable than the CF. Thus, the CB approach based on the *ItemContentLattice* modelling plus the CB-based algorithm was applied. The results obtained by the participating groups (our work is identified as UNED group) are shown in Fig. 3 (in the horizontal axe), sorted by the F-Measure value (range from 0,005 to 0,050). The low results obtained by the different groups' shows the difficulty of the task.

At this point, this low performance can be ascribed to three causes: 1) FCA is not suitable if not for recommendation in general, at least for this given task; 2) the LOD information, although provides an accurate representation of the items, it is not useful in creating a representation of the user preferences, and 3) these low results could be only attributed to the high complexity of the task. The latter is hardly demonstrable; however, we can remove the dependence between the low results and the FCA performance, by applying a "bare" FCA based approach to a different recommendation task (the interest prediction) in order to test its performance.

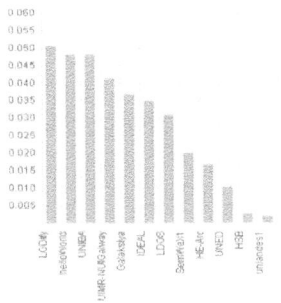
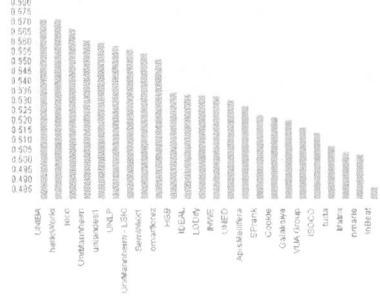

Fig. 3. Reco in the Wild Results   **Fig. 4.** Interest Prediction Results

In the *Interest Prediction task*, given an item set to be recommended, it has to be sorted according to a predicted score, related to the degree of interest of a given item for a given user. In the ESWC2104 Challenge, this scenario is handled by tasks 1 and 2, although we focused our experimentation only on task 2. The use of the previous user behaviours is the best approach to address this task; that is, the application of a CF system to recommend items consumed by the users detected as similar to the target one. As was explained before, the grouping of users has been made through an FCA-based modelling, in the *UserItemLattice*.

The official results released by the *ESWC 2014 Challenge* organizers are shown in the Fig. 4 (ours identified by UNED). This shows the results obtained by all the participant groups, sorted by the F-Measure value (in the vertical axis).As can be seen in the Fig. 4, our results are within the average range (note the bias in the values of the vertical axis); even though no LOD-based expansion technique was applied. Given these results, in the State-of-the-art of the task, it can be concluded that the performance of FCA to organize content can be applied in a recommendation scenario. And even more, the low performance obtained in the previous task does not seem to be attributable to FCA.

4 Conclusions and Future Work

In this paper, two modeling approaches were proposed, one based on a Collaborative-Filtering approach and one based on a Content-Based approach using LOD and FCA theory. A recommendation algorithm that improves the structured model provided by FCA to compute the recommendations was developed for each one.

The experimentation performed in the ESWC2014 *Recommendation Challenge* allows concluding that FCA is a suitable technique to be applied in this kind of recommendation scenario. It seems that an accurate conceptual modelling based on LOD information could lead to better recommendations. However, these experimental results did not clearly confirm that point.

At this point, two future lines of research appear. It has to be proved whether different management of the whole information in the LOD cloud could lead on a better performance approach. Also, it seems that the ESWC 2014 scenario is especially challenging so the application of the approach in other scenarios could offer more representative results and more precise information.

Acknowledgments. This work has been partially supported by projects: MA2VIRMR (S2009/TIC-1542), and HOLOPEDIA (TIN 2010-21128-C02).

References

[1] Eswc 2014, recommendation challenge: http://challenges.2014.eswc-conferences.org/
[2] Balabanovic, M., Shoham, Y.: Fab: content-based, collaborative recommendation. Communications of the ACM 40(3), 66–72 (1997)
[3] Bizer, C., Heath, T., Berners-Lee, T.: Linked data-the story so far. International Journal on Semantic Web and Information Systems 5(3), 1–22 (2009)
[4] Damljanovic, D., Stankovic, M., Laublet, P.: Linked data-based concept recommendation: Comparison of different methods in open innovation scenario. In: Simperl, E., Cimiano, P., Polleres, A., Corcho, O., Presutti, V. (eds.) ESWC 2012. LNCS, vol. 7295, pp. 24–38. Springer, Heidelberg (2012)
[5] Di Noia, T., Mirizzi, R., Ostuni, V.C., Romito, D., Zanker, M.: Linked open data to support content-based recommender systems. In: Proc. of the 8th Int. Conf. on Semantic Systems, pp. 1–8. ACM (2012)
[6] du Boucher-Ryan, P., Bridge, D.: Collaborative recommending using formal concept analysis. Knowledge-Based Systems 19(5), 309–315 (2006)
[7] Ganter, B., Wille, R., Franzke, C.: Formal concept analysis: mathematical foundations. Springer (1997)
[8] Li, X., Murata, T.: A knowledge-based recommendation model utilizing formal concept analysis and association. In: ICCAE, vol. 4, pp. 221–226 (2010)
[9] Ostuni, V.C., Di Noia, T., Di Sciascio, E., Mirizzi, R.: Top-n recommendations from implicit feedback leveraging linked open data. In: Proc. of the 7th ACM Conference on Recommender Systems, RecSys 2013, NY, pp. 85–92 (2013)
[10] Passant, A.: dbrec — music recommendations using DBpedia. In: Patel-Schneider, P.F., Pan, Y., Hitzler, P., Mika, P., Zhang, L., Pan, J.Z., Horrocks, I., Glimm, B. (eds.) ISWC 2010, Part II. LNCS, vol. 6497, pp. 209–224. Springer, Heidelberg (2010)
[11] Ricci, F., Shapira, B.: Recommender systems handbook. Springer (2011)
[12] Schein, A.I., Popescul, A., Ungar, L.H., Pennock, D.M.: Methods and metrics for cold-start recommendations. In: Proc. of the 25th Annual Int. ACM SIGIR Conf. on Research and Development in Information Retrieval, pp. 253–260. ACM, NY (2002)
[13] Senatore, S., Pasi, G.: Lattice navigation for collaborative filtering by means of (fuzzy) formal concept analysis. In: Proc. of the 28th Annual ACM Symposium on Applied Computing, SAC, pp. 920–926. ACM, NY (2013)

Usability Assessment of a Context-Aware and Personality-Based Mobile Recommender System

Matthias Braunhofer, Mehdi Elahi, and Francesco Ricci

Free University of Bozen, Bolzano,
Piazza Domenicani 3, Bolzano, Italy
{mbraunhofer,mehdi.elahi,fricci}@unibz.it
http://www.unibz.it

Abstract. In this paper we present STS (South Tyrol Suggests), a context-aware mobile recommender system for places of interest (POIs) that integrates some innovative components, including: a *personality questionnaire*, i.e., a brief and entertaining questionnaire used by the system to learn users' personality; an *active learning* module that acquires ratings-in-context for POIs that users are likely to have experienced; and a *matrix factorization* based recommendation module that leverages the personality information and several contextual factors in order to generate more relevant recommendations.

Adopting a system oriented perspective, we describe the assessment of the combination of the implemented components. We focus on usability aspects and report the end-user assessment of STS. It was obtained from a controlled live user study as well as from the log data produced by a larger sample of users that have freely downloaded and tried STS through Google Play Store. The result of the assessment showed that the overall usability of the system falls between "good" and "excellent", it helped us to identify potential problems and it provided valuable indications for future system improvement.

Keywords: Recommender systems, context awareness, mobile services, active learning, personality, usability assessment.

1 Introduction

Tourist's decision making is the outcome of a complex decision process that is affected by "internal" (to the tourist) factors, such as personal motivators or past experience, and "external" factors, e.g., advices, information about the products, or the climate of the destination [18]. Context-aware recommender systems can represent and deal with these influencing factors by extending the traditional two-dimensional user/item model that relies only on the ratings given by a community of users to a catalogue of items. This is achieved by augmenting the collected ratings with data about the context of an item consumption and rating [1]. For example, there are places of interest (POIs) that may be liked only if visited on summer (or winter). If the system stores, together with the rating, the situation in which a POI was experienced, it can then use this information to provide more appropriate recommendations in the various future target contextual situations of the user.

The first challenge for generating context-aware recommendations is how to identify the contextual factors (e.g., weather) that are truly influencing the ratings and hence are worth considering [3]. Secondly, acquiring a representative set of in-context ratings (i.e., ratings under various contextual conditions) is clearly more difficult than acquiring context-free ratings. Finally, extending traditional recommender systems to really exploit the additional information brought by in-context ratings, i.e., building a more effective and useful service, is the third challenge for context-aware recommender systems.

In this paper, we focus on the last challenge and we present a concrete mobile context-aware recommender system called STS (South Tyrol Suggests) that is available on Google Play Store. STS recommends places of interest (POIs) in South Tyrol (Italy) by exploiting various contextual factors (e.g., weather, time of day, day of week, location, mood) and an extended matrix factorization rating prediction model. STS can generate recommendations adapted to the current contextual situation, for example, by recommending indoor POIs (e.g., museums, churches, castles) on bad weather conditions and outdoor POIs (e.g., lakes, mountain excursions, scenic walks) on good weather conditions. The user's preference model is learned using two different sources of knowledge: *personality*, in terms of the the Five Factor Model, that the system acquires with a simple questionnaire, and *in context ratings* that the system actively collects from the user. Exploiting the user personality STS can personalize rating requests and recommendations even for new users (cold start). This novel feature for context-aware recommender systems is supported by the fact that user personality is known to be correlated with user tastes and interests [16].

In previous articles we assessed the STS recommendation algorithm and active learning performance by using classical metrics such as Mean Absolute Error and perceived user satisfaction with the recommendations [9,6,5]. In this article we report the results of the system usability in a controlled live user study. Moreover, we have analysed the log data of the system interactions with more than 500 users that have freely downloaded and tried STS through Google Play Store. The outcome is that users largely accept to follow the supported human-computer interaction and find the user interface clear, user-friendly and easy to use. Moreover, we describe here the user feedback, which gives us a valuable indication for future system improvement.

2 Related Work

Adomavicius et al. [1] have identified three context-aware recommendation models: contextual pre-filtering, contextual post-filtering, and contextual modelling. Contextual pre-filtering (or contextualisation of recommendation input) uses information about the current context for selecting the relevant set of rating data and then predicts ratings using any traditional two-dimensional recommendation technique. For instance, one recent example of contextual pre-filtering is

Semantic Pre-Filtering (SPF) proposed by Codina et al. [8]. It exploits a local Matrix Factorization (MF) model trained on the ratings acquired in contextual situations that are identical or influencing the ratings similarly to the target contextual situation.

In contextual post-filtering (or contextualisation of recommendation output) instead, after predicting ratings using any traditional two-dimensional recommender system trained on the entire data set, contextual information is used to adjust the resulting recommendations. Filter Post-Filtering (Filter PoF) and Weight Post-Filtering (Weight PoF), proposed by Panniello et al. [14], are two concrete examples of contextual post-filtering. They filter or weight the recommended items based on their relevance to the user in a specific target context.

Finally, in contextual modelling (or contextualisation of recommendation function), contextual information is directly used in the modelling technique as part of the rating prediction. The Context-Aware Matrix Factorization (CAMF) approach exploited in the ReRex iPhone app [3] and the InCarMusic Android app [2] is an example belonging to this category. It extends traditional MF rating prediction techniques by incorporating additional model parameters (i.e., baselines) that model how the rating for a place of interest (POI) (as for ReRex) or music genre (as for InCarMusic) deviates as effect of context.

An important aspect of context-aware recommender systems, especially those operating on mobile devices, is the supported human-computer interaction. In spite of the widely recognised importance of the recommender system user interface, mainstream research has been focusing mostly on the core rating prediction algorithms that are assessed through offline evaluations. Littler emphasis has been done on issues related to the proper design of the human-computer interaction. As an example of the second type of analysis we mention the work of Park et al. [15]. They proposed a context-aware and group-based restaurant recommender system for mobile devices and evaluated its usability using the System Usability Scale (SUS) [7]. That is a ten-item questionnaire based on a five-point Likert scale that measures the user's perceived quality of the GUI. In their evaluation they involved 13 users and obtained a system SUS score of 70.58. This indicates a good level of usability, when considering that a SUS score above 68 is assumed to be above average [17].

In [11] the authors present a case study of a constraint-based recommender system that was integrated into a travel advisory system, called VIBE, for the Warmbad-Villach spa resort in Austria. Also in their analysis the authors evaluated the system usability and the perceived customer utility using SUS. They collected the replies of 55 users and obtained an average total SUS score of 81.5. Based on these findings they concluded that the users liked the VIBE user interface. Moreover, similarly to what we have done, they were able to identify a number of usability problems that they could address in a next system release.

We believe that system usability must play a crucial role in recommender system development, besides the accuracy of the core recommendation algorithm. Analogously to the two previously discussed research works, we have used the SUS questionnaire in order to measure the user's satisfaction with the system.

STS, the system described in this article, has obtained in our experiments a SUS score of 77.92, i.e., well above the system described in [15] and close to that described in [11]. We must observe that only the first system is mobile while the second not, making the comparison of the scores less significant in this second case.

3 Interaction with the STS System

We describe here a typical system-user interaction and illustrate the main system functions. Let us assume that a tourist is looking for a POI to visit near to Bozen - Bolzano, Italy. After the registration to the system (providing birthdate and gender), the system asks the user to fill out the Ten-Item Personality Inventory (TIPI) questionnaire [10], in order to acquire the user's Big Five personality traits (openness, conscientiousness, extroversion, agreeableness, neuroticism) (see Figure 1, left).

The entered birthdate, gender and personality scores are then used by an active learning component [9,5] to identify, and request the user to rate, a small set of POIs. This information is estimated to best improving the quality of the subsequent recommendations (see Figure 1, right). We note that the system generates personalized rating requests, relying neither on explicit (e.g., ratings) nor implicit feedback (e.g., item views), which is usually not available for newly registered users.

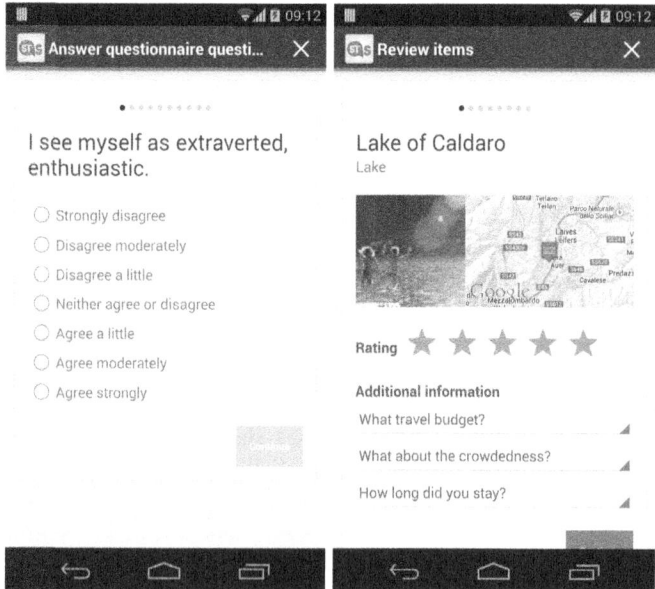

Fig. 1. Active learning

After that preference elicitation phase the system is ready for usage and the user can browse her personalized recommendations through the main application screen (see Figure 2, left). This screen displays a list of four POIs that are considered as highly relevant, considering the current user's and items' contexts. We note that some of these contextual conditions are automatically acquired by the system (e.g., user's distance to the POIs, weather conditions at the POIs), whereas others can be specified by the user through an appropriate system screen (e.g., user's mood and companion), as shown in Figure 2, right.

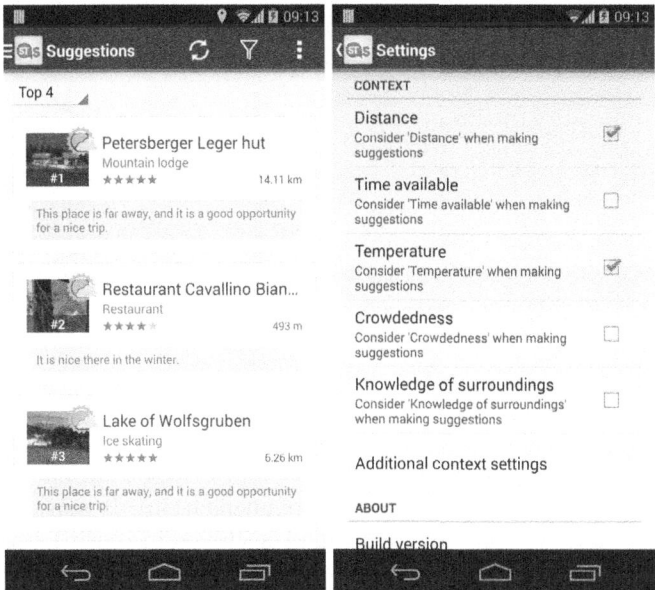

Fig. 2. Context-aware suggestions

If the user is interested in one POI she can click on it and access the POI details window (Figure 3, left). This window presents various information about the POI, such as a photo, its name, a description, its category as well as an explanation of the recommendation based on the most influential contextual condition. Other supported features include the ability to write a review for the POI, to obtain route recommendations to reach the POI (see Figure 3, right) and to bookmark the POI, which then makes it easy and fast to access it later on.

4 Recommendations Computation

STS implements a rich client always-online architecture, i.e., the client has been kept as thin as possible and it works only in a limited way offline. The client application has been developed using the open-source Android platform and

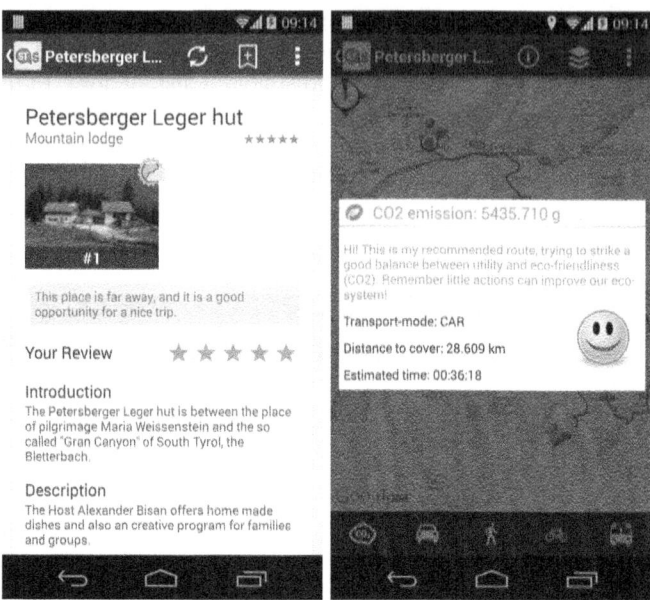

Fig. 3. POI details

implements the presentation layer (GUI and presentation logic). The server application is based on Apache Tomcat server and PostgreSQL database. It implements the data and business logic (recommendation). It makes use of web services and data provided by the Regional Association of South Tyrol's Tourism Organizations (LTS[1]), the Municipality of Bolzano[2] and Mondometeo[3]. These data sources provide descriptions as well as weather forecast information for a total of 27,000 POIs. The server's functionality is exposed via a RESTful web service that accepts and sends JSON objects providing several types of content (suggestions, POIs, reviews/ratings, user profiles).

In order to take into account the current contextual conditions when generating POI recommendations, we have extended the context-aware matrix factorization approach described in [3]. This model, besides the standard parameters (i.e., global average, item bias, user bias and user-item interaction), incorporates baseline parameters for each contextual condition and item pair. Since the original context-aware matrix factorization model fails to provide personalized recommendations for users with no or few ratings (i.e., new user problem), we have enhanced the representation of a user by incorporating user attributes (i.e., age group, gender and the scores for the Big Five personality traits) with a mathematical modelling approach that is analogous to that proposed in [13].

---

[1] LTS: LTS: http://www.lts.it
[2] Municipality of Bolzano: http://www.comune.bolzano.it
[3] Mondometeo: http://www.mondometeo.org

This allows to model the user preferences even if neither implicit nor explicit feedback is available.

The proposed model computes a rating prediction for user u and item i in the contextual situation described by the contextual conditions $c_1, ..., c_k$ using the following rule:

$$\hat{r}_{uic_1,...,c_k} = \bar{i} + b_u + \sum_{j=1}^{k} b_{ic_j} + q_i^\top \cdot (p_u + \sum_{a \in A(u)} y_a), \qquad (1)$$

where q_i, p_u and y_a are the latent factor vectors representing the item i, the user u and the user attribute a, respectively. $\bar{i}$ is the average rating for item i, b_u is the baseline parameter for user u and b_{ic_j} is the baseline for contextual condition c_j and item i. Model parameters are learned offline, once every five minutes, by minimizing the associated regularized squared error function through stochastic gradient descent.

5 System Usability Assessment

We have evaluated STS in a user study that involved 30 participants (students, colleagues, working partners and sportspersons) aged between 18-35. The users were asked to look for attractions or events in South Tyrol. The concrete task procedure is as follows: firstly the participants need to consider the contextual conditions that are relevant to them and specify them in the system settings. They were then asked to browse the attractions and events sections and check whether they could find something interesting for them. Also, they were instructed to browse the system recommendations, select one that they believed could fit their preferences and bookmark it. Finally, users needed to fill out a survey and evaluate the system with regard to the perceived recommendation quality and choice satisfaction, whose measurements are adopted from [12].

The rating prediction accuracy (in terms of Mean Absolute Error-MAE) of our recommendation model as well as the performance of the implemented active learning strategy for eliciting ratings were presented in [6,9,5], with the following conclusions: the recommendation model successfully exploits the weather conditions at POIs and leads to a higher user's perceived recommendation quality and choice satisfaction; and the active learning strategy increases the number of acquired user ratings and the recommendation accuracy in comparison with a state-of-the-art active learning strategy.

Here, we report and discuss the system usability results. Several questionnaires have been proposed for evaluating system usability. We have chosen SUS (System Usability Scale) [7] that has become a standard for such analysis. It has been shown that SUS allows to measure perceived system usability using a small sample population (i.e., 8-12 users) [19]. SUS is composed of 10 statements and users reply on a five points Likert scale ranging from "strongly disagree" (1) to "strongly agree" (5): **Q1**: *I think that I would like to use this system frequently.* **Q2** : *I found the system unnecessarily complex.* **Q3**: *I thought the system was* *easy to use.* **Q4:** *I think that I would need the support of a technical person to be able to use this system.* **Q5:** *I found the various functions in this system were well integrated.* **Q6:** *I thought there was too much inconsistency in this system.* **Q7:** *I would imagine that most people would learn to use this system very quickly.* **Q8:** *I found the system very cumbersome to use.* **Q9:** *I felt very confident using the system.* **Q10:** *I needed to learn a lot of things before I could get going with this system.*

The SUS score is computed by summing the score contributions from each item. Each item's score contribution ranges from 0 to 4. For statements Q1, Q3, Q5, Q7 and Q9 (phrased in an positive way) the score contribution is the scale position (from 1 to 5) minus 1. For statements Q2, Q4, Q6, Q8 and Q10 (phrased in a negative way) the contribution is 5 minus the scale position. Then, the sum of the scores is multiplied by 2.5 to obtain an overall system usability score ranging from 0 to 100. We note that the average SUS score computed in a benchmark of 500 studies is 68 [17]. We considered this as a strong baseline for our system since the systems in the benchmark are not mobile and usability for mobile systems is harder to achieve as it requires to deal with the significant variation among mobile devices such as differences in screen size, screen resolution, CPU performance characteristics, input mechanisms (e.g., soft keyboards, hard keyboards, touch), memory and storage space and installed fonts.

6 Evaluation Results

Figure 4(a) shows the SUS score of each test user; all but one of our subjects scored better than the benchmark. Overall, STS has obtained an average (over the 30 users) SUS score of 77.92, that is well above the benchmark of 68. It has been shown that this SUS score falls between "good" and "excellent" (in terms of the adjectives that the users may use to evaluate the system) [4]. The margin of error of this SUS score for a 99% confidence interval is 2.84. Hence, with 99% confidence the true SUS score of STS is between 75.08 and 80.76, hence significantly higher than the benchmark.

In Figure 4(b) the Box-and-Whisker diagram of the scores of the 10 SUS statements is plotted. It shows the medians and the distributions of the scores of the ten SUS statements. One can see that the medians are 3, 3.5, or 4 which is a substantially good result (4 is the max score). In addition, we have computed the average replies for the 10 SUS statements. We have observed that the highest average scores are for Q2, Q4, and Q10. This implies that the users have evaluated STS as not complex. They also believe that they did not need neither technical help, nor a lot of things to learn, to be able to use the system.

On the other hand, the lowest scores are measured for items Q9, Q7, and Q5. This implies that users were not extremely confident with using the system and thought that most of the people may not learn quickly using the system. They also found some of the functions in the system not well integrated. Our explanation for these issues is that the user interface was not clear enough to let users understand the true motivation and behaviour of certain functions. For

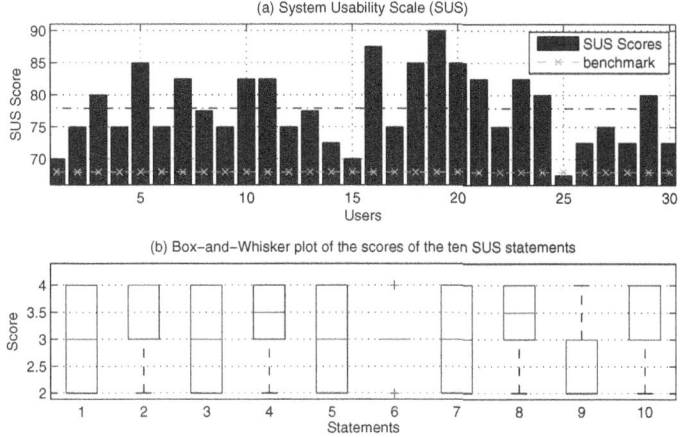

Fig. 4. System Usability Scale (SUS) results

instance, one of our test users mentioned that the personality questionnaire at registration made her mistakenly believe that the app's purpose is to determine her personality type rather than to provide her with relevant POI suggestions based on the current context. We believe that this problem can even worsen if the user is presented with a lengthier questionnaire, which is the reason why we initially decided to use TIPI and not more precise but even more complex approaches.

In order to fix the above-mentioned issues we have improved STS. First of all, we have now replaced the Ten-Item Personality Inventory (TIPI) questionnaire with the Five-Item Personality Inventory (FIPI) questionnaire (see Figure 5, left), which requires less effort. Moreover, we better implemented the active learning process by letting the users to enter their ratings at any moment. The user is presented with a simple and non-invasive in-app notification within the POI suggestions screen informing that better recommendations can be generated if ratings are provided (see Figure 5, right). Finally, we have also improved the user profile page, the instructions, the explanation of the user personality and the presentation of the POI details.

Moreover, in order to better understand the impact of context management on system usability we have compared STS with a similar variant called STS-S. While both variants have similar interfaces, they differ in the way the weather factor is used in the recommender system. More precisely, STS has a user interface where the weather forecast is shown (missing in STS-S) and it exploits the weather condition at the item location for better predicting items' ratings (missing in STS-S). During the experiment, the users were randomly assigned to two groups: one group used STS and the other STS-S. This enabled us to investigate the influence of the incorporation of an important contextual factor, such as the weather, on the usability of the system.

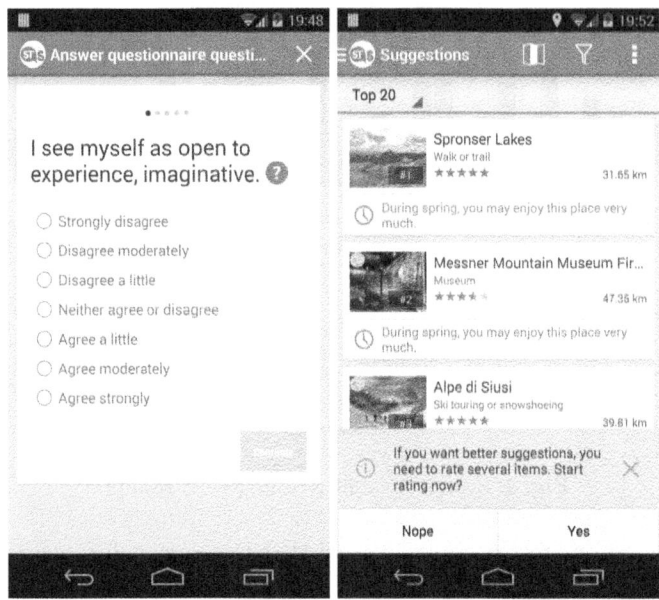

Fig. 5. New user interface design: (left) 5-item personality questionnaire, and, (right) recommendations

STS achieved higher SUS scores compared to STS-S: 78.83 vs 77. Although these two scores are close (and better than the benchmark, i.e., 68) the majority of the users have evaluated STS better than STS-S, in terms of usability. We have computed the t-test, and observed marginal significantly better scores for Q6 and Q10 (see table 1). This indicates that the management of weather forecast data in the proposed mobile context-aware recommender system can increase the system usability in terms of consistency of the system (Q6) and the ability of the users to use the system (Q10). The reason for this is that weather plays an important role in user decision making in tourism application (especially mobile) and also influences the successful adoption of such systems.

Table 1. Comparison of STS and STS-S systems in terms of average scores to SUS statements

	Q1	Q2	Q3	Q4	Q5	Q6	Q7	Q8	Q9	Q10	Overall SUS
STS-S	3.2	3.5	2.8	3.4	2.8	2.8	3.0	3.1	2.8	3.1	77.0
STS	3.0	3.2	3.1	3.3	3.1	3.2	2.8	3.4	2.7	3.4	78.8
p-value	0.27	0.16	0.18	0.40	0.14	**0.08**	0.25	0.19	0.40	**0.11**	0.19

Finally, we would like to note that STS was deployed on Google Play on September 18, 2013, and up to April 6, 2014, 535 users have downloaded and tried the system. Overall, the system has collected 2,528 ratings and many were entered together with a contextual description of the experience. Among the full set of users, 420 (78.5%) have completed the personality questionnaire and 350 (65.42%) went through the active learning phase. This shows that users largely accept to complete the personality questionnaire as well as the active learning phase to obtain better subsequent recommendations.

7 Conclusions and Future Work

In this paper, we have presented a novel mobile context-aware recommender system named STS, which recommends POIs using a set of contextual factors, such as the weather conditions, the time of day, user's location and user's mood. The novelty of our system resides in several aspects that, we believe, have resulted in the high usability score given by the users. First of all, STS learns to predict users' preferences not only using their past ratings, but also exploiting their personality, which is acquired by asking them to complete a brief and entertaining questionnaire as part of the registration process. Second, the user's personality information has been subsequently used for actively acquiring ratings for POIs that the user is likely to have experienced, and ultimately for producing better recommendations for POIs.

We have conducted a live user study where we measured the system's usability. The results of our user study show that STS has a usability score well above standard benchmarks. Its interface was considered simple and intuitive, and no major usability problems were found during the user study. The main limitation of STS was that not enough clearly it lets the users to understand the true motivation and behaviour of certain functions (e.g. the personality test). We addressed this issue by revising the interaction design, whose benefits will be evaluated in a future work, together with other improvements mainly related the the proactive behaviour of the system. Moreover, in the future we would like to extend the used set of contextual factors by taking into account other dimensions, such as the parking availability and the traffic conditions. We are also currently working on a novel explanation mechanism, that exploits the most influential contextual factor for a given POI rating prediction, to justify why the POI is recommended. We believe that this function can even further improve the usability of the system.

References

1. Adomavicius, G., Mobasher, B., Ricci, F., Tuzhilin, A.: Context-aware recommender systems. AI Magazine 32(3), 67–80 (2011)
2. Baltrunas, L., Kaminskas, M., Ludwig, B., Moling, O., Ricci, F., Aydin, A., Lüke, K.-H., Schwaiger, R.: InCarMusic: Context-aware music recommendations in a car. In: Huemer, C., Setzer, T. (eds.) EC-Web 2011. LNBIP, vol. 85, pp. 89–100. Springer, Heidelberg (2011)

3. Baltrunas, L., Ludwig, B., Peer, S., Ricci, F.: Context relevance assessment and exploitation in mobile recommender systems. Personal and Ubiquitous Computing 16(5), 507–526 (2012)
4. Bangor, A., Kortum, P., Miller, J.: Determining what individual sus scores mean: Adding an adjective rating scale. Journal of Usability Studies 4(3) (2009)
5. Braunhofer, M., Elahi, M., Ge, M., Ricci, F.: Context dependent preference acquisition with personality-based active learning in mobile recommender systems. In: Zaphiris, P., Ioannou, A. (eds.) LCT 2014, Part II. LNCS, vol. 8524, pp. 105–116. Springer, Heidelberg (2014)
6. Braunhofer, M., Elahi, M., Ricci, F., Schievenin, T.: Context-aware points of interest suggestion with dynamic weather data management. In: 21st Conference on Information and Communication Technologies in Tourism, ENTER 2014 (2014)
7. Brooke, J.: Sus: A quick and dirty usability scale. Usability Evaluation in Industry 189, 194 (1996)
8. Codina, V., Ricci, F., Ceccaroni, L.: Exploiting the semantic similarity of contextual situations for pre-filtering recommendation. In: Carberry, S., Weibelzahl, S., Micarelli, A., Semeraro, G. (eds.) UMAP 2013. LNCS, vol. 7899, pp. 165–177. Springer, Heidelberg (2013)
9. Elahi, M., Braunhofer, M., Ricci, F., Tkalcic, M.: Personality-based active learning for collaborative filtering recommender systems. In: Baldoni, M., Baroglio, C., Boella, G., Micalizio, R. (eds.) AI*IA 2013. LNCS (LNAI), vol. 8249, pp. 360–371. Springer, Heidelberg (2013)
10. Gosling, S.D., Rentfrow, P.J., Swann Jr., W.B.: A very brief measure of the big-five personality domains. Journal of Research in Personality 37(6), 504–528 (2003)
11. Jannach, D., Zanker, M., Fuchs, M.: Constraint-based recommendation in tourism: A multiperspective case study. Information Technology & Tourism 11(2), 139–155 (2009)
12. Knijnenburg, B.P., Willemsen, M.C., Gantner, Z., Soncu, H., Newell, C.: Explaining the user experience of recommender systems. User Modeling and User-Adapted Interaction 22(4-5), 441–504 (2012)
13. Koren, Y., Bell, R., Volinsky, C.: Matrix factorization techniques for recommender systems. Computer 42(8), 30–37 (2009)
14. Panniello, U., Tuzhilin, A., Gorgoglione, M., Palmisano, C., Pedone, A.: Experimental comparison of pre-vs. post-filtering approaches in context-aware recommender systems. In: Proceedings of the Third ACM Conference on Recommender Systems, pp. 265–268. ACM (2009)
15. Park, M.-H., Park, H.-S., Cho, S.-B.: Restaurant recommendation for group of people in mobile environments using probabilistic multi-criteria decision making. In: Lee, S., Choo, H., Ha, S., Shin, I.C. (eds.) APCHI 2008. LNCS, vol. 5068, pp. 114–122. Springer, Heidelberg (2008)
16. Rentfrow, P.J., Gosling, S.D.: The do re mi's of everyday life: the structure and personality correlates of music preferences. Journal of Personality and Social Psychology 84(6), 1236 (2003)
17. Sauro, J.: Measuring usability with the system usability scale (sus), http://www.measuringusability.com/sus.php (accessed: January 15, 2013)
18. Swarbrooke, J., Horner, S.: Consumer behaviour in tourism. Routledge (2007)
19. Tullis, T.S., Stetson, J.N.: A comparison of questionnaires for assessing website usability. In: Usability Professional Association Conference (2004)

A Linked Data Recommender System Using a Neighborhood-Based Graph Kernel

Vito Claudio Ostuni[1], Tommaso Di Noia[1],
Roberto Mirizzi[2], and Eugenio Di Sciascio[1]

[1] Polytechnic University of Bari, Bari, Italy
[2] Yahoo!, Sunnivale, CA, US
{vitoclaudio.ostuni,tommaso.dinoia,eugenio.disciascio}@poliba.it,
robertom@yahoo-inc.com

Abstract. The ultimate mission of a Recommender System (RS) is to help users discover items they might be interested in. In order to be really useful for the end-user, Content-based (CB) RSs need both to harvest as much information as possible about such items and to effectively handle it. The boom of `Linked Open Data` (LOD) datasets with their huge amount of semantically interrelated data is thus a great opportunity for boosting CB-RSs. In this paper we present a CB-RS that leverages LOD and profits from a *neighborhood-based graph kernel*. The proposed kernel is able to compute semantic item similarities by matching their local neighborhood graphs. Experimental evaluation on the `MovieLens` dataset shows that the proposed approach outperforms in terms of accuracy and novelty other competitive approaches.

1 Introduction

In personalized information access, the role played by recommender systems is growing considerably in importance. Every time we buy a product on Amazon, watch a movie on Netflix, listen to a song on Pandora, just to cite a few, their recommender systems suggest new items we could be interested in. Broadly speaking, existing technologies used to build recommendation engines fall in either of the following two categories: content-based filtering and collaborative filtering ones. In this work we focus on Content-based Recommender Systems (CB-RSs). They are based exclusively on domain knowledge to compute useful recommendations for the end-users by looking at information collected in their profile. On the one hand, when designing and developing a CB-RS, one of the biggest issues to face is the difficulty to get such knowledge. On the other hand, a common problem of this technique is the lack of novelty for recommended items.

The research presented here addresses these two problems by exploiting `Linked Open Data` to get domain knowledge and by proposing a neighborhood-based graph kernel. This is able to effectively handle the graph-based nature of the underlying LOD knowledge and capture the relations existing between items in order to compute accurate and novel recommendations. Once we represent the items by their local graph, that we call *item neighborhood graph*, the kernel computes a weighted count of common entities between two item neighborhood graphs by taking into account their local structure. Finally, we use such kernel with SVM regression to learn the user model and to output a recommendation list.

Main contributions of this work are:

- mining of the semantics associated to items through their LOD-based local graph representation;
- formulation of a neighboorhood-based graph kernel for matching LOD-based item descriptions;
- improvement in accuracy and novelty with respect to existing CB-RSs that leverage LOD;

The rest of this paper is structured as follows. In Section 2 we detail our recommendation approach, specifying how we leverage Linked Open Data and defining a graph-kernel suitable for RDF data. The evaluation of our system and discussion of the results is carried out in Section 3. Then, we present relevant related work in Section 4. Finally, conclusion and future work conclude this paper.

2 Content-Based Recommendation from LOD Using Graph Kernels

A common way of computing content-based recommendations is learning a function that, for each item in the system, predicts the relevance of such item for the user. In a few words, the relevance represents the likelihood that the user is interested in that item [17]. The application of Machine Learning techniques is a typical way to accomplish such task [17]. A *top-N* item recommendation problem in a standard content-based setting is mainly split into two different tasks: (i) given a collection of items for which past user's preferences are available, learn a regression or classification model to predict the relevance associated to unknown items; (ii) eventually, according to such scores, the system recommends the most relevant items to the user.

More formally, let I be the set of items to use in the recommendation. For each user $u \in U$, we assume to have a collection of items $I_u \subset I$, with their associated relevance scores $r_{u,i}$. Depending on the system these scores can be derived from either implicit or explicit feedback. Given a training set for u defined as $T_u = \{(i, r_{u,i}) \text{ with } i \in I_u\}$, the two tasks for the *top-N* recommendation problem, in our setting, consist of:

1. learning a function $f_u : I \to \mathbb{R}$ from T_u which assigns a relevance score to the items in I;
2. using such function to predict the score associated to all the unknown items in $I \setminus I_u$, rank them and recommend the *top-N*.

Due to the underlying data model of RDF datasets, we are particularly interested in those machine learning methods that are appropriate for dealing with objects structured as graphs. A popular class of techniques particularly suited for working with structured data are *Kernel Methods* [19]. Given two input objects i and j, defined in an input domain space D, the basic idea behind Kernel Methods is to construct a **kernel function** $k : D \times D \to \mathbb{R}$, that can be informally seen as a similarity measure between i and j. This function must satisfy $k(i,j) = \langle \phi(i), \phi(j) \rangle$ for all $i, j \in D$, where $\phi : D \to F$ is a mapping function to a inner product[1] feature space F. A kernel function defined in such a way must be symmetric and positive semidefinite in order to be a valid kernel [19]. Then, the classification or regression task involves linear convex methods based exclusively on inner products computed using the kernel in the embedding feature space. These methods provide a powerful framework for decoupling the data representation from the learning task.

In this work we define a novel graph-based kernel and adopt SVM Regression [19] as kernel-based algorithm for learning the user model f_u. We formalize our *top-N* item recommendation problem in a regression setting because a continuous relevance score is needed for computing the final ranking.

Hereafter we describe the way we represent items in I by means of LOD datasets and then we show how such a representation is leveraged in our graph-based kernel.

2.1 Graph-Based Item Representation

Defining an expressive and efficient kernel starting from RDF data is not a trivial task. In the last few years various graph kernel functions have been designed to capture the intrinsic similarity of graphs. Unfortunately many complex kernels, such as the ones based on subgraph isomorphism, maximum common subgraphs, or graph edit distance are appropriate for chemical structures and biological networks but are not suitable for knowledge graphs. Mostly because of the size of those graphs that require computational efficient methods and because they have different properties due to the fact that they are not governed by physical laws [9]. In addition, as pointed out by [11], graphs representing chemical compounds usually have few node labels which occur frequently in the graph and nodes in these graphs have a low degree. In contrast, in RDF graphs node URIs are used as unique identifiers and hence occur only once in a graph. Moreover, nodes in RDF graphs may have a very high degree.

In our approach we condition the computation of the graph kernel to a graph matching problem. We say that two items are similar if they share a similar neighborhood in the RDF graph. The rationale behind our approach is that two items are similar if they are related to similar entities. Each item $i \in I$ is then modelled by extracting a graph-based representation from the underlying RDF data. Given the URI corresponding to i, we perform a breadth-first search (via SPARQL queries) from this item up to a limited depth to extract a subgraph which characterizes the information content associated to i. In the approach presented in this paper, we consider the underlying RDF graph as undirected because we are

---

[1] Following the notation used in the kernel literature, we use $\langle \boldsymbol{x}, \boldsymbol{y} \rangle$ to denote the inner product between the vectors $\boldsymbol{x}$ and $\boldsymbol{y}$.

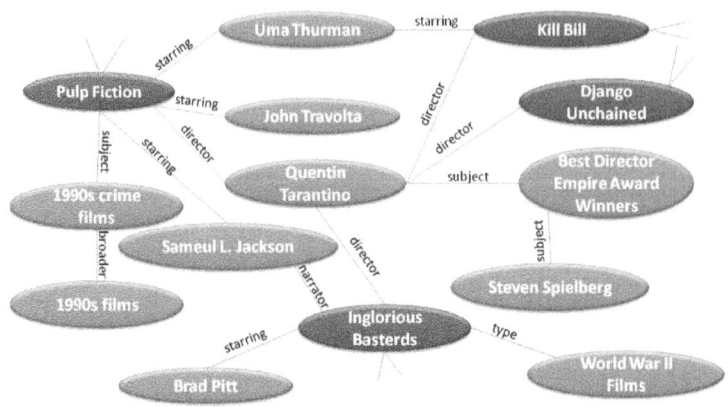

Fig. 1. Fragment of an RDF graph extracted from DBpedia

mostly interested in the entities and not in the relation type in itself. So, given an RDF entity e, we collect all the RDF triples where it appears as either subject or object via a property p. Collecting all the RDF triples extracted starting from each item we build a new undirected graph $G = (E, P)$, where E represents the set of nodes (entities) and $P \subseteq E \times E$ the set of edges. We name each edge in P as $p_k(e_n, e_m)$ to denote that the property p_k connects the two entities e_n and e_m. This means that either the triple (e_n, p_k, e_m) or the triple (e_m, p_k, e_n) belongs to the original RDF graph. We notice that, by construction of G, we have $I \subset E$. In this work, we do not consider literals nor datatype properties in the construction of the graph.

Fig. 1 shows a sketch of the graph G extracted from DBpedia for the movie domain. The nodes in red belong to I and represent movies. As for the other entities in the figure, it is easy to notice they represent actors, directors, narrators, categories, classes. In the actual graph, there are many more properties that allow us to get rich and detailed knowledge about movies.

We introduce now the notion of **h-hop item neighborhood graph** for G. For a generic item i, its h-hop neighborhood graph $G^h(i) = (E^h(i), P^h(i))$ is the subgraph of G induced by the set of entities $E^h(i)$ that are reachable in **at most** h hops from i according to the shortest path. Fig. 2 shows two possible 2-hop item neighborhood graphs for item i and item j, respectively $G^2(i)$ and $G^2(j)$. We see that, if we consider the shortest path, all the entities are no more than 2 hops distant from i and j, respectively.

Finally, we define $\widehat{E}^h(i) = E^h(i) \setminus E^{h-1}(i)$ as the set of entities **exactly** h hops far from i. In other words, these entities are reachable, based on the shortest path, only after h hops. Analogously, we define $\widehat{P}^h(i) = P^h(i) \setminus P^{h-1}(i)$.

In order to clarify how to build $\widehat{E}^h$ and $\widehat{P}^h$, we show an example using the two item neighborhood graphs in Fig. 2. With reference to items i and j, we have:

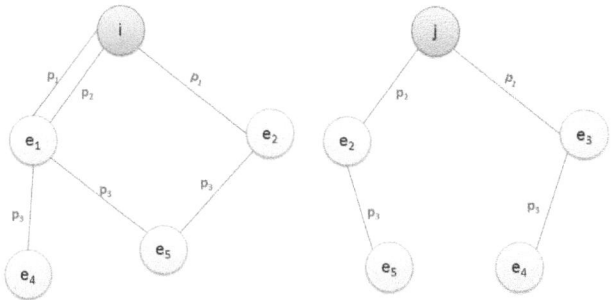

Fig. 2. Two 2-hop item neighborhood graphs

$E^1(i) = \{e_1, e_2\}$ $\quad P^1(i) = \{p_1(i,e_1), p_2(i,e_1), p_1(i,e_2)\}$
$E^2(i) = \{e_1, e_2, e_4, e_5\}$ $\quad P^2(i) = \{p_1(i,e_1), p_2(i,e_1), p_1(i,e_2), p_3(e_1,e_4),$
$\qquad\qquad\qquad\qquad\qquad\qquad p_3(e_1,e_5), p_3(e_2,e_5)\}$
$\widehat{E}^1(i) = \{e_1, e_2\}$ $\quad \widehat{P}^1(i) = \{p_1(i,e_1), p_2(i,e_1), p_1(i,e_2)\}$
$\widehat{E}^2(i) = \{e_4, e_5\}$ $\quad \widehat{P}^2(i) = \{p_3(e_1,e_4), p_3(e_1,e_5), p_3(e_2,e_5)\}$

$E^1(j) = \{e_2, e_3\}$ $\quad P^1(j) = \{p_2(j,e_2), p_1(j,e_3)\}$
$E^2(j) = \{e_2, e_3, e_4, e_5\}$ $\quad P^2(j) = \{p_2(j,e_2), p_1(j,e_3), p_3(e_2,e_5), p_3(e_3,e_4)\}$
$\widehat{E}^1(j) = \{e_2, e_3\}$ $\quad \widehat{P}^1(j) = \{p_2(j,e_2), p_1(j,e_3)\}$
$\widehat{E}^2(j) = \{e_4, e_5\}$ $\quad \widehat{P}^2(j) = \{p_3(e_2,e_5), p_3(e_3,e_4)\}$

As we will see in Section 2.2, $\widehat{E}^h(i)$ and $\widehat{P}^h(i)$ form the basis for our neighborhood-based graph kernel. We may observe that $\widehat{E}^h(i)$ contains information about which entities are associated to item i at a given distance, while $\widehat{P}^h(i)$ about how they occur.

Finally, we can see that if $G^h(i)$ and $G^h(j)$ share at least one entity, then i and j are at most distant $2 \cdot h$ hops. For instance, for a *2-hop item neighborhood graph* as the ones depicted in Fig. 2 we can compute paths of up to length 4 between i and j.

Summing up, let $I = \{i, j, \ldots\}$ be the set of items we want to recommend, as for example movies or musical artists, we represent them by their h-hop neighborhood graph $G^h(i)$. This graph-based data is exploited by our kernel to build a LOD-based recommender system able to suggest relevant resources in I, given T_u.

2.2 Neighborhood-Based Graph Kernel

Based on the notion of *h-hop item neighborhood graph* we define the **h-hop neighborhood-based graph kernel** $k_{G^h}(i,j)$ as:

$$k_{G^h}(i,j) = \langle \phi_{G^h}(i), \phi_{G^h}(j) \rangle \tag{1}$$

where the application of the map function ϕ_{G^h} to the h-hop item neighborhood graph $G^h(i)$ gives us its feature vector representation:

$$\phi_{G^h}(i) = (w_{i,e_1}, w_{i,e_2}, ... w_{i,e_m}, ..., w_{i,e_l})$$

where w weights refer to entities in E. Specifically, w_{i,e_m} represents the weight associated to the entity e_m in $G^h(i)$. Each term is computed using the following formula:

$$w_{i,e_m} = \sum_{l=1}^{h} \alpha_l \cdot c_{\widehat{P}^l(i),e_m}$$

where α_l coefficients are real and non-negative, and:

$$c_{\widehat{P}^l(i),e_m} = |\{p_k(e_n, e_m) \mid p_k(e_n, e_m) \in \widehat{P}^l(i) \wedge e_m \in \widehat{E}^l(i)\}|$$

In particular, $c_{\widehat{P}^l(i),e_m}$ is the number of edges in $\widehat{P}^l(i)$ that involve the node e_m, that is the *occurrence* of the entity e_m in the item neighborhood at distance l. The more the entity e_m appears in paths originated by i, the more it is descriptive of i. Indeed, α_l is a weighting factor depending on the distance l from the item i, whose aim is to up-weight entities closer to the item and to penalize farther entities. It allows us to take into account the *locality* of those entities in the graph neighborhood. The closer an entity e_m to the item i, the stronger its relatedness to it. In other words, α_l can be seen as a decay factor for entities farther from the item i. In Section 3.2 we will show the results of the experimental evaluation for different values of α_l.

To clarify how we compute the weights w in the construction of the ϕ_{G^h} feature vectors we show an example using the two item neighborhood graphs represented in Fig. 2. With respect to item i, we have: $c_{\widehat{P}^1(i),e_1} = 2$, $c_{\widehat{P}^1(i),e_2} = 1$, $c_{\widehat{P}^2(i),e_4} = 1$, $c_{\widehat{P}^2(i),e_5} = 2$. For item j, we have: $c_{\widehat{P}^1(j),e_2} = 1$, $c_{\widehat{P}^1(j),e_3} = 1$, $c_{\widehat{P}^2(i),e_4} = 1$, $c_{\widehat{P}^2(i),e_5} = 1$. All other $c_{\widehat{P}^l(i),e}$ are equal to 0. Once the occurrences $c_{\widehat{P}^l,e}$ are known, the computation of the w scores is straightforward.

Finally, the kernel $k_{G^h}(i,j)$ can be computed by taking the scalar product of the respective feature vectors, $\phi_{G^h}(i)$ and $\phi_{G^h}(j)$. The result of the dot product is essentially the weighted count of the common entities shared by the two item neighborhoods. It is noteworthy that this relatedness measure is based both on *occurrence* and on *locality* of the entities.

In order to uniform different neighborhood sizes, each feature vector is normalized to unit length using the $L2$ norm, hence the dot product corresponds to the cosine similarity measure.

Similarly to [20] and [3], our kernel relies on an explicit computation of the feature vectors. This leads to a sparse vector representation that can speed up the computation with respect to pairwise item computation, allowing us to use fast linear SVM solvers.

3 Experimental Evaluation

In this section we detail the experiments accomplished to evaluate our approach. In particular we are interested in the following two aspects: (i) evaluate the accuracy and novelty of the proposed neighborhood-based graph kernel for recommendations leveraging LOD; (ii) investigate the improvements of the proposed approach with respect to a previous work on LOD-based RSs [4] and a RS based on another graph kernel for RDF [11].

3.1 Experimental Setting

Datasets Description. The evaluation has been carried out on the well known MovieLens[2] dataset. The original MovieLens 1M dataset contains 1,000,209 ratings for 3,883 movies by 6,040 users. Starting from this dataset, we first transformed the 1-5 star ratings to binary relevance scores using 4 as threshold. Then, in order to exploit the knowledge encoded in LOD datasets, we mapped items in MovieLens to their corresponding DBpedia URI. In this work, we leveraged DBpedia 3.9, one of the principal knowledge bases in the the LOD cloud. It currently contains about 4 million resources, out of which 3.22 million are classified in a consistent ontology[3]. For a detailed explanation about the mapping methodology please refer to [15]. The item mappings to DBpedia are available at: http://sisinflab.poliba.it/semanticweb/lod/recsys/datasets/.

Then, for each movie in the dataset we extracted its h-hop neighborhood graph with $h = 2$. This choice is driven by a preliminary analysis where we found out that $h = 2$ is a good compromise between computation time and accuracy of the recommendation. During the search, we considered all the RDF object properties belonging to the DBpedia ontology[4], plus three more properties: rdf:type, dcterms:subject and skos:broader. At the end of the data extraction procedure, the resulting graph contains 121,584 entities.

Evaluation Methodology. In our evaluation we focused on accuracy and novelty performances. We measured accuracy by *Precision@N/Recall@N* [8] and *Mean Reciprocal Rank*, and novelty by *Entropy-Based Novelty* [1].

Precision@N is computed as the fraction of *top-N* recommended items in test set that are relevant for the user. *Recall@N* is the fraction of relevant items in the test set which appear in the *top-N* recommendation list.

Mean Reciprocal Rank (*MRR*) is useful for evaluating how early in the list the first relevant recommended item appears. Specifically, *Reciprocal Rank* is the inverse of the position of the first relevant recommendation. The higher, the better.

In the computation of these accuracy metrics, we considered only the items that appear in the user test set to populate the *top-N* user recommendation list.

As pointed out by [12], the most accurate recommendations according to the standard metrics are sometimes not the recommendations that are most useful to users. In order to assess the utility of a recommender system, it is extremely important to evaluate also its capacity to suggest items that users would not readily discover for themselves, that is its ability to generate novel

---
[2] http://www.grouplens.org/node/73
[3] http://wiki.dbpedia.org/Ontology39
[4] http://mappings.dbpedia.org/server/ontology/classes/Film

and unexpected results. The *Entropy-Based Novelty* (*EBN*) expresses the ability of a recommender system to suggest less popular items, i.e. items not known by a wide number of users. In particular, for each user's recommendation list L_u, the novelty is computed as:

$$EBN_u@N = -\sum_{i \in L_u} p_i \cdot \log_2 p_i$$

where:

$$p_i = \frac{|\{u \in U \mid i \text{ is relevant to } u\}|}{|U|}$$

The lower $EBN_u@N$, the better the novelty.

Table 1 shows some statistics about the dataset used for the experiments. In order to assess the performance of the proposed algorithm for different sizes of the training set, we split the MovieLens dataset in different chunks of training/test data: 20-80%, 40-60% and 80-20%. Evaluating the performance also with a small training set allows us to understand how immune the system is to shortage of information about users i.e., its immunity to cold-start problem for user.

For each training/test partitioning, the task was to use the training set to train the model and generate the *top-N* recommendation list for each user. After the output was produced, we evaluated the system by the metrics previously defined, according to the data in the test set. We repeated the experiment three times for each condition of the training/test partitioning, with randomly selected samples each time. The results presented in Table 2 are averaged across the three runs.

Table 1. Dataset statistics

training/test partitioning	users	items	avg train items per user	avg test items per user
MovieLens 20-80%	6038	3148	29.67	116.78
MovieLens 40-60%	6036	3148	58.98	87.45
MovieLens 80-20%	5992	3148	118.23	29.09

3.2 Results Discussion

The first part of our tests was carried out to tune the α_l coefficients (as defined in Section 2.2) in order to evaluate the effectiveness of the kernel. For this purpose, we performed several experiments by varying the value of the two coefficients α_1 and α_2. We remember that since our experiments have been performed with $h = 2$, we only have these two coefficients. In particular we considered the ratio $\frac{\alpha_1}{\alpha_2}$. The rationale behind our choice is that the higher $\frac{\alpha_1}{\alpha_2}$, the higher is the importance given to the entities directly connected to the items (*1-hop* entities). A value of $\frac{\alpha_1}{\alpha_2} < 1$ means that *2-hop* entities are given more importance than *1-hop* entities. In Table 2 we show the results for several values of the α-ratio.

Accuracy. When we have a few ratings in the training set (as for MovieLens 20-80%), we notice the best accuracy results are reached for values $\frac{\alpha_1}{\alpha_2} \leq 1$. To us, this is quite surprisingly since it means that, if we want to improve the accuracy of recommended items, the contribution carried by entities at a 2-hop distance must be considered more or equally relevant than the one of the 1-hop distant entities. Our interpretation for this behavior is that when the training set is small, the system has to learn the user model based on a few items in the user profile. Hence, up-weighting the entities at 2-hop distance allows the system to better exploit the LOD graph structure by catching implicit relations between items. The situation changes when the training set grows.

Novelty. The best novelty results are achieved when the α-ratio is equal to 1, under all the conditions of partitioning. This means giving the same importance to *1-hop* and *2-hop* entities.

Comparison with Other Methods. In the second part of our experiments we compared our approach with other existing RSs. Table 3 shows the results. NK-α-ratio refers to our Neighborhood-based Kernel approach. VSM is the LOD-based RS presented in [4]. It relies on a bag-of-resources item representation and the well known Vector Space Model. The user model is learned using SVM. Both in [4] and in our approach the C meta-parameter for SVM is chosen via cross-validation. NB uses the same item feature representation as [4], but a different learning algorithm, the Naive Bayes classifier. This is the baseline for our comparison. WK refers to the Walk-based Kernel presented in [11] for dealing with RDF graphs. The procedure to learn the user model is the same, we only replaced the kernel. The results show that our approach performs always better than the others, both in accuracy and in novelty.

Table 2. Accuracy and Novelty results for MovieLens data – kernel calibration

α_1/α_2	MRR	P@1	P@5	P@10	R@1	R@5	R@10	EBN@10	EBN@25	EBN@50
Training set 20% – Test set 80%										
0.25	0.8701	0.7665	0.7708	0.6895	0.0259	0.1300	0.2342	0.3683	0.9110	1.8428
1	0.8454	0.7267	0.7482	0.6712	0.0242	0.1259	0.2304	**0.2919**	**0.7493**	**1.5027**
2	0.8570	0.7473	0.7591	0.6817	0.0249	0.1267	0.2312	0.4417	1.1223	2.3400
5	0.8536	0.7416	0.7551	0.6772	0.0245	0.1257	0.2311	0.3186	0.8239	1.6596
10	0.8541	0.7420	0.7576	0.6824	0.0243	0.1248	0.2310	0.4659	1.0691	1.9882
20	0.8551	0.7430	0.7574	0.6840	0.0245	0.1243	0.2309	0.3642	0.8930	1.8039
Training set 40% – Test set 60%										
0.25	0.8700	0.7662	0.7792	0.6846	0.0351	0.1775	0.3128	0.6298	1.5448	3.0880
1	0.8576	0.7459	0.7671	0.6767	0.0343	0.1770	0.3101	**0.4484**	**1.1523**	**2.3442**
2	0.8676	0.7633	0.7738	0.6822	0.0347	0.1766	0.3110	0.6920	1.7489	3.572
5	0.8626	0.7542	0.7729	0.6787	0.0342	0.1761	0.3096	0.5196	1.3431	2.7098
10	0.8687	0.7637	0.7809	0.6866	0.0344	0.1775	0.3124	0.6955	1.6652	3.1951
20	**0.8726**	**0.7709**	**0.7833**	0.6882	**0.0352**	0.1776	**0.3129**	0.5665	1.4109	2.8935
Training set 80% – Test set 20%										
0.25	0.8574	0.7465	0.7323	0.5737	0.1028	0.4705	0.6320	1.0336	2.5164	4.9358
1	0.8533	0.7393	0.7325	0.5756	0.1026	0.4738	0.6349	**0.6584**	**1.7063**	**3.5096**
2	0.8537	0.7389	0.7347	0.5754	0.1028	0.4739	0.6341	1.0251	2.5985	5.1991
5	0.8536	0.7393	0.7361	0.5777	0.1008	0.4740	0.6351	0.7945	2.0451	4.1497
10	0.8607	0.7505	0.7440	0.5796	0.1030	0.4771	0.6358	0.9947	2.4532	4.8567
20	**0.8678**	0.7625	0.7448	0.5799	**0.1059**	**0.4775**	**0.6359**	0.8489	2.1117	4.3242

Table 3. Accuracy and Novelty results for MovieLens data – comparative approaches

alg	MRR	P@1	P@5	P@10	R@1	R@5	R@10	EBN@10	EBN@25	EBN@50
				Training set 20% – Test set 80%						
NK-0.25	**0.8701**	**0.7665**	0.7708	**0.6895**	**0.0259**	**0.1300**	**0.2342**	0.3683	0.9110	1.8428
NK-1	0.8454	0.7267	0.7482	0.6712	0.0242	0.1259	0.2304	**0.2919**	**0.7493**	**1.5027**
NB	0.7908	0.6577	0.6158	0.6099	0.0222	0.1071	0.2146	0.6817	1.4635	2.5681
VSM	0.8341	0.7101	0.7241	0.6633	0.0233	0.1188	0.2251	0.3543	0.8631	1.6847
WK	0.7948	0.6624	0.6167	0.6063	0.0223	0.1077	0.2143	0.5286	1.2648	2.3743
				Training set 40% – Test set 60%						
NK-1	0.8576	0.7459	0.7671	0.6767	0.0343	0.1770	0.3101	**0.4484**	**1.1523**	**2.3442**
NK-20	**0.8726**	**0.7709**	**0.7833**	**0.6882**	**0.0352**	**0.1776**	**0.3129**	0.5665	1.4109	2.8935
NB	0.7844	0.6452	0.6211	0.6158	0.0298	0.1451	0.2890	1.1050	2.4112	4.2484
VSM	0.8528	0.7392	0.7518	0.6722	0.0329	0.1679	0.3066	0.5329	1.3481	2.6926
WK	0.7911	0.6523	0.6185	0.6085	0.0298	0.1449	0.2883	0.7477	1.8834	3.6366
				Training set 80% – Test set 20%						
NK-1	0.8533	0.7393	0.7325	0.5756	0.1026	0.4738	0.6349	**0.6584**	**1.7063**	**3.5096**
NK-20	**0.8678**	**0.7625**	**0.7448**	**0.5799**	**0.1059**	**0.4775**	**0.6359**	0.8489	2.1117	4.3242
NB	0.7894	0.6506	0.6214	0.5454	0.0918	0.4174	0.6133	1.698	3.7625	6.5729
VSM	0.8509	0.7344	0.7309	0.5741	0.1001	0.4709	0.6340	0.7628	1.9818	4.042
WK	0.7892	0.6475	0.6161	0.5336	0.0923	0.4154	0.6106	0.9915	2.5958	5.0806

4 Related Work

Being our approach content-based and leveraging Linked Open Data, in this section we will overview RSs based on ontologies and on LOD. Part of this section is also reserved to existing literature about graph kernels.

Ontology-Based RSs. *Foxtrot* and *Quickstep* are two ontology-based recommender systems presented in [13]. The definition of semantic user profiles allows the system to compute collaborative recommendations. In [2] the authors propose a hybrid recommendation system, where user preferences and item features are described by semantic concepts to obtain users' clusters corresponding to implicit *Communities of Interest*. In [14] the authors introduce the so called *semantically enhanced collaborative filtering* where structured semantic knowledge about items is used in conjunction with user-item ratings to create a combined similarity measure for item comparisons. In all of these works, experimental evaluation demonstrates that the accuracy is improved especially in presence of sparse datasets.

LOD-Based RSs. In the last years, great interest has been shown by the scientific community in using Linked Open Data for RSs. The authors in [7] were among the first to theoretically propose to use LOD as knowledge base for recommender systems. In [18] the authors use DBpedia to feed a RS based on matrix-factorization. In [4,5] a model-based approach and a memory-based one are presented to compute content-based recommendations leveraging LOD datasets and DBpedia in particular. More recently, two hybrid approaches have been presented: in [15] it is shown how to compute *top-N* recommendations from implicit feedback using linked data sources and in [10] the authors propose an event recommendation system based on linked data and user diversity. In [16] a mobile RS that uses DBpedia as the core for the recommendation is presented.

Graph Kernels. Several graph kernels have been proposed in machine learning. Based on the concept of *Convolution Kernels* [6], many kernel functions work by counting common structures in graphs. While the problem of checking whether two graphs are isomorph is known to be NP-complete, the task of searching for common substructure usually can be done more efficiently. In [20] the authors present a kernel based on the Weisfeiler-Lehman test of graph isomorphism. Basically they compute the number of subtrees shared between two graphs. More recently, some variants of these kernels have been developed in the field of Semantic Web with application to RDF graphs. In [11] graph kernels based on intersection graphs and intersection trees are introduced. Finally, a faster approximation of the Weisfeiler-Lehman graph kernel is presented in [3].

5 Conclusion and Future Work

The high-quality and vast information contained within Linked Open Data datasets, makes LOD the perfect candidate for a new era of knowledge-enabled and content-based recommender systems. In this paper we have presented a content-based recommender system that leverages the knowledge encoded in semantic datasets of the Linked Open Data compass. The innovative aspects of this work are the way we represent items in the knowledge base by their neighborhood graphs, and the usage of a neighborhood-based graph kernel that is able to effectively exploit the local neighborhood of such items. The evaluation shows an improvement in the accuracy and novelty of our system with respect to existing approaches for content-based recommendation. Currently, we are working on other graph kernels which consider different substructures such as partial subtrees.

References

1. Bellogín, A., Cantador, I., Castells, P.: A study of heterogeneity in recommendations for a social music service. In: Proceedings of the 1st International Workshop on Information Heterogeneity and Fusion in Recommender Systems, HetRec 2010, pp. 1–8. ACM Press, New York (2010)
2. Cantador, I., Bellogín, A., Castells, P.: A multilayer ontology-based hybrid recommendation model. AI Commun. Special Issue on Rec. Sys. 21(2-3), 203–210 (2008)
3. de Vries, G.K.D.: A fast approximation of the weisfeiler-lehman graph kernel for RDF data. In: Blockeel, H., Kersting, K., Nijssen, S., Železný, F. (eds.) ECML PKDD 2013, Part I. LNCS (LNAI), vol. 8188, pp. 606–621. Springer, Heidelberg (2013)
4. Di Noia, T., Mirizzi, R., Ostuni, V.C., Romito, D.: Exploiting the web of data in model-based recommender systems. In: Proceedings of the Sixth ACM Conference on Recommender Systems, RecSys 2012, pp. 253–256. ACM, New York (2012)
5. Di Noia, T., Mirizzi, R., Ostuni, V.C., Romito, D., Zanker, M.: Linked open data to support content-based recommender systems. In: Proceedings of the 8th International Conference on Semantic Systems, SEMANTICS 2012, pp. 1–8. ACM, New York (2012)
6. Gärtner, T., Flach, P.A., Wrobel, S.: On graph kernels: Hardness results and efficient alternatives. In: COLT, pp. 129–143 (2003)

7. Heitmann, B., Hayes, C.: Using linked data to build open, collaborative recommender systems. In: AAAI Spring Symposium: Linked Data Meets Artificial Intelligence (2010)
8. Herlocker, J.L., Konstan, J.A., Terveen, L.G., Riedl, J.T.: Evaluating collaborative filtering recommender systems. ACM Trans. Inf. Syst. 22(1), 5–53 (2004)
9. Khan, A., Li, N., Yan, X., Guan, Z., Chakraborty, S., Tao, S.: Neighborhood based fast graph search in large networks. In: Proceedings of the 2011 ACM SIGMOD International Conference on Management of Data, SIGMOD 2011, pp. 901–912. ACM, New York (2011)
10. Khrouf, H., Troncy, R.: Hybrid event recommendation using linked data and user diversity. In: Proceedings of the 7th ACM Conference on Recommender Systems, RecSys 2013, pp. 185–192. ACM, New York (2013)
11. Lösch, U., Bloehdorn, S., Rettinger, A.: Graph kernels for RDF data. In: Simperl, E., Cimiano, P., Polleres, A., Corcho, O., Presutti, V. (eds.) ESWC 2012. LNCS, vol. 7295, pp. 134–148. Springer, Heidelberg (2012)
12. McNee, S.M., Riedl, J., Konstan, J.A.: Being accurate is not enough: How accuracy metrics have hurt recommender systems. In: CHI 2006 Extended Abstracts on Human Factors in Computing Systems, CHI EA 2006, pp. 1097–1101. ACM, New York (2006)
13. Middleton, S.E., Roure, D.D., Shadbolt, N.R.: Ontology-based recommender systems. Handbook on Ontologies 32(6), 779–796 (2009)
14. Mobasher, B., Jin, X., Zhou, Y.: Semantically enhanced collaborative filtering on the web. In: Berendt, B., Hotho, A., Mladenič, D., van Someren, M., Spiliopoulou, M., Stumme, G. (eds.) EWMF 2003. LNCS (LNAI), vol. 3209, pp. 57–76. Springer, Heidelberg (2004)
15. Ostuni, V.C., Di Noia, T., Di Sciascio, E., Mirizzi, R.: Top-n recommendations from implicit feedback leveraging linked open data. In: Proceedings of the 7th ACM Conference on Recommender Systems, RecSys 2013, pp. 85–92. ACM, New York (2013)
16. Ostuni, V.C., Gentile, G., Di Noia, T., Mirizzi, R., Romito, D., Di Sciascio, E.: Mobile movie recommendations with linked data. In: Cuzzocrea, A., Kittl, C., Simos, D.E., Weippl, E., Xu, L. (eds.) CD-ARES 2013. LNCS, vol. 8127, pp. 400–415. Springer, Heidelberg (2013)
17. Pazzani, M.J., Billsus, D.: The adaptive web, pp. 325–341. Springer, Heidelberg (2007)
18. Peska, L., Vojtas, P.: Using linked open data to improve recommending on e-commerce. In: 2nd International Workshop on Semantic Technologies Meet Recommender Systems & Big Data (SeRSy 2013), CEUR-WS (2013)
19. Shawe-Taylor, J., Cristianini, N.: Kernel Methods for Pattern Analysis. Cambridge University Press, New York (2004)
20. Shervashidze, N., Schweitzer, P., van Leeuwen, E.J., Mehlhorn, K., Borgwardt, K.M.: Weisfeiler-lehman graph kernels. J. Mach. Learn. Res. 12, 2539–2561 (2011)

Resource Recommendation in Social Annotation Systems Based on User Partitioning

Jonathan Gemmell, Bamshad Mobasher, and Robin Burke

Center for Web Intelligence
School of Computing, DePaul University
Chicago, Illinois, USA
{jgemmell,mobasher,rburke}@cdm.depaul.edu

Abstract. Social annotation systems have become a staple of the World Wide Web, enabling users to organize their favorite resources with tags. Resource recommenders that exploit these tags to model users and resources have proven to be effective in assisting users navigate complex information spaces, particularly when combined with other approaches. In previous work, we demonstrated the power of a linear weighted hybrid that combines the weighted results of simple component recommenders. While this hybrid was able to learn how to weigh each of the components, it treated all users the same. In this work, we present a framework to automatically discover partitions of users and learn optimal weights for each partition. The experimental results on three real world data sets not only demonstrates an improvement in the accuracy of the algorithm, but also offers unique insights into how social annotation systems are used by various groups of users.

Keywords: User Partitioning, Personalization, Social Annotation Systems, Resource Recommendation, Hybrid Recommenders.

1 Introduction

Social annotation systems have become ubiquitous. Many sites such as Bibsonomy, Citeulike and Delicious are explicitly designed around the application of user-selected tags to online resources. Other sites such as Amazon, YouTube and LastFM have included annotations as part of their repertoire of tools. The complex relationship generated by the tagging process forms a large multidimensional information space, often called a folksonomy. Such an information space offers unique and interesting avenues for the user to navigate, but the sheer size and inherent noise can also make it frustrating. Recommender technologies are key to helping users exploit these systems without becoming encumbered by information overload.

These systems offer many potential forms of recommendation. Tag recommenders can aid users as they annotate resources. User recommenders can connect users with similar tastes. Resource search can help users find new and interesting items related to a particular tag. In this paper, we specifically explore resource recommendation. The system recommends a personalized set of resources for a given user.

Our linear weighted hybrid framework has proven to be effective across several data sets and across varying recommendation tasks. It relies on the output of several simple component recommenders. It then formulates a recommendation set by weighting these outputs in a linear combination. Our experimental work revealed that folksonomies often require a set of weights tuned specifically to their users to produce optimal results.

This insight implies that the structures of the folksonomies are inherently different from data set to data set. In LastFM, for example, a recommender that models resources as a vector of users does well. The same recommender performs relatively poorly in MovieLens, a website devoted to movies. LastFM users appear to be interacting with the system in a way that makes them better modeled by their music than MovieLens users are modeled by their movies, perhaps because users often gravitate to a particular genre of music, but most moviegoers watch the same big budget films.

Observing that user behavior influences the performance the component weights across data sets, we ask ourselves if it is not likely that the characteristics of different user segments may also require different component weights. It may be reasonable to cluster users based on some preconceived notion. However, such a notion for clustering the users may not be applicable to all data sets; we have already seen that data sets have unique characteristics. Moreover, a preconceived notion may not produce optimal separation of the users for the purpose of resource recommendation. In this paper, we integrate a user partitioning algorithm into our linear weighted hybrid framework, learning a different set of weights for each partition.

Our thorough experimental work reveals that the user partitioning hybrid surpasses that of the linear weighted hybrid while remaining efficient, scalable, and extensible. Moreover, examination of the partitions and their component weights underscore the unique characteristics of the data sets generated by the differing user behaviors.

The rest of this paper is organized as follows. We present related work in Section 2. In Section 3, we describe our data model and how we partition users. Section 4 details our experimental evaluation. Finally we offer our conclusions in Section 5.

2 Related Work

Resource recommendation is a well-studied problem. However, the complex structures of social annotation systems present new challenges. Efforts have often focused on adapting traditional methods, such as collaborative filtering, to the problem [5,17]. Graph based algorithms [12] have been proposed, but are computationally expensive when making a query. Matrix factorization models [14] are faster at query time, but are expensive to build. Probabilistic models [18,13] methods have also been proposed.

A common thread in these approaches is the desire to exploit the three dimensional information joining the user, resource and tag spaces. In previous work, we have attempted to tie together this information through the use of hybrid recommenders. Our linear weighted hybrid was composed of simple component recommenders, each of which focused on a particular dimension of the data. The hybrid has been proven to outperform the individual components in many recommendation scenarios [4]. However, this hybrid treated all users as if they were the same.

This paper extends the linear weighted hybrid, by proposing a framework for automatically partitioning users. The technique has already been demonstrated effective for tag recommendation.

3 User Partitioning Resource Recommendation Hybrid

This section begins by presenting the data model often used to describe a folksonomies. We then detail the framework for partitioning users and learning weights for the component recommenders Lastly, we briefly discuss each of the components that are the foundation of the hybrid.

3.1 Data Model

We model a social annotation system and four sets: U, R, T and A. U is the set of all users that employ the system. R is the set of all resources that any of the users have annotated. T is the set of all tags any user has every applied to a resource. Finally, A is the set of all annotations which is defined as a single user, a single resource, and all tags that user has applied to that resource.

Often this data is conceptualized as a three-dimensional matrix, which we call URT. The matrix is binary. An entry in it is 1 if u annotated r with t, and is 0 otherwise. One convenience of this matrix is the ability to generate aggregate projections. While these projections reduce the dimensionality making it easier to work with the data, it also sacrifices some information [11,5].

For example, we can aggregate resources across URT in order to generate UT. An entry $UT(u,t)$ in this projection is the number of times user u has annotated any resource with tag t. It is then possible to model a users as vectors drawn from this projection. Here, a user is modeled as a vector over the tag space, where the weight $w(t_i)$ in dimension i corresponds to the importance of the tag, t_i: $\boldsymbol{u^t} = \langle w(t_1), w(t_2)...w(t_{|T|}) \rangle$. Likewise, it is possible to model tags as column drawn from UT. Two other aggregate projections are possible, UR and RT offering ways to model resources and alternative means to model users or tags. We use these aggregate models in many of the component recommenders with the one caveat that our previous experimentation has shown that a binary version of UR yields better results. For consistency, we continue to use the binary version in this work.

3.2 User Partitioning Hybrid

Previous observations point toward a need to partition users and treat the partitions differently. For example, in a popular social annotation system focusing on music, users often employ generic tags such as "rock" or idiosyncratic tags such as "sawAtConcertWithSally". In this system, recommenders that models users across the tag space fare poorly. However, some users of the systems do indeed reveal their musical preferences by tagging music with more specific tags such as "britishInvasion". If we could partition users and develop a recommendation strategy for each partition, we may be able to outperform a strategy that treats all individuals the same.

When partitioning users, we may rely on some preconceived notion and then purposely design a recommendation strategy for the partitions. The size of the user profile, the variety of their tags, or the types of resources they collect are all potentially useful ways to partition the users. Such notions however have two major drawbacks. First, we cannot be certain that the partitions based on these notions would be optimal for the task of recommending resources. Second, these notions for partitioning users may not generalize across all systems. Instead, we opt to discover optimal partitions by means of an iterative learning process inspired by the K-means clustering algorithm [6].

We begin by randomly assigning users to one of k partitions. We then optimize the recommendation strategy for each partition. Each user is then evaluated using each of the optimized strategies and reassigned to the partition – and thereby the recommendation strategy – that performs best for that user. Again, we optimize the recommendation strategy for each partition, now with a modified set of users. We repeat this process until the partitions stabilize.

While the similarities to K-means clustering is apparent, it is worth pointing out one fundamental difference. The users are not placed into a cluster based on their similarity one another. Rather, they are assigned to a partition after evaluating how well the recommendation strategy of that partition serves their needs. Consequently, users are partitioned based on their performance with regard to the linear combinations of recommendation components.

The recommendation strategy can take on many forms. In this work, we define the generalized notion of a resource recommender as evaluating the function $\psi : U \times Q \times R \to \mathbb{R}$ which operates on a user $u \in U$, a set of requirements $q \in Q = \mathcal{P}(U \cup T \cup R)$, and a resource $r \in R$, and produces a real-valued result p, which is the predicted value of r for u: $\psi(u, q, r) = p$.

This paper specifically evaluates the case of resource recommendation where q is empty. Though it should be noted that the framework can easily be extended to include "more-like-this" recommendations or "tag-query" recommendations where users select a resource or a tag as a requirement. Still other forms are possible [3]. By iterating over all resources and calculating their predicted value, a ranked list of resources can be constructed: $rec(u) = TOP_{r \in R}^n \psi(u, q, r)$.

For each partition, a different recommendation strategy is learned. In the case of a linear weighted hybrid, that means learning a unique set of weights for the component recommenders. The hybrid is composed of simple components, each of which focuses on a particular dimension of the data [1]. All components evaluate the function ψ and the results are aggregated to form the final result.

More technically, the hybrid maintains a set of simple component recommenders C. When queried, the hybrid is given a user u as input. It passes on this user to each of its components. Each component then iterates over the resources generating the predicted values for those resources. The components return the results which are combined together in the function $\psi_h(u, r, t) = \sum_{c \in C} \alpha_c \psi_c(u, q, r)$ where $\psi_h(u, r, t)$ is the relevance score for the hybrid and α_c is the weight given to the component recommender, c. Since scores from the components may not be on the same scale, we normalize the scores so that each $\psi_c(u, r, t)$ falls in the interval [0,1].

An advantage of the hybrid is that it can query any number of components and be trained for unique partitions of users. We train the hybrid on the partitions through a hill climbing technique. We initialize the α vector with random positive numbers. The performance of the holdout set is then evaluated using a holdout set. Many performance measures are possible, among them recall (see Section 4.2).

After randomly perturbing the α vector the holdout set is tested again. The change is kept if the performance is improved. If the change does not improve performance, we reject it and revert the α vector to its former state. In order to ensure we are not trapped in a local maxima, we rarely accept a change even when it does not improve the performance and we occasionally restart the procedure with new alphas. In order to avoid overfitting, validation sets may be used while training the weights.

The user partitioning hybrid maintains several linear weighted hybrids, one for each partition. Once the linear hybrids are trained, the users are then evaluated against them and assigned to the partition in which they perform best. The process repeats until the user partitions stabilize – when the number of the users moving across partitions meets a small threshold. It is in this way, that a unique strategy is developed for each partition of users and users are aggregated in partitions depending on which strategy works best for them.

3.3 Component Recommenders

In this section, we describe the components that are integrated into the user partitioning hybrid. While the framework is extensible and any number of components can be selected, we have purposely chosen simple components that exploit particular aspects of the data. In doing so we hope to illustrate the unique characteristics inherent in different folksonomies can be modeled through a combination of simple components. Moreover, for a partition of users, one component can be given greater importance indicating that those users rely more strongly on the data that component exploits.

Popularity Models. One of the simplest recommendation strategies is merely to promote the most popular resources. This technique is not personalized and is not likely to produce outstanding results. Though, as part of a set of component recommenders it may add to the overall performance of the hybrid. We define $\psi(u,q,r)$ for the popularity recommender, Pop, as $\psi(u,q,r) = \sum_{v \in U} \theta(v,r)$ where $\theta(v,r)$ is 1 if v annotated r and 0 otherwise.

Similarity Based Models. When a user annotates a resource, she is in effect also tagging herself. Observing that both users and resources can be modeled by a vector space model of tags drawn from UT or RT, we can use these models to measure the similarity between users and resources. We calculate $\psi(u,q,r)$ for our $TagSim$ recommender as $\psi(u,q,r) = \sigma(u,r)$ where σ is a similarity function. In this work we rely on cosine similarity.

Collaborative Models. Collaborative filtering is a popular and successful recommendation strategy which assumes that users that have shared preferences in the past will continue to do so in the future. User-based collaborative filtering often draws information from a two dimensional matrix. [7,10,16] The three dimensional model of a folksonomy is not directly applicable to this technique, but the aggregate projections can be used giving us two recommenders: KNN_{ur} and KNN_{ut}. The function takes the form $\psi(u,q,r) = \sum_{v \in N_u} \sigma(u,v)\theta(v,r)$ where N_u is a neighborhood of users and $\sigma(u,v)$ is the similarity of the user a neighbor using either the resource or tags models.

Likewise item-based collaborative filtering [2,15] can be performed by drawing on the RU and RT projections resulting in KNN_{ru} and KNN_{rt}. We define N_r as the

k nearest resources to r drawn from the user profile, u, and then define the relevance score as $\psi(u, q, r) = \sum_{s \in N_r} \sigma(r, s)$.

4 Experimental Evaluation

This section is divided into three parts. First, we look at the data sets used our experiments. Second, the experimental methodology is explained. Lastly, we present our results on the data sets separately before making larger conclusions.

4.1 Data Sets

Four data sets were used in our evaluation. On each data set, we generated a p-core [9] such that each user, resource and tag is guaranteed to occur in at least p annotations While the generation of p-cores eliminates infrequent users, resources and tags, it also focuses on the denser part of the folksonomy. Investigation into the long tail or cold start problem would require a fuller data set, but lie outside the bounds of this paper. We now present each of the data sets.

Bibsonomy is used to collect URL bookmarks and journal articles. The system administrators [8] have made the data available. After taking a 5-core the data set contained 13,909 annotations with 357 users, 1,738 resources and 1,573 tags.

Citeulike is largely used by researches to organize journal articles. Using the 17 February 2009 download available from the site, we computed a 5-core which contained 2,051 users, 5,376 resources, 3,343 tags and a total of 105,873 annotations.

MovieLens allows users to rate and tag movies. It is operated by the GroupLens research lab at the University of Minnesota. We created a 5-core from this data. The result was 35,366 annotations with 819 users, 2,445 resources and 2,309 tags.

LastFM users can upload play lists, share their musical preferences, connect to fans with similar interests, or annotate their music. After scraping the website and generating a p-core of 20 our data set contained 2,368 users, 2,350 resources, 1,141 tags and 172,177 annotations.

4.2 Methodology

We begin by dividing the annotations of the users across five folds. Four folds are used to build the models, while the fifth is used as training examples to tune the parameters. Those parameters include the neighborhood size of the collaborative filtering algorithm as well as the component weights and user assignments of the user partitioning hybrid. The fifth fold is then discarded and we perform four-fold cross validation on the remaining data.

A training example consists of a user u and the all resources annotated by the user in the fold R_{hold}, also known as the holdout set. The user is passed to a recommendation engine and a set of recommended resources R_{rec} is returned. Given these two sets of resources, we can assess the performance of the recommenders.

In this work, we use recall and precision. Recall measures the percentage of items in the holdout set that appear in the recommendation set: $recall = |R_{rec} \cap R_{hold}|/|R_{rec}|$.

Table 1. Contributions of the component recommenders to the the linear weighted hybrid and the user partitioning hybrid in Bibsonomy and Citeulike

Bibsonomy

	n	Pop	$TagSim$	KNN_{ur}	KNN_{ut}	KNN_{ru}	KNN_{rt}
All	357	0.010	0.023	0.431	0.020	0.209	0.307
1	72	0.020	0.227	0.332	0.022	0.151	0.247
2	87	0.088	0.038	0.462	0.030	0.165	0.217
3	65	0.146	0.025	0.248	0.068	0.276	0.236
4	67	0.017	0.196	0.332	0.169	0.109	0.177
5	66	0.059	0.067	0.335	0.025	0.279	0.235

Citeulike

	n	Pop	$TagSim$	KNN_{ur}	KNN_{ut}	KNN_{ru}	KNN_{rt}
All	2,051	0.217	0.184	0.270	0.025	0.162	0.142
1	495	0.211	0.146	0.143	0.055	0.230	0.215
2	360	0.127	0.165	0.155	0.222	0.248	0.083
3	402	0.113	0.262	0.309	0.020	0.151	0.145
4	335	0.270	0.146	0.218	0.130	0.097	0.139
5	459	0.217	0.111	0.354	0.015	0.112	0.191

Precision measures the percentage of items in the recommendation set that appear in the holdout set: $precision = |R_{rec} \cap R_{hold}|/|R_{hold}|$.

Recall and precision are calculated for each user, averaged over all the users, and then again over each fold. The metrics are calculated on recommendation sets of size one through ten and presented in Figures 1 through 4.

4.3 Experimental Results

Tables 1 and 2 show the α vectors as learned through the hill climbing approach for the Bibsonomy, Citeulike, MovieLens and LastFM data sets. The contribution of the component recommenders in the linear weighted hybrid is presented in the first line, labeled "all". In this recommender, a single set of weights is trained for all users. In the next lines, we see the α vectors for each of the partitions in the user partitioning hybrid. Recall that users are partitioned and the weights of the components are optimized for each partition. These α vectors are labeled 1 through 5. For example, the linear weighted hybrid for Bibsonomy did not strongly rely on *pop* (0.010), but the third partition of the user partitioning hybrid did find it useful (0.146).

Figures 1 through 4 report the recall and precision of the algorithm for recommendation sets of size one through ten. For example, we see that KNN_{ur} is the third best performing approach in Citeulike. For a recommendation set of size one, it yield about 2.89% recall and 9.13% precision. A recommendation set of size ten, on the other hand, produces a recall of 14.74% and a precision of 4.86%.

In all four data sets, we observe that the hybrids outperform the component recommenders. We also observe that in all four cases, the user partition hybrid outperforms

Table 2. Contributions of the component recommenders to the the linear weighted hybrid and the user partitioning hybrid in MovieLens and LastFM

MovieLens

	n	Pop	$TagSim$	KNN_{ur}	KNN_{ut}	KNN_{ru}	KNN_{rt}
All	819	0.003	0.269	0.424	0.004	0.153	0.147
1	173	0.078	0.172	0.261	0.007	0.197	0.286
2	157	0.066	0.147	0.385	0.006	0.225	0.171
3	190	0.151	0.164	0.412	0.023	0.163	0.088
4	136	0.027	0.318	0.324	0.104	0.120	0.107
5	163	0.027	0.356	0.362	0.008	0.095	0.153

LastFM

	n	Pop	$TagSim$	KNN_{ur}	KNN_{ut}	KNN_{ru}	KNN_{rt}
All	2,368	0.006	0.153	0.410	0.005	0.425	0.001
1	521	0.004	0.081	0.534	0.004	0.243	0.135
2	363	0.005	0.200	0.356	0.003	0.354	0.082
3	473	0.010	0.084	0.479	0.069	0.315	0.042
4	683	0.008	0.111	0.260	0.007	0.601	0.013
5	328	0.040	0.180	0.209	0.055	0.394	0.122

the linear weighted hybrid, though to a varying degree. We now turn our attention to each of the data sets after which we draw observations that are more general.

Bibsonomy. It is not surprising that when recommending resources to users, the best performing component recommenders are those drawing upon the user-resource relationship. KNN_{ur}, the user based collaborative filtering approach which models users as resources, and KNN_{ru}, the item based approach which models items as users do well. However, the hybrids far surpass the individual components lending credence to the claim that a recommendation strategy should leverage many dimensions of the data.

Analysis of the α vectors tell a similar story. The linear weighted hybrid is largely composed of KNN_{ur} and KNN_{ru}, however KNN_{rt} also plays an important role, again illustrating the need for an integrative approach. However, when we evaluate the α vectors of the user partitioning hybrid we see other trends begin to emerge.

Whereas Pop has little influence in the linear weighted hybrid, it does play a significant role (0.146) in the third partition of the user partitioning hybrid. These users appear more likely to consume popular web pages and journal articles. Partitions 1 and 4 have major contributions by $TagSim$, 0.227 and 0.196 respectively, unlike the linear weighted hybrid which hardly draws upon it at all. These users appear to be employing tags that strongly relate to their areas of interest, making their user model a good way to discover new resources. The forth partition draws heavily on KNN_{ut} again underscoring the utility of tags for recommending resource to the users in this partition.

In sum, all the partitions draw upon KNN_{ur}, KNN_{ru} and KNN_{rt} just as the linear weighted hybrid does. However, the user partition hybrid is able to surpass the linear weighted hybrid by incorporating other components to see the needs of specific to the partitions.

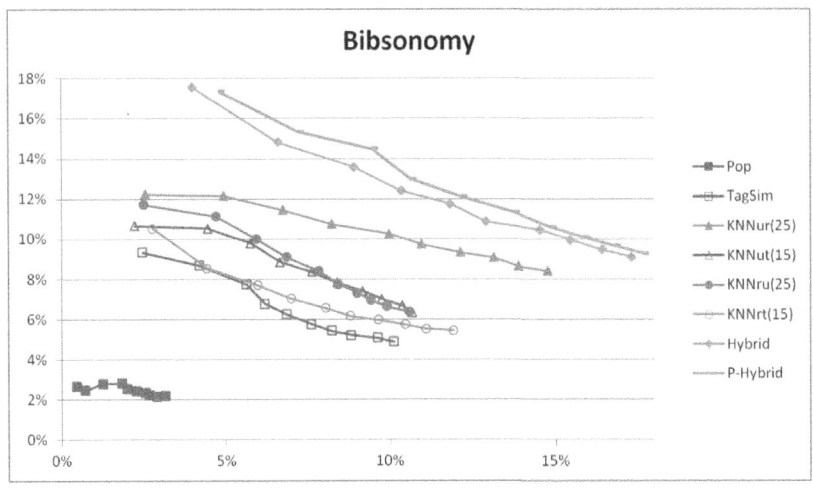

Fig. 1. Bibsonomy: recall versus precision

Citeulike. Citeulike is similar to Bibsonomy in that KNN_{ur} and KNN_{ru} perform well and in that the hybrids outperform all the components. However, the similarities end there. Looking at the α vector of the linear weighted hybrid we see that it exploits almost all of the component recommenders. KNN_{ut} is the only one that is largely ignored. Looking at the α vectors of the partitions we see the same trend. They all draw upon the same five component recommenders, though to slightly varying degrees.

Partition 2 is the only one to break the mold and exploit KNN_{ut}. Since each partition is weighing the components similarly to the linear weighted hybrid itself, we would not expect a great improvement over this technique. In fact, Figure 2 shows only a slight improvement. Partitioning the users offers little benefit; it seems that the users in Citeulike are interacting with the system in similar ways. This is perhaps not surprising since the bulk of the users of Citeulike are researchers annotating journal articles, a user base that share similar motivations for using the system. They often stick to their area of expertise and employ tags taken from that domain.

MovieLens. In this data set, we again see an improvement. The linear weighted hybrid draws almost entirely on $TagSim$, KNN_{ur}, KNN_{ru} and KNN_{rt}, whereas Pop and KNN_{ut} account for almost nothing in the hybrid. The third and fourth partitions of the user partitioning hybrid however incorporate these component recommenders. The third partition of users seems to favor popular resources, while the forth can be modeled by their tags perhaps because users in this partition are more careful about which tags they employ.

The remaining partitions appear to rely on the same components of the linear weighted hybrid, but shift their focus. The first gives more weight to KNN_{rt}. The second gives more weight to KNN_{ur} and the fifth focuses mostly on $TagSim$. These users appear vary slightly in their behavior. In some cases, it seems the tags are playing an increasingly important role. In others, the tag information seems less relevant.

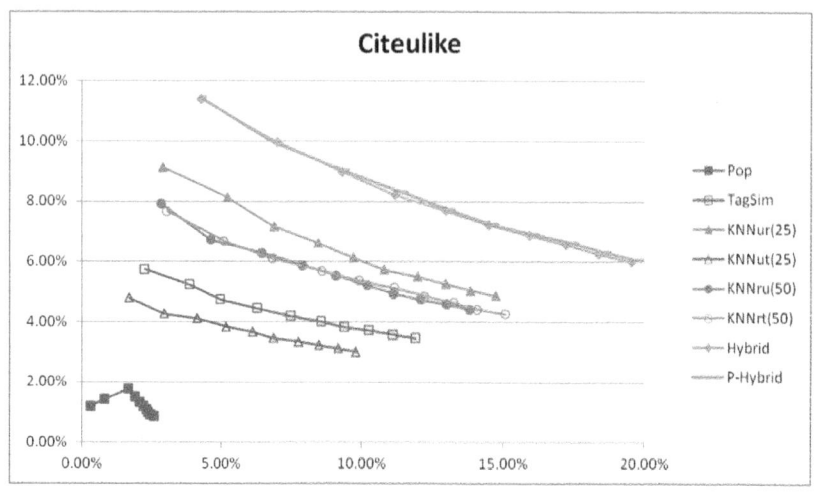

Fig. 2. Citeulike: recall versus precision

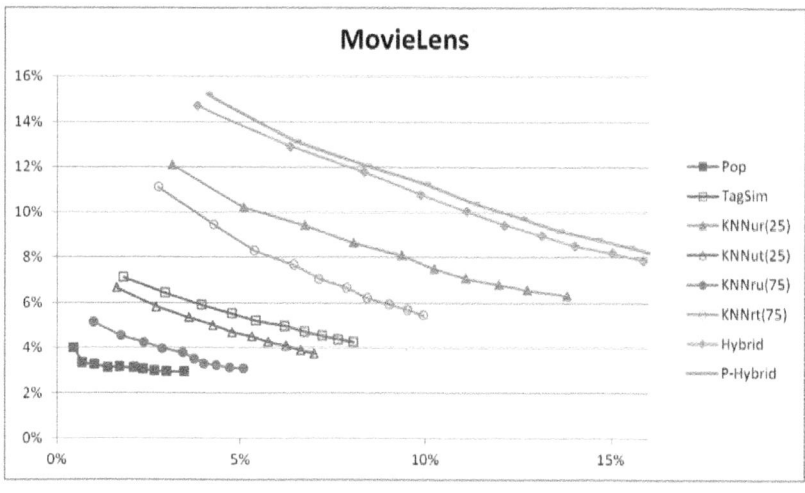

Fig. 3. MovieLens: recall versus precision

LastFM. In LastFM, Pop is remarkably absent in the linear weighted hybrid and all the partitions of the user partitioning hybrid. KNN_{ut} shows a similar trend, though in partitions 3 and 5 it shows up marginally. KNN_{rt}, on the other hand, takes on a much greater role in partitions 1 and 5 of the user partitioning hybrid than it does in the linear weighted hybrid. In general, it seems that tags are not good models for users or resources, but in these partitions, they offer some benefit.

Otherwise, the partitions exploit the same components as the linear weighted hybrid though to differing degrees. Partition 1 focuses on KNN_{ur} over KNN_{ru}, whereas

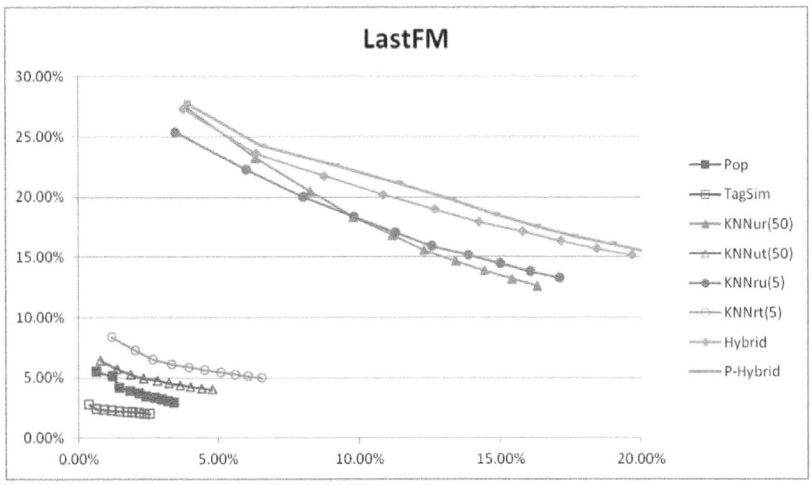

Fig. 4. LastFM: recall versus precision

partition 4 prefers KNN_{ru}. The linear weighted hybrid was forced to balance these components for all users. The user partitioning hybrid, on the other hand, was able to combine the components to meet the specific needs for the users in each partition.

5 Conclusion

This paper presented a framework for automatically partitioning users and developing a resource recommendation strategy for each partition. Users were first randomly placed into a partition. Then the relative contribution of several simple component recommenders was optimized for each of these partitions. Users were reassigned to the partition in which they fared best and the weights of the component optimized again. This procedure was repeated until the partitions stabilized.

Our experimental work shows that the user partitioning hybrid outperformed the linear weighted hybrid which treats all users the same. In cases where users can be partitioned, the improvement is greater. In cases where users seem to be exhibiting similar behaviors, the improvement is only marginal.

These observations offer insights into how users are interacting with the different social annotation systems. As user interactions with online systems continue to increase in complexity, recommendation techniques are needed that can adapt to varying user behavior.

References

1. Burke, R.: Hybrid recommender systems: Survey and experiments. User Modeling and User-Adapted Interaction 12(4), 331–370 (2002)
2. Deshpande, M., Karypis, G.: Item-Based Top-N Recommendation Algorithms. ACM Transactions on Information Systems 22(1), 143–177 (2004)

3. Felfernig, A., Burke, R.: Constraint-based recommender systems: technologies and research issues. In: International Conference on Electronic Commerce, Innsbruck, Austria (2008)
4. Gemmell, J., Schimoler, T., Mobasher, B., Burke, R.: Hybrid tag recommendation for social annotation systems. In: 19th ACM International Conference on Information and Knowledge Management, Toronto, Canada (2010)
5. Gemmell, J., Schimoler, T., Ramezani, M., Mobasher, B.: Adapting K-Nearest Neighbor for Tag Recommendation in Folksonomies. In: 7th Workshop on Intelligent Techniques for Web Personalization and Recommender Systems, Chicago, Illinois (2009)
6. Hartigan, J.A., Wong, M.A.: Algorithm as 136: A k-means clustering algorithm. Journal of the Royal Statistical Society. Series C (Applied Statistics) 28(1), 100–108 (1979)
7. Herlocker, J., Konstan, J., Borchers, A., Riedl, J.: An Algorithmic Framework for Performing Collaborative Filtering. In: 22nd Annual International ACM SIGIR Conference on Research and Development in Information Retrieval, Berkeley, California. ACM (1999)
8. Hotho, A., Jaschke, R., Schmitz, C., Stumme, G.: BibSonomy: A social bookmark and publication sharing system. In: Proceedings of the Conceptual Structures Tool Interoperability Workshop at the 14th International Conference on Conceptual Structures, Aalborg, Denmark (2006)
9. Jäschke, R., Marinho, L., Hotho, A., Schmidt-Thieme, L., Stumme, G.: Tag Recommendations in Folksonomies. In: Kok, J.N., Koronacki, J., Lopez de Mantaras, R., Matwin, S., Mladenič, D., Skowron, A. (eds.) PKDD 2007. LNCS (LNAI), vol. 4702, pp. 506–514. Springer, Heidelberg (2007)
10. Konstan, J., Miller, B., Maltz, D., Herlocker, J., Gordon, L., Riedl, J.: GroupLens: Applying Collaborative Filtering to Usenet News. Communications of the ACM 40(3), 87 (1997)
11. Mika, P.: Ontologies are us: A unified model of social networks and semantics. Web Semantics: Science, Services and Agents on the World Wide Web 5(1), 5–15 (2007)
12. Page, L., Brin, S., Motwani, R., Winograd, T.: The pagerank citation ranking: Bringing order to the web (1998)
13. Plangprasopchok, A., Lerman, K.: Exploiting social annotation for automatic resource discovery. In: Proceedings of AAAI Workshop on Information Integration, Vancouver, British Columbia (2007)
14. Rendle, S., Schmidt-Thieme, L.: Pairwise Interaction Tensor Factorization for Personalized Tag Recommendation. In: Proceedings of the Third ACM International Conference on Web Search and Data Mining, New York (2010)
15. Sarwar, B., Karypis, G., Konstan, J., Reidl, J.: Item-Based Collaborative Filtering Recommendation Algorithms. In: 10th International Conference on World Wide Web, Hong Kong, China (2001)
16. Shardanand, U., Maes, P.: Social Information Filtering: Algorithms for Automating "Word of Mouth". In: SIGCHI Conference on Human Factors in Computing Systems, Denver, Colorado (1995)
17. Tso-Sutter, K., Marinho, L., Schmidt-Thieme, L.: Tag-aware recommender systems by fusion of collaborative filtering algorithms. In: Proceedings of the 2008 ACM Symposium on Applied Computing, Ceara, Brazil (2008)
18. Wetzker, R., Umbrath, W., Said, A.: A hybrid approach to item recommendation in folksonomies. In: ESAIR 2009: Proceedings of the WSDM 2009 Workshop on Exploiting Semantic Annotations in Information Retrieval, Barcelona, Spain (2009)

Active Learning in Collaborative Filtering Recommender Systems

Mehdi Elahi[1], Francesco Ricci[1], and Neil Rubens[2]

[1] Free University of Bozen-Bolzano, Bozen-Bolzano, Italy
{mehdi.elahi,fricci}@unibz.it
http://www.unibz.it

[2] University of Electro-Communications, Tokyo, Japan
neil@hrstc.org
http://www.uec.ac.jp

Abstract. In Collaborative Filtering Recommender Systems user's preferences are expressed in terms of rated items and each rating allows to improve system prediction accuracy. However, not all of the ratings bring the same amount of information about the user's tastes. Active Learning aims at identifying rating data that better reflects users' preferences. Active learning *Strategies* are used to selectively choose the items to present to the user in order to acquire her ratings and ultimately improve the recommendation accuracy. In this survey article, we review recent active learning techniques for collaborative filtering along two dimensions: (a) whether the system requested ratings are personalised or not, and, (b) whether active learning is guided by one criterion (heuristic) or multiple criteria.

Keywords: recommender systems, cold start, active learning.

1 Introduction

This article concisely reviews the state-of-the-art in active learning for collaborative filtering recommender systems. *Active Learning* tackles the problem of obtaining high quality data that better represents the preferences of a user and largely improves the performance of the system. This is done by identifying, for each user, a set of items and requesting the user to rate them. The ultimate goal is to acquire ratings that will enable the system to generate effective recommendations. However, users are typically uninterested and reluctant to enter many ratings: this activity represents a cognitive cost for the user. This is why, it is important to carefully design a strategy to choose, the smallest in number, and the greatest in informativeness, of instances (ratings) to train the system. In other words, in collaborative filtering an active learning *Strategy* for rating elicitation is a precise procedure for selecting which items to present to the user for rating elicitation.

So far, several active learning strategies have been proposed and evaluated for collaborative filtering recommender systems. These strategies hold different features and implement various heuristics in selecting the useful items to be presented to the users to rate. Heuristics are strategies that instead of directly minimising the system prediction error try to improve other system properties that are indirectly influencing the error. For instance, acquiring more ratings for popular items (as the popularity-based strategy does) tends to reduce the system error but may also acquire too many high ratings that can erroneously bias the system towards high rating predictions [8,6].

The classification of these strategies with respect to descriptive and discriminative dimensions can give a useful overview and become a practical resource for practitioners and researchers in the field of recommender systems. For that aim, we have identified two important dimensions that have been addressed by several research works [17,18,11,19,12,10], and then, analyzed and classified the active learning strategies along these two dimensions, namely:

- **Personalisation:** that address the extent to which the personalisation is performed when selecting the list of candidate items for the users to rate. Hence, this dimension classifies the strategies into *Non-Personalzied*, and *Personalised*. Non-personalized strategies are those that ask all the users to rate the same list of items. Personalized strategies, on the other hand, ask different users to rate different items. Personalization is an important aspect in active learning since the users have different tastes, preferences and experiences, hence, the usefulness of the ratings for the same set of items could vary greatly from user to user. Moreover, selecting items to be rated with regards to preferences of each user, may provide a more pleasant experience for the user (e.g. by presenting them with items that they can actually rate), and at the same time may be more informative for the system.
- **Hybridization:** reflects whether the strategy takes into account a single heuristic (criterion) for selecting the items for the users to rate or combines several heuristics in order to create a more effective strategy. In this regard, the strategies can be classified into *Single-heuristic (or Individual)* and *Combined-heuristic (or Combined)* strategies. Single-heuristic strategies are those that implement a unique item selection rule and select items only based on that heuristic. Combined-heuristic strategies hybridize single-heuristic strategies by aggregating and combining a number of strategies and utilize multiple item selection rules in order to better estimate which items are more useful for improving the system performance and therefore should be presented to the user for rating.

We note that the main contributions of this article are: (1) novel dimensions for classification of active learning strategies in collaborative filtering, i.e., personalisation and hybridization in active learning, (2) comprehensive analysis and classification of more than 24 strategies (see Fig. 2) as well as the brief description of potential pros and cons of these strategies, (3) sub-classification of the strategies for an even better and more informative description and discrimination of them, e.g., static combined-heuristic or adaptive combined-heuristic strategies.

The remainder of the article is structured as follows: section 2 gives a summary on typical user-system interaction and an illustrative example of active learning in collaborative filtering; section 3 introduces several non-personalized active learning strategies that can also be either single-heuristic or combined-heuristics; section 4 presents an analogue analysis of personalized strategies; and finally, section 5 concludes this survey article.

2 Active Learning in Collaborative Filtering

The first research works in active learning for recommender systems have been motivated by the need to implement more effective sign up processes for the classical collaborative filtering systems [4]. In fact, these works assume the *Standard Interaction Model* [3] for user-system interaction in collaborative filtering, i.e., selecting and proposing to users a set of items to rate only during the sign up process, until the user rates a sufficient number of items. An example of the works dealing with this interaction model is [17] where the authors focus explicitly on the sign up process, i.e., when a new user starts using a collaborative filtering recommender system and must rate some items in order to provide the system with some initial information about her preferences.

A more recent alternative interaction model is the *Conversational and Collaborative* [3], i.e., the user is supposed to rate items during the sign-up process, but is also invited to rate additional items whenever she is motivated to provide more ratings. In [3] the authors propose a set of techniques to intelligently select items to rate when the user is particularly motivated to provide such information.

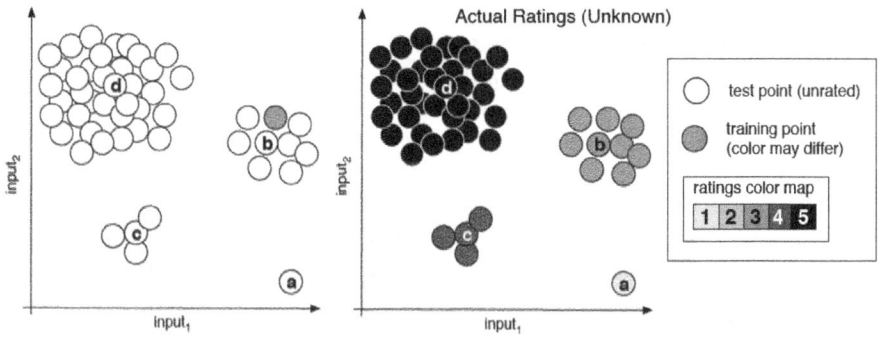

Fig. 1. Active learning, an illustrative example [19]

Figure 1 illustrates an example of active learning in recommender systems [19]. The left chart in the figure, represents the starting state, in which the system has requested the user to rate just a movie within the upper right group, say the Sci-Fi genre. The right chart shows the actual ratings of the user (color coded) but the system is not aware of these preferences. The chart is also showing four possibilities for selecting the next movie to be rated, i.e., movie *a, b, c* or *d*. If the system selects the movie a, say a very peculiar movie, it may not influence prediction accuracy, since, no any other movie is located nearby. However, if the movie b is selected, it may let the system to make prediction for the movies within the same area. However, it has already some information for predicting movies within this area. If the movie c is selected, the system is able to make new predictions, but only for the other three movies in this area, say Zombie movies. Ultimately, by selecting movie d, the system will be able to make predictions for a large number of movies that are located nearby, in the same area (say Comedy movies). Therefore, selecting movie d is likely to be the ideal choice as it allows the system to improve the accuracy of the predictions for the largest number of movies [19].

3 Non-Personalised Active Learning

Simpler active learning strategies do not take into account users previously expressed preferences and request users to rate the same set of items. We refer to these strategies as non-personalized. In this case, the heuristic for the item selection process does not depend on the profiles of individual users. For example, a non-personalized strategy may select items based on their popularity. Note that popularity criterion is not affected by preferences of users who haven't yet experienced the item; hence all of the users would be presented with the same item to rate (regardless of their preferences). We have identified two sub-categories within this group: single and combined heuristic.

3.1 Single-Heuristic Strategies

Uncertainty-Reduction. The strategies within this group, favour items that have received controversial feedback from the users (i.e., more diverse ratings). Hence, the system is more uncertain about user's opinion on them. Asking the user to rate such items can bring useful (discriminative) information about the user's preferences.

Variance [20,19,9,10]. It considers the ratings' variance as the indication of the uncertainty of the system about the rating prediction of an item. This strategy asks the users to rate the items with the highest variance of the ratings in the dataset. Hence, it favours the items that have been rated diversely.

Entropy of Ratings [17,1,20,9,12]. Entropy measures the dispersion of the ratings of the users for an item [18]. Entropy of ratings is computed by using the relative frequency of each of the five possible rating values (1-5) [17]. A variant of this strategy, *Entropy0* [18,9,10], tries to solve a limitation of the entropy strategy, i.e., its tendency to select unpopular items. Entropy0 tackle this problem by considering the unknown ratings as a new rating value, equal to 0, and hence considering a rating scales between 0 to 5. In such a way, a high frequency of the 0 rating (i.e., many unknown ratings) tends to decrease Entropy0 [18].

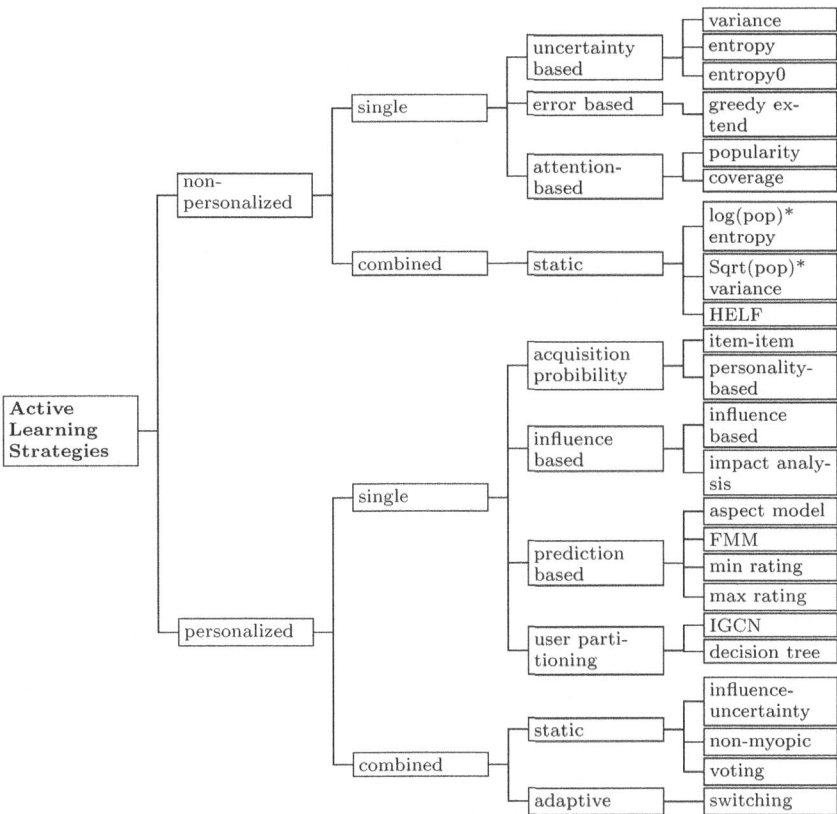

Fig. 2. Classification of active learning strategies in collaborative filtering

Error Reduction. In this group of strategies items are considered useful if they enhance the predictive accuracy of the system. While items with diverse rating may seem informative, they may not be necessarily the best items to request to rate if the rating prediction error is the primary concern. Indeed, error reduction is the main goal of any active learning strategy [19] since it is known to be strictly (negatively) correlated to the user satisfaction.

Greedy Extend [9,10]. Lets us denote with A the prediction algorithm (e.g. Factor Model), and with $F(A)$ the performance measure of A, i.e., RMSE (estimated on the training set). The goal of greedy extend is to obtain an item list L, whose ratings should be elicited from the users, such that RMSE is minimised: $L = argmin_{L \subset I_u, |L|=N}\{F(A_L)\}$ where A_L is the prediction algorithm A trained only on the ratings given for the items in the list L, I_u is the subset of the all items whose ratings are not known to the system, and may therefore be selected by the strategy to acquire ratings, and N is the maximum number of items that the strategy should return.

Attention-Based. The attention-based strategies are simple and easy to implement, and they were used as the initial attempts to solve the cold start problem in collaborative filtering [17,3]. They are considered as baseline strategies in several analyses of active learning in recommender systems [16,12,9,15].

Popularity [17,3,20,18,9,12]. This strategy selects the items that have received the highest number of ratings. Hence, it is more likely that the user is able to rate these items and consequently the size of the rating dataset can be increased [3]. However, popular items are typically widely liked and already rated high by the users. Therefore, their ratings may bring a little information to the system.

Coverage [9]. This strategy selects the items that are highly co-rated by the users, and hence, eliciting their ratings may improve the prediction accuracy for the other items [9]. Here, $Coverage(i) = \sum_j n_{ij}$, where n_{ij} is the number of users who co-rated the items i and j. The heuristic used by this strategy is that collaborative filtering recognizes patterns across the items that are co-rated and hence correlated. These items are supposed to be the most useful ones in the sense that they help the system to better learn the users' preferences.

3.2 Combined-Heuristic Strategies

Combined-heuristic strategies hybridize single strategies in order to achieve a range of objectives, e.g., accuracy improvement, coverage widening, or user satisfaction. Such hybridization can be done in various ways: a certain number of strategies can vote for items and the most voted ones are selected; a certain number of strategies assign selection scores to each item and the total score is the product of these scores; a number of strategies select sets of items and the union or intersection of the selected items is chosen.

Log(popularity)*Entropy [17,3,20,16]. This strategy scores an item by computing the logarithm of the popularity multiplied by the entropy of the ratings given to the item. Hence, this strategy tries to combine the effect of the popularity score, which is discussed above, with the heuristics that favours items with more diverse ratings (larger entropy), which may provide more useful (discriminative) information about the user's preferences [3]. There is also a variation of this strategy proposed in [9] which uses $\sqrt{popularity}$ instead of $log(popularity)$, and *variance* instead of *entropy*.

HELF [18,9,10]. HELF stands for Harmonic mean of Entropy and Logarithm of Frequency. HELF aims at combining popularity with informativeness. As mentioned before (see uncertainty based strategies) the entropy strategy tends to select obscure items that are rarely rated. Hence, HELF attempts to solve this problem by selecting informative items that are also rated frequently by the users. Here entropy and popularity scores are combined to select the items that are familiar for a larger number of users and at the same time the users widely disagreed on them [18]: $HELF(i) = \frac{2 \times LF_i \times H(i)}{LF_i + H(i)}$ where, LF_i denotes for the normalized logarithm of the rating frequency of item i, and $H(i)$ denotes for the normalized entropy of item i.

4 Personalised Active Learning

The second major category of active learning strategies for collaborative filtering comprises strategies that ask different users to rate different items (personalisation). The strategies in this group can also be either single or combined heuristic.

4.1 Single-Heuristic Strategies

Acquisition Probability Based. Strategies in this group focus on improving the performance of the system by maximizing the probability that the selected items are familiar to the user, hence are ratable. By proposing more familiar items to the users, these strategies tend to collect more ratings. For example if the user has not watched a movie, read a book, listened to a music track, or visited a touristic place, it is better for the system not to ask the user to rate them. In fact, it is important that the active learning strategy estimates and considers the probability that a user is able to rate an item before proposing it for rating.

Item-Item Strategy [17,18]. This strategy selects the items with the highest similarity to the previously rated items. Hence, after acquiring at least one rating from a user (e.g., by requesting her to rate in the sign-up process), the similarity values between her rated item(s) and the other unrated items are computed, and the items most similar to the rated ones are presented to the user to rate. Since this strategy does not care about the informativeness of the items and it can acquire the ratings of less useful items, hence may fail to improve the system in terms of prediction accuracy [17].

Personality-Based Binary Prediction [5,2]. This strategy first transforms the rating matrix to a matrix with the same number of rows and columns, by mapping null entries to 0 and not null entries to 1. Hence, the new matrix models only whether a user rated an item or not, regardless of its value. Then, this new matrix is used to train an extended version of the matrix factorization algorithm. This model can also profile users not only in terms of the binary ratings, but also using known user attributes, for instance, the Big Five personality traits scored on a scale from 1 to 5. Given a user u, an item i and the set of user attributes $A(u)$, it predicts which items have been experienced by the user by using the following rule: $\hat{pr}_{ui} = \bar{i} + b_u + q_i^\top \cdot (p_u + \sum_{a \in A(u)} y_a)$ where $\hat{pr}_{ui}$ is the computed estimation of the probability that user u has experienced item i, and, p_u, q_i and y_a are the latent factor vectors associated with the user u, the item i and the user attribute a respectively [5]. The model parameters are then learnt, as it is common in matrix factorization, by minimizing the associated regularized squared error function through stochastic gradient descent.

Influence Based. Eliciting the ratings for the items that the system is more uncertain about the users' evaluation, can be beneficial for the system to better predict the ratings of these particular items. However, that will not necessarily end up with the reduction of the uncertainty of the rating prediction for other items. Influence based strategies select items, in the attempt to minimize the rating prediction uncertainty for all the items.

Influence Based [20]. This strategy estimates the influence of item's ratings on the rating prediction of other items and selects the items with the largest influence. First the rating prediction $\hat{r}_{u,i}$ for user u and an unrated item i, is computed. Then, the rating prediction $\hat{r}_{u,i}$ is decreased by 1 unit: $\hat{r}'_{u,i} = \hat{r}_{u,i} - 1$. Finally two prediction models are generated, one adding $\hat{r}_{u,i}$ and another adding $\hat{r}'_{u,i}$ to the traing set, and the absolute value of the differences of theirs predictions for the ratings of all the items different from i are computed. The influence of i is estimated by summing up all these differences. Finally, the items with the highest influence are selected for active learning [20].

Impact Analysis [16]. This strategy selects the items whose ratings have the highest impact on the prediction of the other ratings. In order to get the gist of this strategy, let us consider a graph-based representation of the rating dataset, where users and items are nodes of the graph. A rating can be seen as a link between a user and an item. In order to make a recommendation for a user using a user-based nearest neighbour model there should be at least a four-node path being created. A four-node path between the users u_1, u_2 and items p_1, p_2 is found when the user u_1 has rated item p_1 and p_2, and user u_2 has co-rated p_2. In this case, the nearest neighbour model can generate a prediction of the rating of u_2 for p_1. Hence, the more four-node paths are created the better the prediction may become. For that reason, this strategy attempts to discover and elicit the ratings of items that produces more new four-node paths.

Prediction Based. These are strategies that use a rating prediction model in order to identify which items are better to propose to the users to rate. Items are ranked according to their predicted ratings and the top items are selected for rating elicitation. The prediction models used by these strategies may differ. Hence, we can partition these strategies according to the prediction model they use. One of the advantages of these strategies is that they are typically less bothersome to the user since they request to rate items that are predicted as relevant for the user. Hence, the user may even enjoy seeing and rating them. Moreover, since they are relevant for the user, they are also likely to have been experienced by her.

Aspect Model [13,11,19,14]. This strategy determines a latent space model for each user, i.e., models the user as a mixture of multiple interests (aspects). Every user $u \in U$ has a probabilistic membership in multiple aspects $z \in Z$, and users in the same group are assumed to have similar rating patterns. The probability that the user u rates r the item i is estimated by: $p(r|u,i) = \sum_{z \in Z} p(r|z,i)p(z|u)$ where $p(z|u)$ models how likely the user u will belong to the group z and $p(r|z,i)$ models how likely the users in group z will rate r the item i. An extension of this strategy uses *Flexible Mixture Model (FMM)* [13,11] and determines two sets of latent aspects z_u and z_i: every user u is considered to be a mixture of multiple interests (user aspects) but also every item i is considered to be a mixture of patterns (item aspects).

MinRating [15]. This strategy selects, for the user to rate, the items with the smallest predicted ratings. It is argued that when a new user is registered, since the system has no or few ratings of that user, the model parameters computed for this user can be inaccurate and considerably different from the optimal parameters. Therefore, it could be better to choose the items whose ratings are more erroneously predicted. On the other hand, since most of the ratings given by the users are large (users tend to rate the items they like) the prediction error for the items with low predicted ratings is expected to be high. Hence, eliciting low ratings should reveal large prediction errors and may impose significant changes into the model parameters.

MinNorm [15]. This strategy uses a prediction model (i.e., matrix factorization) to compute the latent factors of each item and then selects the items whose latent factor vectors have the smallest Euclidean norm. The reason is that when active learning has acquired a number of ratings, in matrix factorization, it could be better to stabilise the prediction model and avoid large changes in the latent factors. This is because the system has already achieved a certain level of accuracy that may be better to keep it. In order to do that, the change of the factors (gradient) should be minimized. While the system has less control on the prediction error, minimising the item factors may result in the minimum gradient and more stable prediction model.

User Partitioning. The heuristic guiding the strategies within this group is to first partition the existing users into a number of clusters, where the users of each cluster posses similar tastes and affinities. Then it selects the items whose rating will better reveal to which cluster the user belongs.

Information Gain through Clustered Neighbours (IGCN) [18]. This strategy constructs a decision tree where each leaf node represents a cluster of users and each internal node stores a test for a specific item that is proposed to a user to rate. Users are clustered according to their similarity values that are measured using a neighbourhood based collaborative filtering approach. Starting from the root node, a new user is proposed to rate a sequence of items, according to the built decision tree, until she reaches one of the leaf nodes. Hence, the most informative items, which belong to the tree, are those whose ratings will enable to better classify the user in her representative cluster.

Decision Tree [10,21]. Also this strategy uses a decision tree whose nodes, either internal or leaf, represents groups of users. Given an internal node, a candidate partitioning movie, divides the users into three groups based on the ratings of the users: *Lovers* (who rated the item high), *Haters* (who rated the item low), and *Unknowns* (who did not rate the item). When the tree is built, for each of these groups, the rating predictions of their unrated items are estimated. The estimated RMSE is computed as the squared root of the deviation of the predicted ratings from the true ratings. Finally, the total prediction error is computed by summing up the *RMSE* in the three groups and the movie with minimal total error is selected for active learning. This process is iterated within each of the three previously built groups, to select the next movies and corresponding users partitions.

4.2 Combined-Heuristic Strategies

Personalized Combined-heuristic strategies hybridise personalized single-heuristic strategies by combining them in order to leverage the advantages that each method provides.

Influence and Uncertainty Based [20]. This strategy combines influence-based (see section 4.1) and variance strategy (see section 3.1). It selects items based on the influence that the rating of an item may have on the rating prediction of the other items and the variance of the item's ratings (as a measure of system prediction uncertainty): $argmax_i\{Var(i)\,I(i)\}$ where $I(i)$ is the influence of item i (see section 4.1).

Non-Myopic [15]. This strategy combines two prediction based strategies: Min-Rating and MinNorm. At the beginning, when the first requests are made by the system, the items are selected mainly by MinRating strategy, which is supposed to work better in the early stages of the system, when the users have not rated many items (see the description of MinRating strategy). As more requests are made by the system, and more ratings are elicited, the system tends to use more the MinNorm strategy since MinNorm is supposed to work better in the late stage of the system evolution, e.g., when the users have already rated many items (see the description of MinNorm) [15].

Voting [8,6]. This strategy scores an item i with the number of votes given by a committee of strategies. Each strategy produces its top candidate items for rating elicitation (strategy votes) and then the items appearing more often in these lists are selected. We stress that the voting strategy depends on the selected voting strategies. For example, including random strategy may impose an exploratory behaviour that could improve the system coverage [8].

Combined with Switching [7]. Every time this strategy is applied, a certain percentage of the users (called exploration group) are randomly selected for choosing the best performing individual strategy, then this winning strategy is applied on the remaining users. Each individual strategy is tested to an equal number of random users in the exploration group: it selects items to be rated by these users, and acquires their ratings (if available). Based on the ratings acquired by the system, a factor model is trained and its MAE and NDCG for these newly acquired ratings are computed. Then the observed probability for each individual strategy to acquire ratings for the selected items is also computed by estimating the ratio of the number of acquired ratings over the number of items requested to be rated. Finally, the score of each individual strategy is calculated by multiplying this probability either by the rating prediction error (MAE) on the acquired ratings, if MAE is the target metric to minimize, or by (1 - NDCG) in the other case. The strategy with the highest score is then selected. Hence, the combined switching strategy is selecting the individual strategy that is able to acquire from the exploration group the largest number of ratings for items whose system rating prediction is currently most erroneous [7].

5 Conclusion

In this article we provided a concise review of the state-of-the-art on active learning in collaborative filtering recommender systems. We have performed a comprehensive analysis and classified a wide range of active learning techniques, called *Strategies*, along the two dimensions: how personalised these techniques are, and how many different item selection criteria (heuristics) are considered by these strategies in their rating elicitation process.

It is worth noting that active learning for collaborative filtering is a multi disciplinary field, overlapping with a broad range of topics such as machine learning, data mining, information retrieval and filtering, recommender systems, human computer interaction and cognitive science. Such a broad range of disciplines, makes it difficult to cover all the works related to them. However, in this paper, we have conducted a comprehensive analysis of the literature by covering almost the main research works in the field. To our knowledge no paper before has performed such an analysis.

However, there are a number of interesting topics that have not been addressed so far and can be considered for future works. Firstly, it is important to survey works that have been done in active learning for other types of recommender systems, such as content-based and context-aware. Secondly, it is important to analyze active learning techniques based on their applicability to specific application domains. Indeed, the majority of the works in this field have tested active learning techniques in the movie domain (in offline settings). Finally, we must stress the importance of conducting more live user studies where active learning benefit can be better assessed.

References

1. Boutilier, C., Zemel, R.S., Marlin, B.: Active collaborative filtering. In: Proceedings of the Nineteenth Annual Conference on Uncertainty in Artificial Intelligence (UAI 2003), Acapulco (2003)
2. Braunhofer, M., Elahi, M., Ge, M., Ricci, F.: Context dependent preference acquisition with personality-based active learning in mobile recommender systems. In: Zaphiris, P., Ioannou, A. (eds.) LCT 2014, Part II. LNCS, vol. 8524, pp. 105–116. Springer, Heidelberg (2014)
3. Carenini, G., Smith, J., Poole, D.: Towards more conversational and collaborative recommender systems. In: Proceedings of the 8th International Conference on Intelligent User Interfaces, IUI 2003, pp. 12–18. ACM, New York (2003)
4. Desrosiers, C., Karypis, G.: A comprehensive survey of neighborhood-based recommendation methods. In: Ricci, F., Rokach, L., Shapira, B., Kantor, P.B. (eds.) Recommender Systems Handbook, pp. 107–144. Springer (2011)
5. Elahi, M., Braunhofer, M., Ricci, F., Tkalcic, M.: Personality-based active learning for collaborative filtering recommender systems. In: Baldoni, M., Baroglio, C., Boella, G., Micalizio, R. (eds.) AI*IA 2013. LNCS, vol. 8249, pp. 360–371. Springer, Heidelberg (2013)
6. Elahi, M., Repsys, V., Ricci, F.: Rating elicitation strategies for collaborative filtering. In: Huemer, C., Setzer, T. (eds.) EC-Web 2011. LNBIP, vol. 85, pp. 160–171. Springer, Heidelberg (2011)

7. Elahi, M., Ricci, F., Rubens, N.: Adapting to natural rating acquisition with combined active learning strategies. In: Chen, L., Felfernig, A., Liu, J., Raś, Z.W. (eds.) ISMIS 2012. LNCS, vol. 7661, pp. 254–263. Springer, Heidelberg (2012)
8. Elahi, M., Ricci, F., Rubens, N.: Active learning strategies for rating elicitation in collaborative filtering: a system-wide perspective. ACM Transactions on Intelligent Systems and Technology 5(1) (2014)
9. Golbandi, N., Koren, Y., Lempel, R.: On bootstrapping recommender systems. In: Proceedings of the 19th ACM International Conference on Information and Knowledge Management, CIKM 2010, pp. 1805–1808. ACM, New York (2010)
10. Golbandi, N., Koren, Y., Lempel, R.: Adaptive bootstrapping of recommender systems using decision trees. In: Proceedings of the Fourth ACM International Conference on Web Search and Data Mining, WSDM 2011, pp. 595–604. ACM, New York (2011)
11. Harpale, A.S., Yang, Y.: Personalized active learning for collaborative filtering. In: SIGIR 2008: Proceedings of the 31st Annual International ACM SIGIR Conference on Research and Development in Information Retrieval, pp. 91–98. ACM, New York (2008)
12. He, L., Liu, N.N., Yang, Q.: Active dual collaborative filtering with both item and attribute feedback. In: AAAI (2011)
13. Jin, R., Si, L.: A Bayesian approach toward active learning for collaborative filtering. In: Proceedings of the 20th Conference in Uncertainty in Artificial Intelligence, UAI 2004, Banff, Canada, July 7-11, pp. 278–285 (2004)
14. Karimi, R., Freudenthaler, C., Nanopoulos, A., Schmidt-Thieme, L.: Active learning for aspect model in recommender systems. In: CIDM, pp. 162–167. IEEE (2011)
15. Karimi, R., Freudenthaler, C., Nanopoulos, A., Schmidt-Thieme, L.: Non-myopic active learning for recommender systems based on matrix factorization. In: IRI, pp. 299–303. IEEE Systems, Man, and Cybernetics Society (2011)
16. Mello, C.E., Aufaure, M.-A., Zimbrao, G.: Active learning driven by rating impact analysis. In: Proceedings of the Fourth ACM Conference on Recommender Systems, RecSys 2010, pp. 341–344. ACM, New York (2010)
17. Rashid, A.M., Albert, I., Cosley, D., Lam, S.K., Mcnee, S.M., Konstan, J.A., Riedl, J.: Getting to know you: Learning new user preferences in recommender systems. In: Proceedings of the 2002 International Conference on Intelligent User Interfaces, IUI 2002, pp. 127–134. ACM Press (2002)
18. Rashid, A.M., Karypis, G., Riedl, J.: Learning preferences of new users in recommender systems: an information theoretic approach. SIGKDD Explor. Newsl. 10, 90–100 (2008)
19. Rubens, N., Kaplan, D., Sugiyama, M.: Active learning in recommender systems. In: Ricci, F., Rokach, L., Shapira, B., Kantor, P. (eds.) Recommender Systems Handbook, pp. 735–767. Springer (2011)
20. Rubens, N., Sugiyama, M.: Influence-based collaborative active learning. In: Proceedings of the 2007 ACM Conference on Recommender Systems, RecSys 2007, pp. 145–148. ACM, New York (2007)
21. Zhou, K., Yang, S.-H., Zha, H.: Functional matrix factorizations for cold-start recommendation. In: Proceedings of the 34th International ACM SIGIR Conference on Research and Development in Information Retrieval, SIGIR 2011, pp. 315–324. ACM, New York (2011)

Personality-Aware Collaborative Filtering: An Empirical Study in Multiple Domains with Facebook Data

Ignacio Fernández-Tobías and Iván Cantador

Universidad Autónoma de Madrid, 28049 Madrid, Spain
{ignacio.fernandezt,ivan.cantador}@uam.es

Abstract. In this paper we investigate the incorporation of information about the users' personality into a number of collaborative filtering methods, aiming to address situations of user preference scarcity. Through empirical experiments on a multi-domain dataset obtained from Facebook, we show that the proposed personality-aware collaborative filtering methods effectively –and consistently in the studied domains– increase recommendation performance, in terms of both precision and recall. We also present an analysis of relationships existing between user preferences and personality for the different domains, considering the users' gender and age.

Keywords: recommender systems, collaborative filtering, personality, user similarity.

1 Introduction

Collaborative filtering has been shown to be one of the most successful approaches for providing personalized recommendations. It has, however, limitations when there is a scarcity of user preferences, which leads to a restricted coverage of the user-item preference space (sparsity problem) and a weak capability of recommending items to a new user (cold start problem).

Aiming to address this situation, approaches have been proposed to exploit additional information about users and items, increasing the density of the user-item preference space or capturing user similarities that do not (merely) depend on personal preferences. Among the existing input signals that have been exploited to establish those similarities, psychological aspects –such as emotions, moods and personality– have been gaining increasing attention by the recommender systems community [12].

Personality, as defined in psychology, is an organized and dynamic set of characteristics possessed by a person that uniquely influence his or her cognitions, motivations, emotions and behaviors in certain situations. In particular, recent studies have shown that personality –accounting for user response patterns– correlates with user preferences in different domains, such as music [14, 16], movies and TV shows [3, 13], books and magazines [2, 15], and websites [10]. These correlations are the basis with which traits and types of personality may help explain why people prefer one option to other, and could be used to improve personalization services.

In fact, several authors [9, 11, 17, 18] have already explored how user personality can be exploited to improve collaborative filtering recommendations. However, due to the current difficulty of obtaining information about both user preferences and personality, proposed approaches have been evaluated with relatively small datasets in single domains. Addressing these limitations, in this paper we present an empirical study comparing state of art and novel personality-aware collaborative filtering methods with a large multi-domain dataset obtained from Facebook. We show that the proposed methods effectively –and consistently in the studied domains– increase recommendation performance, in terms of both precision and recall. Moreover, differently to previous work, we present an analysis of relationships between user preferences and personality in several domains, considering the users' gender and age. We show that these demographic attributes lead to different user preference-personality patterns, which calls for further work in the personality-aware recommendation research agenda.

The reminder of the paper is organized as follows. Section 2 reviews related work. Section 3 presents the evaluated personality-aware collaborative filtering methods, and Section 4 reports and discusses obtained experimental results. Complementing these results, Section 5 analyzes relationships between user preferences and personality in the studied domains. Finally, Section 6 ends with conclusions and future research lines.

2 Related Work

2.1 Personality Modeling

Different models have been proposed to characterize and represent human personality. Among them, the Five Factor (FF) model [4] is considered one of the most comprehensive, and has been the mostly used to build user personality profiles [9]. The FF model establishes five broad domains or dimensions –called factors and commonly known as the Big Five– to describe human personality: *openness, conscientiousness, extraversion, agreeableness* and *neuroticism*.

The openness (OPE) factor reflects a person's tendency to intellectual curiosity, creativity and preference for novelty and variety of experiences. The conscientiousness (COS) factor reflects a person's tendency to show self-discipline and aim for personal achievements, and have an organized (not spontaneous) and dependable behavior. The extraversion (EXT) factor reflects a person's tendency to seek stimulation in the company of others, and put energy in finding positive emotions. The agreeableness (AGR) factor reflects a person's tendency to be kind, concerned, truthful and cooperative towards others. Finally, the neuroticism (NEU) factor reflects a person's tendency to experience unpleasant emotions, and refers to the degree of emotional stability and impulse control.

The measurement of the FFs comprises items that are self-descriptive sentences or adjectives, commonly presented in the form of short tests. In this context, the International Personality Item Pool[1] (IPIP) is a publicly available collection of items for use in psychometric tests, and the 20-100 item IPIP proxy for Costa and McCrae's

---

[1] International Personality Item Pool (IPIP), http://ipip.ori.org

NEO-PI-R test [5] is one of the most popular and widely accepted questionnaires to measure the Big Five in adult men and women without overt psychopathology.

In this paper we use the FF model to represent user personality. In particular, we utilize the dataset provided by myPersonality project[2] [1], which has personality and entertainment preference profiles of Facebook users. The dataset contains the FF scores of 3.1 million users, collected by using 20 to 336 item IPIP questionnaires. With this dataset we aim to exploit the relationships between user preferences and personality for recommendation.

2.2 Relationships between User Preferences and Personality

Personality influences how people make their decisions [12]. In particular, it has been shown that people with similar personality characteristics are likely to have similar preferences. In [16] Rentfrow and Gosling investigated how music preferences are related with personality in terms of the FF model, showing that "reflective" people with high openness usually have preferences for jazz, blues and classical music, and "energetic" people with high degree of extraversion and agreeableness usually appreciate rap, hip-hop, funk and electronic music. Also in the music domain and using the FF model, Rawlings and Ciancarelli [14] observed that openness and extraversion are the personality factors that best explain the variance in personal preferences. They showed that people with high openness tend to like diverse music styles, and people with high extraversion are likely to have preferences for popular music.

In the movie domain, Chausson [3] presented a study showing that people open to experiences are likely to prefer comedy and fantasy movies, conscientious individuals are more inclined to enjoy action movies, and neurotic people tend to like romantic movies. Afterwards, Odi et al. [13] explored the relationships between personality factors and induced emotions in movies for different social contexts –e.g. watching a movie alone or with someone else–, and observed different patterns in experienced emotions as functions of the extraversion, agreeableness and neuroticism factors.

Extending the spectrum of analyzed domains, in [15] Rentfrow et al. investigated the relations between personality factors and user preferences in several entertainment domains, namely movies, TV shows, books, magazines and music. They focused their study on five personality-based content categories: aesthetic, cerebral, communal, dark and thrilling. The authors observed positive and negative relationships between such categories and some of the personality factors, e.g., they showed that aesthetic contents relate positively with agreeableness and negatively with neuroticism, and that cerebral contents correlate with extraversion. Also considering several domains – movies, TV shows, books and music–, in [2] we presented a preliminary study on the relations between personality types and entertainment preferences. Analyzing a large dataset of personality factor and domain genre preference user profiles, we extracted personality-based user stereotypes for each genre, and inferred association rules and similarities between types of personality of people with preferences for particular genres. Finally, in the multi-domain scenario of the Web, Kosinski et al. [10]

---

[2] myPersonality project, http://mypersonality.org

presented a study revealing meaningful psychologically relationships between user preferences and personality for certain websites and website categories.

Continuing our previous work [2], in this paper we analyze the relationships between user preferences and personality in multiple entertainment domains. Here we extend the number of considered domain genres and, differently from other studies, conduct the analysis by clustering the user profiles according to demographic attributes, namely gender and age. We show that there are differences in the correlations between user preferences and personality depending on such attributes.

2.3 Personality-Aware Recommender Systems

Once extracted, personality factors could be used to build personality-based user profiles that may be exploited by personalized information retrieval and filtering approaches [8, 11]. In [18] Tkalčič et al. applied and evaluated three user similarity metrics for the heuristic-based collaborative filtering strategy: a typical rating-based similarity, a similarity based on the Euclidean distance with FF data, and a similarity based on a weighted Euclidean distance with the FF data. Their reported results showed that approaches using FF data perform statistically equivalent or better than the rating-based approach, especially in cold-start situations. In her PhD dissertation [11], Nunes explored the use of personality user profile composed of NEO-IPIP items and facets in addition to the Big Five factors, showing that fine-grained personality user profiles help achieve better recommendations. Following the findings of Rentfrow and Gosling [16], in [9] Hu and Pu presented a collaborative filtering approach based on the correlations between personality types and music preferences, in which the similarity between two users is estimated by means of the Pearson's correlation coefficient on the users' FF scores. Combining this approach with a rating-based collaborative filtering, the authors showed significant improvements over the baseline of considering only ratings data. In [17] Roshchina proposed an approach that extracts FF-based profiles by analyzing hotel reviews written by users, and incorporates these profiles into a nearest neighbor algorithm to enhance personalized recommendations. Finally, in [6] Elahi et al. presented an active learning technique that exploits user personality to accurately acquire user ratings for collaborative filtering in cold-start situations.

Instead of using the Euclidean distance as done in [18], in this paper we propose to use the cosine-based distance to establish (dis)similarities between users in the collaborative filtering strategy for both preference- and personality-based user profiles. Similarly to [11], we explore alternative representations of personality user profiles, but focusing on Big Five data instead of considering the large number of NEO-IPIP items and facets. For comparison purposes, we implement and evaluate the Pearson-based user similarity presented in [9], but we also assess a user similarity based on Spearman's correlation, aiming to capture non-linear relationships between user personality factors. Finally, as done in [17], we evaluate collaborative filtering strategies based on nearest neighbors, but differently to that work, in this paper we report recommendation performance results for several neighborhood sizes, and evaluate hybrid approaches that combine user preference and personality data.

3 Personality-Aware Collaborative Filtering Methods

In the recommender systems literature, the preference of a user $u \in \mathcal{U}$ for certain item $i \in \mathcal{I}$ is commonly represented as a rating $r_{u,i} \in \mathcal{R}$, where $\mathcal{R}$ is a totally ordered set, e.g. non negative integers or real numbers within a certain range. For each user u, a recommender system aims to predict ratings $r_{u,i}$ of items i unrated by u, and suggest the items with the highest predicted ratings $\tilde{r}_{u,i}$.

In particular, heuristic-based collaborative filtering strategies compute $\tilde{r}_{u,i}$ as an aggregate of the ratings of some other (usually, the most similar) users v. More formally, $\tilde{r}_{u,i} = \text{aggr}_{v \in \mathcal{N}_u} r_{v,i}$, where $\mathcal{N}_u$ denotes the set of N users who are the most similar to u, and is usually referred as the set of neighbors or neighborhood. Several aggregation functions aggr have been proposed in the literature. One of the most widely used, and that we adopt in this paper (for unary/binary ratings) is:

$$\tilde{r}_{u,i} = \bar{r}_u + \kappa \sum_{v \in \mathcal{N}_u} sim(u,v) \cdot (r_{v,i} - \bar{r}_v)$$

where $sim(u,v)$ is a function that measures the similarity between two users u and v, $\bar{r}_u$ is the average value of user u'ratings, and κ is a normalization factor, which is usually set as $\kappa = 1/\sum_{v \in \mathcal{N}_u} sim(u,v)$.

Together with the rating aggregate function, the user similarity function is a central component that characterizes a collaborative filtering strategy. A standard similarity metric is based on the Pearson's correlation coefficient:

$$sim(u,v) = \frac{\sum_{i \in \mathcal{I}_u \cap \mathcal{I}_v}(r_{u,i} - \bar{r}_u)(r_{v,i} - \bar{r}_v)}{\sqrt{\sum_{i \in \mathcal{I}_u \cap \mathcal{I}_v}(r_{u,i} - \bar{r}_u)^2 \sum_{i \in \mathcal{I}_u \cap \mathcal{I}_v}(r_{v,i} - \bar{r}_v)^2}}$$

where $\mathcal{I}_u \subseteq \mathcal{I}$ is the set of items rated by user u. This metric is not applicable when the ratings are either unary (such as the Facebook's likes) or binary (such as the YouTube's thumps up/down). In these cases, a user similarity based on the Jaccard's coefficient is commonly used:

$$sim_{pref}(u,v) = \frac{|\mathcal{I}_u \cap \mathcal{I}_v|}{|\mathcal{I}_u \cup \mathcal{I}_v|} \quad (1)$$

This is in fact the similarity metric we consider as baseline in our experiments. We shall refer the collaborative filtering strategy that utilizes $sim_{pref}(u,v)$, without considering the users' personality, as CF. Analogously to [9], in order to incorporate personality information into the recommendation process, we shall study a hybrid recommendation strategy that linearly combines $sim_{pref}(u,v)$ with a personality-based user similarity $sim_{pers}(u,v)$ as follows:

$$sim(u,v) = \lambda \cdot sim_{pref}(u,v) + (1-\lambda) \cdot sim_{pers}(u,v) \quad (2)$$

where $\lambda \in [0,1]$ controls the influence of user preferences and personality on the recommendation process. For λ values close to 1, user preferences are more relevant, while for λ values close to 0, personality gets higher relevance. In the subsequent sections, we propose several formulations of $sim_{pers}(u,v)$ that yield the personality-aware collaborative filtering methods we empirically compare.

Let $p_u = \{p_{u,ope}, p_{u,cos}, p_{u,ext}, p_{u,agr}, p_{u,neu}\}$ be the user u's personality-based profile composed of u's Big Five scores. Previous approaches have considered the components $p_{u,k}$ ranging in a numeric interval, e.g. [1,5] and [1,100], as derived from the IPIP questionnaires. Here, we consider this representation as well, and refer it as *continuous* personality profile. Nonetheless, aiming to explore simpler personality-aware user profiles and similarities, we also propose to study a personality representation in which each component $p_{u,k}$ takes one of a limited set of categorical values –namely low, medium, and high–, obtained from the corresponding original Big Five scores. We refer this representation as *discrete* personality profile.

3.1 Cosine-Based Personality User Similarity Methods (COS)

The first personality-based user similarity we evaluate is the cosine-based similarity:

$$sim_{pers\_cos}(u,v) = \frac{\sum_k p_{u,k} \cdot p_{v,k}}{\sqrt{\sum_k p_{u,k}^2} \sqrt{\sum_k p_{v,k}^2}} \quad (3)$$

Its incorporation in formula (2) produces a recommendation method that we call COS. Depending on whether continuous or discrete personality profiles are used, we shall refer to COS-c and COS-d methods, respectively. These methods will have different implementations depending on the λ value used, i.e., COS-c-λ and COS-d-λ, with $0 < \lambda < 1$. The case of $\lambda = 1$ (exploiting only user preferences) is equivalent to the CF method, and the case of $\lambda = 0$ will be referred as COS-c-pers and COS-d-pers, since only user personality information is exploited.

3.2 Pearson-Based Personality User Similarity Methods (PEA)

The second personality-based user similarity we evaluate was proposed by Hu and Pu in [9], and is based on the Pearson's correlation coefficient:

$$sim_{pers\_pea}(u,v) = \frac{\sum_k (p_{u,k} - \overline{p_u})(p_{v,k} - \overline{p_v})}{\sqrt{\sum_k (p_{u,k} - \overline{p_u})^2 \sum_k (p_{v,k} - \overline{p_v})^2}} \quad (4)$$

Its integration in (2) produces a recommendation method that we call PEA. Similarly to the COS case, for the PEA similarity, we shall evaluate the PEA-c-per, PEA-d-per, PEA-c-λ and PEA-d-λ methods, with $0 < \lambda < 1$.

3.3 Spearman-Based Personality User Similarity Methods (SPE)

The third and last personality-based user similarity we propose is based on the Spearman's correlation coefficient:

$$sim_{pers\_spe}(u,v) = \frac{\sum_k (s_{u,k} - \overline{s_u})(s_{v,k} - \overline{s_v})}{\sqrt{\sum_k (s_{u,k} - \overline{s_u})^2 \sum_k (s_{v,k} - \overline{s_v})^2}} \quad (5)$$

where $s_{u,k}$ is the position of $p_{u,k}$ in the decreasing order ranking of u's Big Five scores. Analogously to previous cases, the incorporation of this similarity into (2) produces a recommendation method that we call SPE, and which will be instantiated and evaluated in the SPE-c-per, SPE-d-per, SPE-c-λ and SPE-d-λ methods.

4 Experiments

4.1 Dataset

The dataset used in our experiments is part of the database made publicly available in myPersonality project [1]. myPersonality is a Facebook application with which users take psychometric tests and receive feedback on their scores. The users allow the application to record personal information from their Facebook profiles, such a demographic and geo-location data, *likes*, status updates, and friendship relations, among others. In particular, as of March 2014, the tool has let record a database with 46 million Facebook likes of 220,000 users for 5.5 million items of diverse nature – people (actors, musicians, politicians, sportsmen, writers, etc.), objects (movies, TV shows, songs, books, games, etc.), organizations, events, etc.–, and the Big Five scores of 3.1 million users, collected using 20 to 336 item IPIP questionnaires.

Due to the size and complexity of the database, in this paper we restrict our study to a subset of its items. Specifically, we selected all likes (ratings) associated to items belonging to one of the following 3 categories: Movie genre, Book genre, and Musical genre. Thus, for instance, selected items belonging to the Movie genre category are movie genres such as comedy, action, adventure, drama, and science fiction. Note that we do not take into account a large number of potential valuable items, such as particular movies preferred by users. Next, we selected those users of the dataset that had ratings for the considered items. Once the items and users were selected, we conducted text processing operations to consolidate morphological derivations of certain item names (e.g. science fiction, science-fiction, sci-fi, and sf). Table 1 shows some statistics about the number of users, items and ratings in the considered domains. The minimum, maximum, and average (standard deviation) numbers of ratings per user were: 1, 19 and 1.73 (1.14) for movies, 1, 15 and 1.57 (1.08) for books, and 1, 61 and 3.68 (3.66) for music. In the table, users are grouped by gender and by age according to Erikson's psychosocial stages [7] (see Table 2).

Table 1. Statistics of the used dataset (gender and age of some users were not declared)

Domain	#users						
	all	female	male	adolescent	young adult	middle-aged adult	advanced-aged adult
movies	16168	9827	6341	2833	3086	1610	189
books	15251	9919	5332	2672	2916	1577	202
music	17980	10924	7056	3164	3467	1898	234

Domain (#Items)	#likes (sparsity)						
	all	female	male	adolescent	young adult	middle-aged adult	advanced-aged adult
movies (268)	27921 (99.36%)	17073 (99.35%)	10848 (99.36%)	4850 (99.36%)	5192 (99.37%)	2643 (99.39%)	289 (99.43%)
books (305)	23882 (99.49%)	15717 (99.48%)	8165 (99.50%)	4105 (99.50%)	4478 (99.50%)	2493 (99.48%)	336 (99.45%)
music (1175)	66079 (99.69%)	38898 (99.70%)	27181 (99.67%)	11628 (99.69%)	12055 (99.70%)	5876 (99.74%)	654 (99.76%)

As explained in Section 3, we propose to evaluate the recommendation methods utilizing both continuous and discrete user personality profiles. Specifically, for building the discrete profiles, we transform each original personality factor score in [1, 5] into one of the following categories: "low", "medium", and "high." Considering the distribution of personality factor scores of all users in the dataset, for each personality factor, the *low* category is assigned to those scores that are below the 33th percentile, the *medium* category is assigned to those scores that are between the 33th and 66th percentiles, and the *high* category is assigned to those scores that are between the 66th and 100th percentiles. Table 2 shows the obtained intervals.

Table 2. Considered categories for user ages (left) and personality factors (right)

Age category	Age interval
adolescent	< 20 years old
young adult	[20, 39]
middle-aged adult	[40, 50]
advanced-aged adult	> 50 years old

Personality factor	Personality factor categories and intervals		
	low	medium	high
OPE	[1.00, 3.75)	[3.75, 4.25)	[4.25, 5.00]
COS	[1.00, 3.05)	[3.05, 3.75)	[3.75, 5.00]
EXT	[1.00, 3.25)	[3.25, 4.00)	[4.00, 5.00]
AGR	[1.00, 3.25)	[3.25, 4.00)	[4.00, 5.00]
NEU	[1.00, 2.50)	[2.50, 3.10)	[3.10, 5.00]

4.2 Results

In our experiments we empirically compared 61 methods: CF, COS-c-λ, COS-d-λ, PEA-c-λ, PEA-d-λ, SPE-c-λ, and SPE-d-λ, with $\lambda = 0, 0.1, 0.2, ..., 0.9$. The methods were evaluated in the three considered domains, by means of their precision, recall and F-measure values for the top k recommendations –P@k, R@k and F@k– with $k = 1,...,5$, averaged by 5-times 5-fold cross validation. All methods were executed with neighborhood sizes of 5, 10, 15, 20 and 25. Tables 3, 4 and 5 show the methods' configurations with best results (in terms of average F-measure values). All differences with CF's values are statistically significant (2-tailed Wilcoxon, p≤0.05).

Table 3. Avg. P@k, R@k and F@k values achieved by the best performing methods in the movies domain. Values higher than CF's are in bold, and the highest values are underlined.

Method	Neighbors	P@1	P@2	P@3	P@4	P@5	R@1	R@2	R@3	R@4	R@5	F@1	F@2	F@3	F@4	F@5
CF	20	.146	.382	.350	<u>.480</u>	.490	.025	.140	.247	.268	.298	.043	.205	.290	.344	.371
COS-c-pers	5	.099	.242	.290	.339	.353	**.099**	.241	**.284**	**.292**	.294	**.099**	.241	.287	.314	.321
COS-c-0.3	15	**.154**	**.400**	**<u>.488</u>**	.463	.460	.024	.119	.242	**.306**	.291	.042	.183	**.324**	**.368**	.356
COS-d-pers	10	.068	.228	.282	.252	.298	**.068**	**.228**	**.282**	.252	.298	**.068**	**.228**	.282	.252	.298
COS-d-0.1	10	**.149**	**.405**	**.433**	.456	**.532**	.062	.213	**.306**	**.276**	**.313**	**.088**	**.279**	**.359**	.345	**.394**
PEA-c-pers	5	.095	.267	.337	.375	.373	**.095**	<u>.267</u>	**.333**	**.343**	**.323**	**.095**	.267	**.335**	**.358**	.346
PEA-c-0.2	10	**<u>.178</u>**	**<u>.442</u>**	**.466**	.439	.372	.071	.236	**.350**	**.340**	**.314**	**.102**	**<u>.308</u>**	**<u>.400</u>**	**.383**	.341
PEA-d-pers	5	.061	.210	.302	.280	.321	**.061**	**.209**	**.294**	.267	**.315**	**.061**	**.209**	.298	.273	.318
PEA-d-0.1	10	**.149**	**.400**	**.436**	.476	**<u>.540</u>**	.075	.221	**.311**	**.284**	**<u>.317</u>**	**.100**	**.285**	**.363**	**.356**	**<u>.399</u>**
SPE-c-pers	5	.102	.243	.351	.357	.261	**<u>.102</u>**	.240	**.331**	**.316**	.223	**.102**	.241	**.341**	.335	.241
SPE-c-0.1	10	**.162**	.380	**.429**	.463	.300	.089	.257	**.322**	**<u>.347</u>**	.227	**<u>.115</u>**	**<u>.307</u>**	**.368**	**<u>.397</u>**	.258
SPE-d-pers	5	.057	.226	.299	.296	.330	**.050**	**.200**	**<u>.266</u>**	.237	.254	**.053**	**.212**	.282	.263	.287
SPE-d-0.2	10	.139	**.406**	**.455**	.463	.410	**.047**	**.188**	**<u>.297</u>**	**.288**	.261	**.070**	**.257**	**.359**	**.355**	.319

Table 4. Avg. P@k, R@k and F@k values achieved by the best performing methods in the books domain. Values higher than CF's are in bold, and the highest values are underlined.

Method	Neighbors	P@1	P@2	P@3	P@4	P@5	R@1	R@2	R@3	R@4	R@5	F@1	F@2	F@3	F@4	F@5
CF	15	<u>.097</u>	.146	.189	.227	.291	.026	.081	.129	.199	.245	.041	.104	.153	.212	.266
COS-c-pers	5	.052	.102	.152	.201	.243	**.052**	**.102**	**.150**	.187	.196	**.052**	.102	.151	.194	.217
COS-c-0.1	15	.095	**.150**	**.235**	**.292**	.270	**.027**	**.081**	**.147**	**.254**	.219	**.042**	**.105**	**.181**	**.272**	.242
COS-d-pers	10	.035	.098	.163	.236	.286	**.035**	**.098**	**.163**	<u>**.236**</u>	**.286**	.035	.098	**.163**	<u>**.236**</u>	**.286**
COS-d-0.3	10	.087	**.153**	<u>**.236**</u>	<u>**.266**</u>	**.342**	**.029**	**.085**	**.164**	**.205**	**.276**	**.044**	**.109**	<u>**.194**</u>	**.232**	**.305**
PEA-c-pers	10	.050	.088	.130	.208	.266	<u>**.050**</u>	**.088**	**.130**	**.208**	**.266**	**.050**	.088	.130	.208	**.266**
PEA-c-0.2	10	.087	**.159**	**.196**	**.263**	.277	**.041**	**.103**	**.150**	**.216**	.242	<u>**.056**</u>	**.125**	**.170**	**.237**	.258
PEA-d-pers	10	.043	.100	.164	.231	.256	**.043**	**.100**	**.164**	**.231**	**.256**	.043	.100	**.164**	**.231**	.256
PEA-d-0.5	10	.077	**.164**	**.221**	**.248**	<u>**.381**</u>	.023	**.090**	**.144**	**.209**	<u>**.298**</u>	.035	**.116**	**.174**	**.227**	<u>**.334**</u>
SPE-c-pers	5	.040	.105	.170	.164	.218	**.040**	**.104**	<u>**.169**</u>	.158	.197	.040	**.104**	**.169**	.161	.207
SPE-c-0.5	20	.092	**.156**	.184	**.229**	.272	**.036**	<u>**.112**</u>	**.164**	**.221**	**.272**	**.052**	<u>**.130**</u>	**.173**	**.225**	**.272**
SPE-d-pers	10	.036	.083	.141	**.242**	.272	**.032**	.076	**.129**	**.218**	**.255**	.034	.079	.135	**.229**	.263
SPE-d-0.3	10	.086	**.157**	**.222**	**.249**	**.355**	**.031**	**.087**	**.152**	.173	**.260**	**.046**	**.112**	**.180**	.204	**.300**

Table 5. Avg. P@k, R@k and F@k values achieved by the best performing methods in the music domain. Values higher than CF's are in bold, and the highest values are underlined.

Method	Neighbors	P@1	P@2	P@3	P@4	P@5	R@1	R@2	R@3	R@4	R@5	F@1	F@2	F@3	F@4	F@5
CF	5	.130	.192	.230	.250	.247	.066	.118	.148	.169	.172	.088	.146	.180	.202	.203
COS-c-pers	5	.033	.066	.083	.094	.107	.033	.065	.083	.094	.106	.033	.066	.083	.094	.106
COS-c-0.8	5	**.135**	**.197**	**.238**	.248	**.247**	**.069**	**.120**	**.151**	.167	**.172**	**.092**	**.149**	**.184**	.200	**.203**
COS-d-pers	5	.067	.073	.081	.080	.089	.067	.073	.081	.080	.088	.067	.073	.081	.080	.088
COS-d-0.7	5	**.130**	.189	.219	.222	.236	<u>**.070**</u>	**.119**	**.149**	.164	**.182**	**.091**	**.146**	.177	.189	**.206**
PEA-c-pers	5	.032	.058	.073	.090	.099	.032	.058	.073	.090	.098	.032	.058	.073	.090	.098
PEA-c-0.9	5	**.131**	**.194**	**.234**	.244	<u>**.255**</u>	**.067**	.115	**.149**	.167	<u>**.184**</u>	**.089**	.144	**.182**	.198	<u>**.214**</u>
PEA-d-pers	5	.064	.071	.081	.079	.091	.064	.071	.081	.078	.088	.064	.071	.081	.078	.089
PEA-d-0.9	5	**.134**	**.194**	.228	<u>**.250**</u>	.248	**.069**	**.119**	.144	<u>**.169**</u>	**.177**	**.091**	**.148**	.177	<u>**.202**</u>	**.206**
SPE-c-pers	5	.024	.060	.081	.096	.101	.024	.059	.081	.095	.099	.024	.059	.081	.095	.100
SPE-c-0.9	5	**.130**	**.193**	.227	.241	.241	**.067**	.115	.145	.163	**.177**	**.088**	.144	.177	.194	**.204**
SPE-d-pers	5	.070	.074	.073	.073	.089	.063	.067	.066	.067	.079	.066	.070	.069	.070	.084
SPE-d-0.9	5	**.133**	**.196**	.224	.245	.240	.063	.108	.133	.155	.162	.086	.139	.167	.190	.193

In general, for the three domains, the proposed hybrid recommendation methods that exploit information about the users' **personality** outperform the baseline CF method. It has to be noted that, probably due to the scarcity of user preferences (see Table 1), those methods that give more weight to user personality (i.e., those methods with λ values close to 0) obtain the highest precision and recall values. This is not the case in the music domain, where the average number of rated items per user is larger than in the movies and books domains (see Section 4.1), and the relationships between user preferences and personality are the weakest ones (as will be shown in Section 5).

In terms of average F-measure values, for most cases in the movies and books domains, the **discrete profiles** let obtained better results than the continuous profiles. Regarding the **user similarities**, there is no consensus on which is the best alternative for the studied domains. While in the music domain the COS methods are the best performing, in the movies and books domains the PEA and SPE methods respectively achieve the highest precision and recall values.

4.3 Discussion

The obtained results show that the proposed 3-category personality profiles let generate better recommendations than those obtained with numeric personality profiles, which are the ones used previously in the literature. The discretization process of the Big Five presented in this paper follows a simple approach based on the personality factor distributions in the whole dataset. Approaches dependent on the target domain, considering a different number of personality factor categories, or based on certain user aspects may help improve generated recommendations.

The nature of the utilized dataset, which comprises *like* preferences for domain genres, entailed the use of the Jaccard user similarity (formula 1) in the heuristic-based collaborative filtering strategy for the top N recommendation task. If either binary *like/unlike* records or numeric ratings were available as user preferences, more elaborated collaborative filtering methods –e.g. those based on the Pearson's and Spearman's correlation coefficients– could be investigated for both the top N and rating prediction recommendation tasks.

Moreover, although precision and recall metrics are appropriate and widely used for evaluating the top N recommendation task, other metrics could be explored when assessing personality-aware collaborative filtering methods. In particular, measuring recommendation diversity may be of special interest. As shown in previous studies [2, 14], people open to experience tend to have preferences for more diverse types of items.

5 Relationships between User Preferences and Personality

As done in previous work (see Section 2.2), here we report relationships existing between user preferences and personality. Tables 6 and 7 show linear correlation values between preference- and personality-based user similarities for all distinct pairs of users in each domain. We report such correlation values for different groups of users based on their gender and age, as explained in Section 4.1. All values marked with asterisk (*) are statistically significant at $p<0.05$.

When considering **all users** in a domain, it can be seen that correlation values are close to 0, meaning that there is no (linear) relations between user preferences and personality factors. If we consider **age-based groups**, the relations are strong for adolescent users in the movies domain, and are moderate for middle-aged adults in the movies and music domains. On the other hand, if we consider **gender-based groups**, we can observe that the correlation values are higher between female users in the movies domain and, in less degree, in the books domain. In the music domain, there is no clear distinction for correlations between male and female users. Finally, we note that there are no clear patterns between the correlations obtained with the cosine- and Pearson/Spearman-based personality profiles.

Table 6. Linear correlations between preference- and personality-based user similarities

Domain	minimum #likes per user	Cosine-based Personality User Profiles											
		all ages			adolescent			young adult			middle-aged adult		
		all	female	male	all	female	male	all	female	male	all	female	male
movies	4	.039* (792920)	.053* (296846)	.032* (119804)	.143* (23065)	.155* (7562)	.155* (4182)	.043* (21101)	.045* (7223)	.066* (3586)	.034* (5105)	.074* (2177)	-.084* (605)
	5	.067* (137646)	.080* (47735)	.064* (23125)	**.213*** (3364)	**.356*** (933)	.115* (733)	-.027 (3793)	-.082* (1352)	.060 (597)	.059 (1094)	.067 (388)	-.126 (169)
	6	.120* (19408)	.136* (5867)	.128* (3891)	**.267*** (435)	**.545*** (91)	.150 (120)	.095 (605)	.124 (158)	.083 (136)	**.212*** (153)	**.420*** (28)	.007 (45)
books	4	.037* (230644)	.043* (107132)	.043* (24008)	.058* (5911)	.074* (2495)	.097* (746)	.014 (7012)	.013 (2484)	.031 (909)	.080* (2270)	.118* (1149)	.124* (197)
	5	.042* (58495)	.054* (26688)	.017 (6238)	.037 (729)	.043 (271)	-.013 (112)	.077* (2073)	.099* (855)	.113 (252)	.057* (757)	.107* (374)	.050 (65)
	6	.033* (15926)	.062* (7196)	-.058* (1691)	.060 (279)	.060 (144)	-.419 (17)	.010 (489)	.018 (225)	.169 (46)	.048 (110)	.125 (28)	.115 (23)
music	4	.022* (13962828)	.024* (5065849)	.019* (2248669)	.027* (433486)	.022* (146624)	.033* (77412)	.030* (428909)	.034* (150762)	.015* (73019)	-.008* (12311)	.009* (42641)	-.008* (12311)
	8	.040* (1763904)	.048* (597027)	.037* (311186)	.056* (51022)	.084* (17597)	.038* (8726)	.028* (52463)	.003* (15661)	.045* (10877)	.037* (1025)	.115* (2851)	.037* (1025)
	16	.025* (41503)	.011 (9672)	.038* (11090)	.116* (1375)	.125* (344)	.169* (335)	.083* (1113)	-.096 (153)	**.229*** (421)	-.156 (15)	**.464*** (19)	-.156 (15)

Table 7. Linear correlations between preference- and personality-based user similarities

Domain	minimum #likes per user	Spearman-based Personality User Profiles											
		all ages			adolescent			young adult			middle-aged adult		
		all	female	male	all	female	male	all	female	male	all	female	male
movies	4	.006* (767201)	.001 (288179)	.028* (115290)	.032* (22263)	.013 (7233)	.099* (4061)	.022* (20130)	.010 (7029)	.047* (3326)	.032* (4909)	.046* (2083)	-.106* (593)
	5	.024* (133411)	.012* (46436)	.049* (22387)	.137* (3260)	**.210*** (902)	.098* (706)	.005 (3616)	-.067* (1321)	.134* (548)	.047* (1061)	.074 (377)	-.137 (169)
	6	.063* (18982)	.046* (5754)	.098* (3787)	**.248*** (424)	**.574*** (89)	.094 (112)	.103* (594)	-.063 (157)	.273* (135)	-.008* (149)	.113 (28)	-.025 (45)
books	4	.037* (224332)	.034* (104144)	.050* (23385)	.029* (5766)	.033 (2429)	.058 (731)	.011 (6823)	-.007 (2790)	.027 (881)	.103* (2210)	.119* (1119)	.066 (184)
	5	.042* (56869)	.041* (25946)	.027* (6064)	.053 (728)	.083 (266)	-.019 (111)	.006 (2023)	-.019 (841)	.038 (243)	.134* (734)	.115* (363)	-.001 (64)
	6	.027* (15477)	.039* (6998)	-.015 (1639)	.086 (273)	.101 (140)	-.457 (17)	-.017 (477)	-.089 (222)	.168 (43)	.097 (107)	-.066 (27)	.064 (23)
Music	4	-.001* (13552095)	.007* (4928335)	-.008* (2175265)	-.007* (147674)	-.017* (142927)	.005 (75410)	.001 (415860)	.008* (147105)	-.006 (70182)	.002 (97066)	.013* (41223)	-.012 (12012)
	8	.014* (1712038)	.025* (580695)	.004* (301306)	.015* (48739)	.014 (17132)	.004 (8511)	.028* (50968)	.040* (15304)	.027* (10495)	.056* (7152)	.080* (2803)	.017* (1009)
	16	-.030* (40470)	-.012 (9453)	-.043* (10774)	.046 (1341)	-.004 (337)	.052 (329)	.063* (1095)	.005 (153)	.113* (413)	-.048 (72)	.263 (19)	-.403 (14)

6   Conclusions and Future Work

In this paper we have presented an empirical study comparing several collaborative filtering methods that effectively exploit information about the users' personality. In addition to evaluating state of the art approaches, we have assessed new personality-aware recommendation strategies and user profiles, and have used large datasets in several domains. Moreover, we have analyzed relationships between user preferences and personality considering the users' gender and age, which has revealed differences in the preference-personality patterns, calling for further work in the future.

In our study, however, we have focused on broad representations of the users' personality by assuming the same relevance for all the Big Five personality factors. As previous work has shown [3, 14, 16], personality factors may influence differently on user preferences for certain types of items. In the future we shall investigate how fine grained relationships between user preferences and personality factors can be exploited in recommendation. Moreover, we also envision the consideration of personality facets (in addition to or instead of personality factors) as a potential way to exploit personality information in collaborative filtering.

Our investigation has revealed there are differences in the relationships between user preferences and personality according to the users' gender and age. Nonetheless, we have not exploited such particularities for recommendation purposes yet. In this context, other user attributes, such as educational attainment, could be taken into account as well.

Finally, we also plan to evaluate new personality-aware collaborative filtering approaches, e.g. methods based on factor models, and strategies focused on neighbor selection and rating matrix enrichment, instead of on user similarities.

References

1. Bachrach, Y., Kohli, P., Graepel, T., Stillwell, D.J., Kosinski, M.: Personality and Patterns of Facebook Usage. In: Proceedings of the 4th Web Science Conference (WebSci 2012), pp. 24–32 (2012)
2. Cantador, I., Fernández-Tobías, I., Bellogín, A.: Relating Personality Types with User Preferences in Multiple Entertainment Domains. In: Proc. of the 1st Workshop on Emotions and Personality in Personalized Services, pp. 13–28 (2013)
3. Chausson, O.: Who Watches What? Assessing the Impact of Gender and Personality on Film Preferences. myPersonality project, University of Cambridge (2010)
4. Costa, P.T., McCrae, R.R.: Revised NEO Personality Inventory (NEO-PI-R) and NEO Five-Factor Inventory (NEO-FFI) Manual. Psychological Assessment Resources (1992)
5. Goldberg, L.R., Johnson, J.A., Eber, H.W., Hogan, R., Ashton, M.C., Cloninger, C.R., Gough, H.G.: The International Personality Item Pool and the Future of Public-Domain Personality Measures. Journal of Research in Personality 40, 84–96 (2006)
6. Elahi, M., Braunhofer, M., Ricci, F., Tkalcic, M.: Personality-Based Active Learning for Collaborative Filtering Recommender Systems. In: Baldoni, M., Baroglio, C., Boella, G., Micalizio, R. (eds.) AI*IA 2013. LNCS (LNAI), vol. 8249, pp. 360–371. Springer, Heidelberg (2013)
7. Erikson, E.H.: Childhood and Society. W. W. Norton and Company (1950)
8. Hu, R., Pu, P.: A Study on User Perception of Personality-Based Recommender Systems. In: De Bra, P., Kobsa, A., Chin, D. (eds.) UMAP 2010. LNCS, vol. 6075, pp. 291–302. Springer, Heidelberg (2010)
9. Hu, R., Pu, P.: Enhancing Collaborative Filtering Systems with Personality Information. In: Proceedings of the 5th ACM Conference on Recommender Systems, pp. 197–204 (2011)
10. Kosinski, M., Stillwell, D.J., Kohli, P., Bachrach, Y., Graepel, T.: Personality and Website Choice. In: Proceedings of 4th ACM Conference on Web Science, pp. 251–254 (2012)
11. Nunes, M.A.S.N.: Recommender Systems based on Personality Traits: Could Human Psychological Aspects Influence the Computer Decision-making Process? VDM Verlag (2009)

12. Nunes, M.A.S.N., Hu, R.: Personality-based Recommender Systems: An Overview. In: Proceedings of the 6th ACM Conference on Recommender Systems, pp. 5–6 (2012)
13. Odić, A., Tkalčič, M., Tasič, J.F., Košir, A.: Personality and Social Context: Impact on Emotion Induction from Movies. In: Proc. of the 1st Workshop on Emotions and Personality in Personalized Services (2013)
14. Rawlings, D., Ciancarelli, V.: Music Preference and the Five-Factor Model of the NEO Personality Inventory. Psychology of Music 25(2), 120–132 (1997)
15. Rentfrow, P.J., Goldberg, L.R., Zilca, R.: Listening, Watching, and Reading: The Structure and Correlates of Entertainment Preferences. Journal of Personality 79(2), 223–258 (2011)
16. Rentfrow, P.J., Gosling, S.D.: The Do Re Mi's of Everyday Life: The Structure and Personality Correlates of Music Preferences. Journal of Personality and Social Psychology 84(6), 1236–1256 (2003)
17. Roshchina, A.: TWIN: Personality-based Recommender System. MSc thesis, Institute of Technology Tallaght, Dublin (2012)
18. Tkalčič, M., Kunaver, M., Košir, A., Tasič, J.F.: Addressing the New User Problem with a Personality Based User Similarity Measure. In: Proc. of the 2nd Workshop on User Models for Motivational Systems (2011)

Modelling User Preferences from Implicit Preference Indicators via Compensational Aggregations

Ladislav Peska and Peter Vojtas

Faculty of Mathematics and Physics
Charles University in Prague
Malostranske Namesti 25, Prague, Czech Republic
{peska,vojtas}@ksi.mff.cuni.cz

Abstract. In our work, we focus on recommending for small or medium-sized e-commerce portals. Due to high competition, users of these portals lack loyalty and e.g. refuse to register or provide any/enough explicit feedback. Furthermore, products such as tours, cars or furniture have very low average consumption rate preventing us from tracking unregistered user between two consecutive purchases. Recommending on such domains proves to be very challenging, yet interesting research task. We will introduce new method for learning user preferences based on their implicit feedback. The method is based on aggregating various types of implicit feedback with parameterized fuzzy T-norms and S-norms. We have conducted several off-line experiments with real user data from travel agency confirming competitiveness of our method, however further optimizing and on-line experiments should be conducted in the future work.

Keywords: Recommender Systems, Implicit Feedback, Fuzzy T-norms and S-norms, User Preference, E-Commerce.

1 Introduction and Related Work

We face the growth of information on the web with an increasing offer of products, information and services. Automation of web content processing is necessary. Several solutions are available, ranging from search engines to e-shops, aggregation shops and recommender systems. The main problem we are interested in is the personalization of web information processing by user preference mining. Our main starting point is using fuzzy (many valued) logic and interpreting each fuzzy value as a degree of user preference. In the area of e-commerce, we are especially interested in recommending for small e-commerce sites without dominant position on the market. Moreover we are interested in domains, where an average customer do not purchase an item very often (e.g. once a year). The competition of such sites is usually very high, so the users tend not to be very loyal, visit more sites comparing offers and do not provide any data about themselves (e.g. register or rate products). We need to deal with recommendation for a non-registered user based on very little information.

1.1 Related Work

Due to the space reasons, we will provide only a few references to the nearest related work in the area of user preferences and fuzzy systems.

User Preferences: Contrary to the explicit feedback, usage of implicit feedback requires no additional effort from the user. Monitoring implicit feedback varies from simple binary user visit or play counts to more sophisticated scrolling or mouse movement tracking, click stream etc. One of the first approaches to deal with implicit user feedback was Claypool et al. [1]. Their study involved multiple implicit preference indicators and containing idea to combine them in order to achieve better results. In our early work [6], we conducted an online experiment corroborating that using multiple implicit indicators improves recommendation quality. Indicators proposed in [1] served as a starting point to our model of user feedback. Implicit feedback is often taken as positive only. One of the few papers aiming (similarly as us) to infer negative preference from implicit feedback is Lee and Brusilovsky [5]. Hu, Koren and Volinsky [3] raised question of how to interpret real-valued implicit indicator in their work on TV recommender. Their paper brings an idea of decomposing user preference into the polarity and intensity which we use in one part of our method.

Fuzzy Systems: The area of fuzzy systems is closely related to our work. Having multiple types of user feedback, resulting into the multiple preferences, we need an aggregation function to create single value representing user preference on the given object. Such aggregation could be the weighted average, a fuzzy T-norm S-norm or similar functions. Zimmermann and Zysno [9] described human decision making process and suggested parameter for the level of compensations for aggregating functions. Yager [8] suggested using noble reinforced S-norms to cope with the same problem. T-norms and S-norms are a generalization of the usual two-valued logical conjunction and disjunction for fuzzy logics. Usually four axioms are used to define T-norms and S-norms. Besides commutativity and associativity, T-(co)norms keep monotonicity: $T(x,y) \leq T(x,z) IFF y \leq z$ and boundary condition: for T-norms: $T(x,1) = x$ and S-norms: $T(x,0) = x$. Several parametrized families of T-(co)norms were introduced, where level of compensations are determined with parameter λ.

Frank, Schweizer-Sklar, Sugeno-Weber, Yager and Hamacher T-(co)norms are used in this work and are fully described in [4]. As an example, following formula depicts Sugeno-Weber T-norm and S-norm (also called T-conorm).

$$T_{sw}(x,y) = \max\left(0, \frac{x + y + \lambda xy - 1}{1 + \lambda}\right) \qquad S_{sw}(x,y) = \min(1, x + y + \lambda xy)$$

1.2 Main Contribution

The main contributions of this paper are:

- Proposing method for learning user preference from multiple implicit indicators using families of fuzzy T-(co)norms.
- Comparing usability of binary and many-valued feedback.
- Introducing negative user preference based on implicit feedback.
- Off-line experiments on travel agency dataset.

2 User's Implicit Preference Indicators in E-Commerce

We have collected usage data from one of the major Czech travel agencies. Data were collected from December 2012 to January 2014. Travel agency is typical e-commerce enterprise, where customers buy products only once in a while (most typically once a year). The site does not force users to register and so we can track unique users only with cookies stored in the browser. User typically either land straight on the intended object via search engine (less interesting case), or browses through several categories, compares objects (possibly on more websites) and eventually buys an object.

Unlike the majority of research groups we had access to the source codes, so we could (after approval) tailor user feedback mining to suit our needs. Table 1 contains full description of used implicit indicators. Note that indicators are stored on user×object bases. Feedback dataset contains approx. 350 000 user×object records with 0.07% density of user×object matrix and in average 1.6 visited objects per user (220 000 distinct users and 2300 objects). For the purpose of the experiment, the dataset was then restricted to only users with at least one purchased and 4 visited objects leaving over 3500 records from 364 users (in the original dataset there are in total 2000 purchases and approx. 16000 users with 4 or more visited objects).

Table 1. Description of the considered implicit feedbacks for user visiting an object

Factor	*Description*
F_1: *PageView*	Count(*OnLoad()* event on object page)
F_2: *Mouse*	Count(*OnMouseOver()* events on object page)
F_3: *Scroll*	Count(OnScroll() events on object page)
F_4: *Open*	Count(Item was opened from the list of recommended objects)
F_5: *Time*	Sum(time spent on object page – in seconds)
p_{uo}: *Purchase*	1 IFF user bought the item, 0 OTHERWISE

As our previous work corroborated [7], using purely collaborative filtering methods on such a sparse dataset comes up with poor results, so content-based algorithms were used in the experiments. The travel agency domain allows defining fairly reasonable nominal content-based features e.g. *type of the tour*, *destination country*, *types* of *accommodation*, *transportation* or *meal* accompanied by the numeric *price* attribute.

3 Modeling User Preference from Implicit Indicators

In this section, we will first describe our motivation and assumptions which are behind the preference model and then describe the model itself.

First, our deep belief is that using only binary preference (like vs. dislike) leads to the large loss of important and interesting information. After trying several other approaches, we tend to accept preference model described e.g. by Hu et al. [3], where user preference is two-dimensional feature with binary preference $p \in \{0,1\}$ (like, dislike) and numerical intensity of the preference c. This model allows us to easily modify c with e.g. importance of indicator and express negative preference easily as well.

Second, there are several types of user behavior, which can be recognized as indicator of preference; we will further call them as implicit indicators. Those indicators can be used directly e.g. for recommendation, omitting the concept of user preference, but we would rather use them to define user preference, because afterwards any standard recommending algorithm can be used and the user preference itself can be processed for other purposes.

Finally we want to express user preference on each implicit indicator separately and then combine them together. One of the benefits of such approach is that we can define usefulness of each indicator and use this for improved monitoring of user behavior.

3.1 Two-step Model of User Preferences

The major approach in e-commerce systems without explicit feedback is to use business-like point of view and state that user positively prefers the object(s) which he/she has *purchased*. This user preference is binary (0/1) function denoted as $p_{u,o}$. The problem of $p_{u,o}$ is that the purchase actions are very sparse. The vast majority of users did not purchase any object, so $p_{u,o}$ is useless to create any personalized recommendations. However we can use other indicators to express *purchase* behavior. This will be done in two steps: In the first step called *local preference learning*, every feedback indicator value is ordered using a fuzzy set $\hat{f}_i : D_{Fi} \to [0,1]$, where D_{Fi} is the domain of the indicator F_i. With these fuzzy sets, the original space of feedback indicators (also called data cube) $\prod_{i=1}^{N} D_{Fi}$ is transformed into a preference cube $[0,1]^N$.

In the second step, called *global preference*, the local preferences are aggregated into the overall user preference over the item using an aggregation function @: $[0,1]^N \to [0,1]$. The resulting score $\overline{p_{u,o}}$ is a final product of analysis of user behavior and further passed to the content-based recommending algorithm.

Local Preferences: The basic idea behind local preferences is to project user rating (purchasing behavior in case of current dataset) into the domain of each implicit indicator. All currently used implicit indicators are numerical, so we can use some regression method to model relationship between rating and implicit indicator. There are other options like discretizing indicator's domain, but these methods performed poorer in our preliminary experiments. *Linear*, *Quadratic* and *Peak* [2] regressions were included in the experiments.

Global Preferences: There are several ways how to construct global preferences. Probably the most common approach is using weighted average; however weighted average is not compensatory: a single bad value among the indicators can significantly decrease the resulting user preference. This problem is known in the area of decision making and fuzzy systems, where S-norms are suggested. However using solely S-norms may overestimate resulting user preference, so some combination of T-norm and S-norm is needed. While we get local preferences $\hat{f}_i \in [0,1]$, they are first transformed into our internal model of user preferences (polarity p, intensity c).

$p_{i,u,o} = 1$ IFF $\hat{f}_{i,u,o} \geq avg(\hat{f}_i)$; $p_{i,u,o} = -1$ IFF $\hat{f}_{i,u,o} < avg(\hat{f}_i)$
$c_{i,u,o} = |\hat{f}_{i,u,o} - avg(\hat{f}_i)|$

At this point, intensity can be adjusted using importance for each implicit indicator. Now we need to set proper λ for T-norm and S-norm. For each user and object average polarity is computed: $pol_{u,o} := \sum_{\forall i} p_{i,u,o} * c_{i,u,o}$. The higher the polarity is, the more compensatory S-norms and less restrictive T-norms will be used. The midpoint ($pol_{u,o} = 0$) is set to correspond with λ_{prod} for which current family of T-(co)norm equals product T-(co)norm $T_{prod}(x,y) = x * y$; $S_{prod}(x,y) = x + y - x * y$ (e.g. $\lambda_{prod}=1$ for Frank T-(co)norm). Other values are linearly normalized into interval [λ_{prod}, λ_{max}] if $pol_{u,o} > 0$ or [λ_{prod}, λ_{min}] if $pol_{u,o} < 0$. Value λ_{max} (value for which current family of S-norms is most compensatory and T-norm least restrictive) corresponds with sum of maximal intensities c_i seen in the dataset. Vice versa for λ_{min}:

$pol_{u,o}^{max} = \sum_{\forall i} 1 * argmax_{\forall u,o}(c_{i,u,o})$.

After finding the right λ, the aggregations $T_{u,o}$ and $S_{u,o}$ are computed and their values aggregated into $\overline{p_{u,o}}$. *Arithmetic average* and several weighting schemes were tested. The best results achieved *average polarity* weights:

$w_{S-norm} := (pol_{u,o} + pol_{u,o}^{max})/(2 * pol_{u,o}^{max})$
$w_{T-norm} := 1 - w_{S-norm}$

Combined all together, the formula to infer user preference $\overline{p_{u,o}}$ from local preferences $\hat{f}_i$ is as follows: $\overline{p_{u,o}} = w_{T-norm} * T_{\lambda T}(\hat{f}_1, ..., \hat{f}_n) + w_{S-norm} * S_{\lambda S}(\hat{f}_1, ..., \hat{f}_n)$

4 Experiments

In this section we will provide details about our experiments with the two step user preference model on real production data from a travel agency. Our final goal is to provide recommendations (list of top-k objects) to the user, so in the following experiment we were focused on the ranking based metrics. Three experiments were conducted: in the first one were examined local preference methods, the second focused on evaluating two-step user model applied on implicit indicators and the last experiment simulated recommending top-k objects to the user.

4.1 Evaluating Local Preference Methods for Implicit Preference Indicators

Local preference methods transforms data cube into the preference cube. Global preference methods operate on the preference cube $[0,1]^N$ and transform it into $[0,1]$, keeping the partial ordering created by local preference methods. So, no global preference method can reverse an error inherited from the local preference method if all local preferences $\hat{f}_i$ are ordered wrongly. Similarly no global preference method can introduce an error if all local preferences were correctly ordered. Hence, for a given user u, objects o_1 and o_2 we distinguish three possible ordering:

- *Correct* IFF $\forall i: \widehat{f}_i(u, o_1) \leq \widehat{f}_i(u, o_2)$ and $p_{u,o1} < p_{u,o2}$ (or vice versa).
- *Incorrect* IFF $\forall i: \widehat{f}_i(u, o_1) \geq \widehat{f}_i(u, o_2)$ and $\exists i$: the inequality is strict.
- *Incomparable* if nothing from the above applies (possibly correct or incorrect depending on the global preference method).

Table 2. Results of local preference methods evaluation: Results are shown in percentage of all applicable pairs of objects

Method	Incorrect	Correct	Incomparable
Linear	4.2%	57.8%	38.0%
Peak	4.4%	60.4%	35.2%
Quadratic	4.2%	57.9%	37.9%

Table 2 contains results of evaluation of local preference methods. The implicit indicators seem to be well designed as majority of evaluated pairs are correctly ordered and only less than 5% are ordered incorrectly. Differences between evaluated methods appear to be small, but they may still occur in the further phases as we cannot evaluate features of group of incomparable pairs now.

4.2 Evaluating Global Preference Methods for Implicit Preference Indicators

Now we can move to the evaluation of resulting $\overline{p_{u,o}}$ preferences. In this phase we have also included results of SVM and M5P[1] decision tree methods to be compared with our two-step preference model. As we are still interested in ranking oriented metrics, we decided to use Kendall Tau correlation to compare list of objects ordered according to $p_{u,o}$ and $\overline{p_{u,o}}$. As the lists may contain ties, there are two variants for Kendall's Tau: Tau-A with original formulation:

$$\tau_A := \frac{\#concordant - \#discordant}{\frac{1}{2} * n * (n-1)}$$

Where #concordant (#discordant) is a number of pairs whose ratings for both $p_{u,o}$ and $\overline{p_{u,o}}$ strictly agree (disagree). Tau-B coefficient then introduces compensations for ties.

Table 3. Results of global preference methods evaluation

Method	Tau-A	Tau-B
Linear+Hamacher	**0.129**	0.332
M5P	**0.129**	0.346
SVM	0.127	0.327
Linear+Yager	0.115	**0.403**
Quadratic+Sugeno-Weber	0.082	0.212

---

[1] We used default WEKA implementation of SVM for regression and M5P decision tree, see weka.sourceforge.net/doc.dev/weka/classifiers/trees/M5P.html and weka.sourceforge.net/doc.dev/weka/classifiers/functions/SMOreg.html

More than 50 methods varying in local preference method, fuzzy family, or aggregation of T-norms and S-norms were evaluated. Table 3 shows results of some representatives. The methods can be divided into three groups: methods performing poorly in both ranks (e.g. all methods with Schweizer-Sklar family) and methods performing well in either Tau-A (Hamacher, Frank, some Sugeno-Weber families) or Tau-B (Yager, some SugenoWeber families) and (below)average in the other. Generally methods performing well in Tau-B tend to produce more ties in $\overline{p_{u,o}}$ rating, so we expect them to perform poorer in the recommending scenario.

4.3 Recommending Top-K Scenario with Content-Based Recommender

In the last part of the experiments, we will simulate the typical situation of recommending on e-commerce sites: The user comes to the website. Usually this is a new user, or we might have limited historical knowledge about him/her. The user browses a few objects/categories and then decides to buy something or leave and continue searching somewhere else. We have selected two algorithms for recommending: SVM for regression and our own content-based "Statistical"[2] recommending method [2].

The experiment was designed in the following way: We selected train set sizes from 3 up to 10. For each train set size K and each user, we randomly selected K objects he/she had visited as a training set, compute $\overline{p_{u,o}}$ and provide it to the recommending algorithm. The rest of visited objects served as test set. The top-k list of items was formed according to the ratings received from the algorithm. According to the scenario, we are interested in the position of object(s) from the test set, which had current user bought. The *Average Position* (AP) metrics computes average position of purchased objects in the list of recommended objects. We also use the *nDCG* metrics as it is mainly influenced by the objects in the front positions (it does not matter whether the good object is on position #500 or #1000 – both cases are quite as bad).

Table 4. Some representative results of recommending scenario: Results are ordered according to the average position of purchased object in the list

Method	Recommender	AP	nDCG
Peak+Sugeno-Weber	Statistical	**107.7**	0.221
Linear+Hamacher	Statistical	111.1	0.223
Quadratic+Frank	Statistical	118.4	0.240
M5P	Statistical	129.8	**0.245**
SVM	Statistical	166.2	0.233
Linear+Yager	Statistical	209.9	0.217
Binary implicit feedback	**Statistical**	**379.1**	**0.136**
SVM	SVM	387.4	0.173
Linear+Hamacher	SVM	392.0	0.166
M5P	SVM	393.2	0.174

---

[2] Implementation of Statistical method as well as our evaluation environment can be downloaded from: https://github.com/alaneckhardt/PrefWork-2/

Table 4 contains the result of recommending scenario. Results show that our preference model is comparable with standard machine learning methods or even slightly better. Methods scoring well in Tau-A also scores well in both AP and nDCG. All methods clearly outperform Binary implicit feedback (defining $\overline{p_{u,o}}$ as 1 if user visits the object and 0 otherwise). Hamacher and Frank T-(co)norms performed best in absolute numbers and also seems to be the quite stable for various settings of other components, so we can suggest using these T-(co)norms. We cannot conclude on the best local preference method, as the differences in results caused by other components were substantially higher than those inflicted by local preference methods.

5 Conclusions and Future Work

In this paper, we have discussed the problem of using implicit feedback as indicators of user preference. We have presented model of user preference and two-step method for learning them from implicit indicators. Each phase of the two-step model was extensively evaluated and the experiments shown that using multiple interest indicators is valuable addition to the commonly used binary user preference based on implicit feedback and that two-step model can be successfully deployed and outperform standard machine learning algorithms.

For future work, there is still many ways how to tune our model (e.g. finding right λ, combining T-norms and S-norms, using other fuzzy families, choice of recommending algorithm etc.). Our long-term goal is to deploy the system on real e-commerce portal and perform A/B testing with real-world success metrics.

Acknowledgments. This work was supported by the grant SVV-2014-260100, P46 and GAUK-126313.

References

1. Claypool, M., Le, P., Wased, M., Brown, D.: Implicit interest indicators. In: IUI 2001, pp. 33–40. ACM, New York (2001)
2. Eckhardt, A., Vojtáš, P.: Learning user preferences for 2CP-regression for a recommender system. In: van Leeuwen, J., Muscholl, A., Peleg, D., Pokorný, J., Rumpe, B. (eds.) SOFSEM 2010. LNCS, vol. 5901, pp. 346–357. Springer, Heidelberg (2010)
3. Hu, Y., Koren, Y., Volinsky, C.: Collaborative Filtering for Implicit Feedback Datasets. In: ICDM 2008, pp. 263–272. IEEE Computer Society, Washington, DC (2008)
4. Klement, E.P., Mesiar, R., Pap, E.: Triangular Norms. Springer, Netherlands (2000)
5. Lee, D.H., Brusilovsky, P.: Reinforcing Recommendation Using Implicit Negative Feedback. In: Houben, G.-J., McCalla, G., Pianesi, F., Zancanaro, M. (eds.) UMAP 2009. LNCS, vol. 5535, pp. 422–427. Springer, Heidelberg (2009)
6. Peska, L., Vojtas, P.: Evaluating Various Implicit Factors in E-commerce. In: RUE (RecSys) 2012. CEUR, vol. 910, pp. 51–55 (2012)
7. Peska, L., Vojtas, P.: Recommending for Disloyal Customers with Low Consumption Rate. In: Geffert, V., Preneel, B., Rovan, B., Štuller, J., Tjoa, A.M. (eds.) SOFSEM 2014. LNCS, vol. 8327, pp. 455–465. Springer, Heidelberg (2014)
8. Yager, R.R.: Noble Reinforcement in Disjunctive Aggregation Operators. IEEE Transactions on Fuzzy Systems 11, 754–767 (2003)
9. Zimmermann, H.J., Zysno, P.: Latent connectives in human decision making. Fuzzy Sets and Systems 4, 37–51 (1980)

Using Dependency Bigrams and Discourse Connectives for Predicting the Helpfulness of Online Reviews

Matthias Mertz, Nikolaos Korfiatis, and Roberto V. Zicari

Big Data Laboratory,
Goethe-University Frankfurt, Germany
Robert-Mayer-Str. 10, 60325 Frankfurt am Main
mertz@cs.uni-frankfurt.de,
korfiatis@em.uni-frankfurt.de,
zicari@informatik.uni-frankfurt.de
http://www.bigdata.uni-frankfurt.de

Abstract. Helpfulness prediction represents an interesting research topic with immediate practical applications both from a data mining and marketing perspective. In this study we evaluate the performance of two text-based features that have not been used in that context, namely (a) a variation of the bigram feature, utilizing grammatical dependencies and (b) discourse connectives. By treating helpfulness prediction as a binary classification task we show that both features contain valuable information but however they should be used with caution due to the restrictive experimental setup. The study serves as a ground for future work regarding the usefulness of the proposed features in review helpfulness prediction.

Keywords: Online reviews, Review helpfulness prediction, Text-based features, Feature engineering.

1 Introduction

Consumer reviews contribute significantly to the success of online retailers by reducing product uncertainty and exercising a strong influence on consumers' decision to purchase thus increasing product sales as shown e. g. by Chevalier and Mayzlin [1]. Nonetheless not all reviews are equally helpful in aiding potential customers decide to buy or not a particular item, and retailers stand to benefit from including a review helpfulness filter system [2]. This is currently done by asking users to up and down-vote helpful and unhelpful reviews, respectively. This approach contains certain disadvantages, most obviously the need for a few user votes for each review before a helpfulness measure can be established.

There has been considerable research in the last years on automatically determining the helpfulness of consumer reviews using both textual and numerical features based on the available data (review text and rating). The focus of this study is to examine features extracted from the review text, motivated also by its influence on review helpfulness [3]. In this study preliminary experiments with two text-based features that have not been used in the context of consumer review helpfulness prediction before are reported: (a) dependency bigrams and (b) discourse connectives. Our contribution relies on the experimental evaluation of the accuracy obtained with these textual features, in comparison with a baseline feature stemmed from review rating (as shown by Kim et al. [4]). To this end this paper is structured as follows: Sec. 2 reviews related work on the domain of review helpfulness prediction. Experimental setup and feature extraction is documented in Sec. 3 and experimental results are discussed in Sec. 4. The paper concludes in Sec. 5 by addressing limitations and future research.

2 Related Work

Zhang and Varadarajan [5] introduced the task of automatically estimating the helpfulness of consumer reviews by using various features obtained from the review text such as word counts in certain word classes, lexical subjectivity measures, or the lexical similarity between the review and the product description. The authors identified the importance of "shallow syntactic features" determined by part-of-speech tagging as a proxy of the linguistic style of a review, which in turn is a good indicator for its utility.

Kim et al. [4] used support vector regression for estimating the helpfulness of consumer reviews using structural features such as sentence length, review length and formatting properties as well as lexical features composed of unigrams and bigrams. In addition syntactic features consisting of aggregate word frequencies in different word classes and semantic features based on the occurrence of *important* words were associated with each review as an additional "meta-data feature". Unigrams performed better than bigrams with syntactic and the semantic features not improving results if added in addition to the unigrams. Liu et al. [6] used support vector machines to treat helpfulness prediction as a binary classification problem (bad or good). In their approach they criticized the use of helpfulness votes as a method for obtaining ground truth and used a manual annotation of helpfulness from domain experts instead into three categories: (a) *informativeness* (b) *readability*[7] and (c) *subjectivity*. The authors evaluated the performance in terms of accuracy, i.e. the percentage of correctly classified reviews. The informativeness features perform the best with the readability features improving this result marginally ,and subjectiveness features resulting in non-significant change.

On the other hand, Ghose and Ipeirotis [8] used reviewer-based features such as the usefulness of past reviews of the reviewer and the amount of self-disclosed identity information the reviewer provides in his profile. Reviewer-based features in general are beyond the scope of this paper, but these are certainly interesting ideas that might improve the performance of a helpfulness prediction system further.

3 Data and Feature Extraction

3.1 Review Data and Classes

Review data were retrieved from Amazon.com. From the numbers of positive and negative helpfulness votes of a review r, we can determine its *helpfulness ratio* $h(r)$, which is constrained to lie between 0 (minimum helpfulness) and 1 (maximum helpfulness). Following the notation from Kim et al. [4], it is defined as

$$h(r) = \frac{rating_+(r)}{rating_+(r) + rating_-(r)} . \qquad (1)$$

Only taking the mean of multiple votes introduces some measure of objectiveness and reliability into the helpfulness ratio, because each individual vote is highly subjective. Since the reliability rises along with the number of total helpfulness votes, we only used reviews with at least ten votes for the experiments. We conducted some preliminary experiments with the best feature combination from Kim et al. [4] in a regression setup and similar correlation values were obtained. However, after closer examination of the results, we felt that the average prediction error was too large to use the regression setup as a reasonable environment for testing the new features. This led us to approach the prediction task as a classification problem, which has the added advantage that some inaccuracy of the helpfulness ratio is removed once it is mapped to discrete classes. We split each dataset into three classes, namely *bad*, *uncertain* and *good* reviews. Reviews from class uncertain were not used for any experiments, thus again improving the reliability of the ground truth labeling. Given two thresholds t_b and t_g, the class of a review r is defined by

$$\text{class}(r) = \begin{cases} \text{bad} & h(r) \leq t_b \\ \text{uncertain} & t_b < h(r) < t_g \\ \text{good} & h(r) \geq t_g . \end{cases} \qquad (2)$$

The thresholds are initially set to $t_b = 0.3$ and $t_g = 0.7$, which generally leads to classes bad and good of different size. We then adapt the threshold of the larger class until both classes are approximately equally sized. Finally, exactly same-sized classes are constructed by random sampling without replacement. After removing all reviews with less than ten helpfulness votes and splitting the remaining ones into the three classes, only five categories contained enough reviews for conducting reliable experiments. Table 1 shows some details of these datasets and product category.

3.2 Dependency Bigrams

Dependency bigrams are a variation of the classical bigram feature, which is constructed by counting the number of occurrences of each pair of contiguous words. The proposed dependency bigrams use grammatical dependencies between words instead of spatial adjacency in order to construct features from pairs of words.

Table 1. For the product categories used for the experiments: Number of reviews after removing all reviews with less than ten helpfulness votes, the adapted thresholds t_b and t_g, and the corresponding numbers of reviews in the classes bad and good

Category	≥ 10 V.	t_b	Bad R.	t_g	Good R.
Digital Cameras	19547	0.3	2342	1.0	3709
Laptops	6306	0.3	1105	0.96	1114
MP3 Players	6258	0.3	1258	0.93	1309
Tablets & Netbooks	9467	0.27	3420	0.7	3375
Televisions	8363	0.3	1227	0.98	1227

Grammatical dependencies between word pairs can be automatically extracted from review text with the Stanford Parser [9] and its Java implementation was used to construct the features for our experiments. To illustrate the concept of dependency bigrams, we can examine a short sentence taken from a laptop review. *"The battery life is much longer."* parses to the following dependency pairs:

```
det(life, The)              nn(life, battery)
nsubj(longer, life)         cop(longer, is)
advmod(longer, much)        root(ROOT, longer)
```

The term in front of the parentheses encodes the type of dependency between the two following words. This dependency type could provide additional information for the experiments, but we decided not to include it in the features because it would make them more sparse. The new element *ROOT* is related to the one word that is the root of the dependency tree built by the parser. We can see that a few word pairs were extracted that would not have been captured by traditional bigrams. For example, the words *longer* and *life* are not adjacent in the sentence, but now form a dependency bigram.

3.3 Discourse Connectives

A potential indicator of review helpfulness could be the amount of internal discourse in a review text. That is, how different parts of the text related to each other. Such relations are called discourse relations, and the frequencies of various types of discourse relations might be a useful set of features.

Webber and Joshi [10] state that "[t]he two main types of evidence for discourse relations in English are the presence of a discourse connective and sentence adjacency." Sentence adjacency is not suited well for generating meaningful features in this context. Discourse connectives, on the other hand, are a non-trivial indicator of discourse presence and can be extracted automatically from text. Prasad et al. [11] give a detailed description of the concepts of *explicit* and *implicit* discourse connectives. Explicit discourse connectives are words such as "and", "or" and "but" or short phrases like "then again" and "as well as" which link two clauses in a text to each other and can be extracted from review text using regular expression matching for the individual words and phrases. Implicit discourse connectives were not used for the experiments in this paper because they are hard to extract reliably.

4 Experiments

Five datasets with equally-sized classes of helpful and unhelpful reviews were constructed. The experiments were performed with the SVMlight support vector machine implementation [12]. The kernel parameter γ of the RBF kernel and the cost parameter C were tuned by grid-search as suggested by Hsu et al. [13]. Each dataset was used as both training and test data in a ten-fold cross-validation scheme, and ten iterations for each dataset and feature combination provided close confidence bounds. While it is interesting to see the absolute classification accuracy of the proposed features, it is also helpful to compare them to other, more established features. As aforementioned, we used the best-performing combination of star rating, review length and unigram features from Kim et al. [4] as a baseline for this purpose. The star rating turned out to be a very powerful indicator of review helpfulness in exploratory experiments, so we introduced it as a separate baseline. Interestingly, if we use only the star rating $rating(r)$ to determine the predicted helpfulness of a review r according to

$$\text{pred}(r) = \begin{cases} \text{bad} & \text{rating}(r) \in \{1,2,3\} \\ \text{good} & \text{rating}(r) \in \{4,5\}, \end{cases} \quad (3)$$

we can already achieve classification accuracies between eighty and ninety percent on the five datasets of electronics products.

Table 2. Accuracy achieved with different feature combinations on the five datasets. The best result for each dataset is highlighted.

Features used	Digital Cameras	Laptops	MP3 Players	Tablets & Netbooks	Televisions
Star Rating Baseline	81.6%	90.3%	80.5%	82.7%	88.2%
Unigrams	**91.7%**	**94.3%**	90.2%	**87.6%**	92.6%
Bigrams	90.2%	92.9%	89.5%	87.2%	91.3%
Bigrams + Unigrams	**91.7%**	**94.3%**	**90.5%**	87.5%	92.9%
Connectives	89.3%	93.3%	87.2%	85.8%	91.5%
Connectives + Unigrams	91.5%	**94.3%**	90.4%	87.5%	**93.0%**

Table 2 shows the classification performance in terms of accuracy. The reported results for the discourse connective features are those achieved with sense level two, which performed a bit better than levels one and three. All SVM results outperform the simple star rating baseline on any given dataset. Still, that simple baseline already obtains good results. The results with the different feature combinations are not that conclusive. The unigram features do achieve a bit higher accuracy than either the dependency bigrams or the discourse connective features. But this difference is very small. Combining any of the two new features with the unigrams does not improve upon the unigram baseline significantly.

5 Conclusions, Limitations and Future Research

The two proposed new features perform quite well in terms of absolute classification accuracy. Alas, they cannot significantly improve upon the unigram baseline in this setup. It might be that the accuracy is already at its maximum due to the strong restrictions of the setup. Future experimental work could evaluate whether a less restrictive setup brings out stronger differences in the results obtained with different feature combinations. To loosen the restrictions, broader product categories for the datasets could be used in addition to studying the helpfulness prediction task as a regression problem.

Results also confirm that the star rating can serve as a very powerful predictor of review helpfulness. There seems to be a strong correlation between high star ratings and helpful reviews, at least after the applied data filtering. Nonetheless, it can be questioned whether the star rating feature should be used for review helpfulness prediction. While it improves the bottom-line accuracy, it does introduce a bias into the prediction system in that it generally favors reviews which rate the product positively. Future research could also examine how a more accurate extraction method for discourse relations affects the experimental results with the discourse connective features.

References

1. Chevalier, J.A., Mayzlin, D.: The effect of word of mouth on sales: Online book reviews. Journal of Marketing Research 43(3), 345–354 (2006)
2. Korfiatis, N., García-Bariocanal, E., Sánchez-Alonso, S.: Evaluating content quality and helpfulness of online product reviews: The interplay of review helpfulness vs. review content. Electronic Commerce Research and Applications 11(3), 205–217 (2012)
3. Liu, B.: Sentiment analysis and opinion mining. Synthesis Lectures on Human Language Technologies 5(1), 1–167 (2012)
4. Kim, S.M., Pantel, P., Chklovski, T., Pennacchiotti, M.: Automatically assessing review helpfulness. In: Proceedings of the ACL Conference on Empirical Methods in Natural Language Processing, pp. 423–430 (2006)
5. Zhang, Z., Varadarajan, B.: Utility scoring of product reviews. In: Proceedings of the 15th ACM International Conference on Information and Knowledge Management, pp. 51–57 (2006)
6. Liu, J., Cao, Y., Lin, C.Y., Huang, Y., Zhou, M.: Low-quality product review detection in opinion summarization. In: Proceedings of the Joint Conference on Empirical Methods in Natural Language Processing and Computational Natural Language Learning, pp. 334–342 (2007)

7. Korfiatis, N., Rodríguez, D., Sicilia, M.-Á.: The impact of readability on the usefulness of online product reviews: A case study on an online bookstore. In: Lytras, M.D., Damiani, E., Tennyson, R.D. (eds.) WSKS 2008. LNCS (LNAI), vol. 5288, pp. 423–432. Springer, Heidelberg (2008)
8. Ghose, A., Ipeirotis, P.G.: Estimating the helpfulness and economic impact of product reviews: Mining text and reviewer characteristics. IEEE Transactions on Knowledge and Data Engineering 23(10), 1498–1512 (2011)
9. Klein, D., Manning, C.D.: Fast exact inference with a factored model for natural language parsing. In: Advances in Neural Information Processing Systems, pp. 3–10 (2002)
10. Webber, B., Joshi, A.: Discourse structure and computation: past, present and future. In: Proceedings of the ACL 2012 Special Workshop on Rediscovering 50 Years of Discoveries, pp. 42–54. Association for Computational Linguistics (2012)
11. Prasad, R., Miltsakaki, E., Dinesh, N., Lee, A., Joshi, A., Robaldo, L., Webber, B.L.: The penn discourse treebank 2.0 annotation manual. Technical report, The PDTB Research Group (2007)
12. Joachims, T.: Making large-scale support vector machine learning practical. In: Advances in Kernel Methods. MIT Press (1999)
13. Hsu, C.W., Chang, C.C., Lin, C.J.: A practical guide to support vector classification. Technical report, Department of Computer Science, National Taiwan University (2003)

Customer Load Strategies for Demand Response in Bilateral Contracting of Electricity

Fernando Lopes* and Hugo Algarvio

LNEG–National Research Institute, Est. Paço do Lumiar 22, Lisbon, Portugal
{fernando.lopes,hugo.algarvio}@lneg.pt

Abstract. Electricity markets are systems for affecting the purchase and sale of electricity using supply and demand to set energy prices. Electricity can be traded in organized markets or by negotiating forward bilateral contracts. Demand response (DR) refers to participation by customers in electricity markets, seeing and responding to prices as they change over time. Customers may adopt several basic load response strategies, notably foregoing electricity usage at times of high prices without making it up later, and shifting or rescheduling usage away from times of high prices to other times. This article describes on-going work that uses the potential of agent-based technology to develop a computational tool for supporting bilateral contracting in electricity markets with demand response. From the perspective of end-use customers, it investigates how foregoing and shifting affect the energy and monetary outcomes of consumers applying DR during bilateral contracting.

Keywords: Energy markets, multi-agent systems, bilateral contracting, demand response, load response strategies, trading strategies.

1 Introduction

Electricity markets (EMs) are systems for effecting the purchase and sale of electricity using supply and demand to set energy prices. Two major market models are often considered: electricity pools and bilateral contracts. The system price in a typical day-ahead market is frequently determined by matching offers from suppliers to bids from consumers to develop a classic supply and demand equilibrium price, usually on an hourly interval. Market participants have a balance responsibility, meaning that they should deliver or consume in accordance with their bids. For instance, if utility companies produce less than declared they will probably have to buy more power (in external markets) at higher prices.

---

* This work was performed under the project MAN-REM (FCOMP-01-0124-FEDER-020397), supported by both FEDER and National funds through the program "COMPETE–Programa Operacional Temático Factores de Competividade" and "FCT–Fundação para a Ciência e a Tecnologia".

Bilateral contracts are negotiable agreements on delivery and receipt of power between two traders—they involve mainly the sale of large amounts of power (hundreds or thousands of megawatts) over long periods of time (several months to years). Market participants set the terms and conditions of agreements independent of a market operator, i.e., the negotiating parties specify their own contract terms [1]. Typically, bilateral contracts have the advantage of price predictability in comparison to uncertain pool prices.

Demand response (DR), defined broadly, refers to participation by customers in electricity markets, seeing and responding to prices as they change over time. DR may be defined more definitively as changes in electric usage by end-use customers from their normal consumption patterns in response to changes in the price of electricity over time, or to incentive payments designed to induce lower electricity use at times of high wholesale market prices or when system reliability is jeopardized [2]. From the perspective of the electric system as a whole, the emphasis of DR is on reductions in usage at critical times.

Demand response programs enable customers to manage their consumption of electricity in response to supply conditions. Several basic categories of demand response programs (or options) have been considered, notably incentive-based and price-based programs. Incentive-based DR programs offer customers some monetary bonus to reduce load upon operators request. These programs represent contractual arrangements to elicit demand reductions from customers at critical times—incentives may be in the form of explicit bill credits or payments for pre-contracted or measured load reductions. Price-based DR programs allow customers to voluntarily adjust their demand based on electricity prices, to take advantage of lower-priced periods and/or avoid consuming when prices are higher. Customer response is typically driven by an internal economic decision-making process and any load modifications are entirely voluntary. This work is being developed in the context of price-based DR programs.

Customers participating in demand response programs may adopt one or more of the following three basic load response strategies:

1. *Foregoing*: reducing the electricity usage at times of high prices without changing the consumption pattern during other periods.
2. *Shifting*: rescheduling usage away from times of high prices to other times.
3. *Onsite Generation*: turning on onsite or backup emergency generators to supply some or all electricity needs.

We are developing this study in the context of both foregoing and shifting responses.

Agent-based modeling and simulation (ABMS) has generated lots of excitement in recent years because of its promise as a new paradigm for designing and implementing complex software systems (see, e.g., [3]). The major motivations for the increasing interest in ABMS research include the ability to solve problems that have multiple problem solving entities and multiple problem solving methods. Conceptually, a multi-agent approach in which autonomous agents are capable of flexible action in order to meet their design objectives is an ideal fit to the naturally distributed domain of a deregulated energy market.

This paper describes on-going work that uses the potential of agent-based technology to develop a computational tool to support bilateral contracting in electricity markets with demand response. From the perspective of end-use customers, it investigates how different load response strategies affect the energy and monetary outcomes of consumers applying DR during bilateral contracting. Specifically, it studies the influence of both foregoing and shifting on electricity prices and consumption using the ABMS approach.

The work presented here is a natural extension of our previous work in the area of automated negotiation [4–7, 11]. It also refines and extends our previous work in the area of multi-agent electricity markets with demand response [8–10]. In particular, Lopes et al. [8, 9] formalize two novel strategies: a "price management" strategy, for producers/retailers, and a "volume management" strategy, for end-use consumers, associated with the shifting load response, and thus enabling customers to promote demand response. The authors also present a case study on forward bilateral contracts: a retailer agent (seller) and a customer agent (buyer) negotiate a 6-rate tariff using the two novel strategies. Lopes et al. [10] pay special attention to the preferences of the negotiating agents, notably the additive and multiplicative models to rate and compare incoming offers and counter-offers. They also present a case study on forward bilateral contracting involving DR management and a 24h-rate tariff.

2 Bilateral Contracting in Multi-agent Energy Markets

This section describes the process of forward bilateral contracting involving a seller agent and a buyer agent. The agents exchange offers and counter-offers until they reach an agreement or one of the agents decides to opt out of the negotiation. Negotiation includes the determination of prices and quantities of energy, and is executed on a long term, usually six months or more. A brief description of the key features of a negotiation model that handles two-party and multi-issue negotiation follows (see [6] for an in-depth discussion).

Pre-Negotiation. Pre-negotiation is the process of preparing and planning for negotiation and involves mainly the creation of a well-laid plan specifying the activities that negotiators should attend to before actually starting to negotiate. Accordingly, we describe below various activities that negotiators make efforts to perform in order to carefully prepare and plan for negotiation. We consider a set $\mathcal{A} = \{a_s, a_b\}$ of autonomous agents (negotiating parties). The negotiation issues $\{x_1, \ldots, x_n\}$ are quantitative in nature and defined over continuous domains $\{D_1, \ldots, D_n\}$, respectively. The negotiating agenda is the set $\mathcal{I} = \{x_1, \ldots, x_n\}$ of issues to be deliberated during negotiation. For each issue x_k, the range of acceptable values is represented by the interval $D_k = [min_k, max_k]$. In particular, let $[P^s_{k_{min}}, P^s_{k_{max}}]$, $k = 1\ldots n$, denote the range of values for price that are acceptable to the seller agent a_s. Also, let $[P^b_{k_{min}}, P^b_{k_{max}}]$ and $[V^b_{k_{min}}, V^b_{k_{max}}]$, $k = 1\ldots n$, denote the range of values for price and volumes that are acceptable to the buyer agent a_b.

Effective pre-negotiation requires that negotiators prioritize the issues and define the limits. Priorities are set by rank-ordering the issues, i.e., by defining the most important, the second most important, and so on. The priority prt_k^i of an agent $a_i \in \mathcal{A}$ for an issue $x_k \in \mathcal{I}$ is a number that represents the importance of x_k. The weight w_k^i is a number that represents the preference for x_k. The limit lim_k^i or resistance point is the ultimate fallback position for x_k, the point beyond which a_i is unwilling to concede on x_k.

Additionally, effective pre-negotiation requires that negotiators agree on an appropriate protocol that defines the rules governing the interaction. We consider an alternating offers negotiation protocol [12]. This protocol models the iterative exchange of offers and counter-offers. At any given period of negotiation, an agent may accept an offer, send a counter-offer, or end the negotiation. If a counter-offer is submitted, the process is repeated until one of the agents accept or abandon the negotiation. Thus, the agents a_s and a_b bargain over the division of the surplus of $n \geq 2$ issues by alternately proposing offers at times in $\mathcal{T} = \{1, 2, ...\}$. This means that one offer is made per time period $t \in T$, with an agent offering in odd periods and the other agent offering in even periods. A proposal $p_{i \rightarrow j}^t$ submitted by an agent $a_i \in \mathcal{A}$ to an agent $a_j \in \mathcal{A}$ in period $t \in \mathcal{T}$ is a vector of issue values: $p_{i \rightarrow j}^t = (v_1, \ldots, v_n)$, where v_k, $k = 1 \ldots n$, is a value of an issue $x_k \in \mathcal{I}$. As noted, the agents have the ability to unilaterally opt out of the negotiation when responding to a proposal.

Negotiators should also express their own preferences to rate and compare incoming offers and counter-offers. We consider that each agent $a_i \in \mathcal{A}$ has a continuous utility function, denoted as U_i. Accordingly, when the utility for a_i from one outcome is greater than from another outcome, we assume that a_i prefers the first outcome over the second. The additive model is probably the most widely used in multi-issue negotiation [13]: the agents determine weights for the issues at stake, assign scores to the different levels on each issue, and take a weighted sum of them to get an entire offer evaluation. The additive model is simple and intuitive, but assumes two types of independence, namely additive independence and utility independence. In particular, the additive independence assumption is usually not acceptable when there are specific interactions among issues. This seems to be the case of the present work, since agents negotiate prices and volumes of energy, variables that are interdependent. The multiplicative utility function is the most well-known function handling interactions among issues. It accommodates inter-dependencies by considering a specific interaction constant and interaction terms involving the multiplication of the weighted scores together (see, e.g., [14]). However, for it to be valid, every pair of issues must be utility independent of the remaining issues.

Actual Negotiation. The actual negotiation process involves basically an iterative exchange or offers and counter-offers. The negotiation protocol marks branching points at which agents have to make decisions according to their strategies. Accordingly, this subsection describes two groups of strategies that have attracted much attention in negotiation research, namely [15]:

1. *concession making or yielding*: negotiators reduce their demands or aspirations to accommodate the opponent;
2. *problem solving or integrating*: negotiators maintain their aspirations and try to find ways of reconciling them with the aspirations of their opponent.

Concession strategies are functions that model typical patterns of concessions throughout negotiation. The host of existing concession strategies includes the following:

1. *starting high and conceding slowly*: negotiators adopt an optimistic opening position and make small concessions throughout negotiation;
2. *starting reasonable and conceding moderately*: negotiators adopt a realistic opening position and make substantial concessions during the course of negotiation.

Problem solving behaviour aims at finding agreements that appeal to all sides, both individually and collectively. Two representative problem solving strategies are as follows:

1. *logrolling*: two parties agree to exchange concessions on different issues, with each party yielding on issues that are of low priority to itself and high priority to the other party;
2. *nonspecific compensation*: one party achieves its goals and pays off the other for accommodating its interests.

Lopes and Coelho [6] present a formal definition of relevant concession strategies and important logrolling strategies.

3 Bilateral Contracting with Demand Response

This section presents strategies for promoting demand response, namely two different types of load response strategies: foregoing (or curtailment) and shifting. Demand response refers to participation by customers in electricity markets in response to prices as they change over time, and typically involves customer behavioral changes. During the trading process (involving an iterative exchange or offers and counter-offers), we consider that customers may respond to changes in retailers' prices either by foregoing usage at times of high prices (proposed by retailers) without making it up later or by shifting their energy usage from periods of high prices (again, offered by retailers) to the remaining hours. Customers are equipped with strategic models allowing them to minimize cost, through DR actions. On the other hand, seller agents are equipped with strategic models allowing them to maximize benefit.

Customer Load Response Strategies. These strategies have the main goal of minimizing the energy cost of customers through DR actions. Thus, through this type of actions, customers can manage their energy consumption in response to high prices for different periods of the day.

Foregoing or Curtailment Response Strategy. This strategy involves reducing energy usage away from times of high prices without making it up later. It aims at minimizing the cost C^b of the customer agent a_b, by considering the prices P_k^s, $k=1\ldots n$, proposed by the seller agent a_s, and determining appropriate values for the volumes V_k^b of a_b. The mathematical formulation of the problem is as follows:

$$Minimize\ C^b = \sum_{k=1}^{n} P_k^s \times V_k^b \qquad (1)$$

subject to:

$$V_{k_{min}}^b \leq V_k^b \qquad (2)$$

$$\sum_{k=1}^{n} V_k^b = (1 - CR) \times V_{tot}^b \qquad (3)$$

The constraint expressed by (2) assures that the volumes considered by a_b may only decrease to admissible values. Also, the constraint (3) guarantees that the total quantity of energy considered by a_b is reduced to a particular level defined by a curtailment response constant CR.

Shifting Response Strategy. This strategy involves involves rescheduling energy usage away from times of high prices to other times. Similarly to the foregoing strategy, it aims at minimizing the cost of a_b by considering the prices proposed by a_s and determining appropriate values for the volumes (see also [8–10]):

$$Minimize\ C^b = \sum_{k=1}^{n} P_k^s \times V_k^b \qquad (4)$$

subject to:

$$V_{k_{min}}^b \leq V_k^b \leq V_{k_{max}}^b \qquad (4)$$

$$\sum_{k=1}^{n} V_k^b = V_{tot}^b \qquad (5)$$

The constraint expressed by (4) assures that the volume considered by a_b is in the range of its acceptable values. Also, the constraint (5) assures that the total quantity of energy V_{tot}^b either does not change or remains close to its initial value (for convenience).

At this stage, it is important to mention that a customer load response strategy considering both the foregoing and the shifting responses could be defined by considering the constraints (3) and (4) simultaneously. The problem for a_b is stated in a similar way and is therefore omitted (see, however, the case study on forward bilateral contracting with demand response described in the next section).

The optimization problem is resolved through a linear programming method called simplex using lp_solve, a Mixed Integer Linear Programming solver.[1] lp_solve is a free linear (integer) programming solver based on the revised simplex method and the Branch-and-bound method for integers. It solves pure linear, (mixed) integer/binary, semi-continuous and special ordered sets models.

Beyond the volumes of energy, the customer also negotiates prices. The prices offered in a new proposal are obtained by the following formula:

$$P^b_{k_{new}} = P^b_{k_{prev}} + Ct \times P^b_{k_{prev}}, \quad k = 1..n \tag{6}$$

where $P^b_{k_{new}}$ is the (new) price to send by a_b, $P^b_{k_{prev}}$ is the (previous) price sent by a_b and not accepted by a_s, and $Ct \in [0, 1]$ is a constant.

Price Management Strategy for Seller. This strategy aims at maximizing the benefit B^s of a_s, by considering the cost of production C_k, $k=1\ldots n$, and the volumes V^b_k proposed by the buyer agent a_b, and determining appropriate valuers for the prices P^s_k of a_s. Thus, we consider that a_s accept the volumes proposed by a_b. The mathematical formulation of the problem is as follows:

$$Maximize\ B^s = \sum_{k=1}^{n} (P^s_k - C_k) \times V^b_k \tag{7}$$

subject to:

$$P^s_k \geq C_k \tag{8}$$

The constraint expressed by (8) assures that the cost of production does not exceed the price of energy considered by a_s.

4   A Case Study on Customer Response Strategies

David Owen, CEO of the SCO Bank, agrees to meet with Tom Britton and John Adams, representatives in Portugal and specialists in operational efficiency. In the meeting, David Owen requests a solution to reduce 5% of the electricity costs in the bank headquarter, located in Lisbon. The corresponding building is constituted by 4 floors, where 200 employees work a five-day week to cope with normal demands. The main sources of consumption are 200 computers, 8 printers, 200 electric lamps, 12 HVAC systems, 3 lifts, 4 kitchens and 4 televisions. Other sources of consumption, such as surveillance cameras, the alarm system and other critical equipment, are not considered. David Owen requests to both Tom Britton and John Adams to negotiate a more beneficial tariff and mainly to find a technical and efficient solution for reducing consumption without affecting the normal activity of the bank. The major objective is to determine the possible five-days workweek electricity cost savings.

---
[1] lpsolve.sourceforge.net

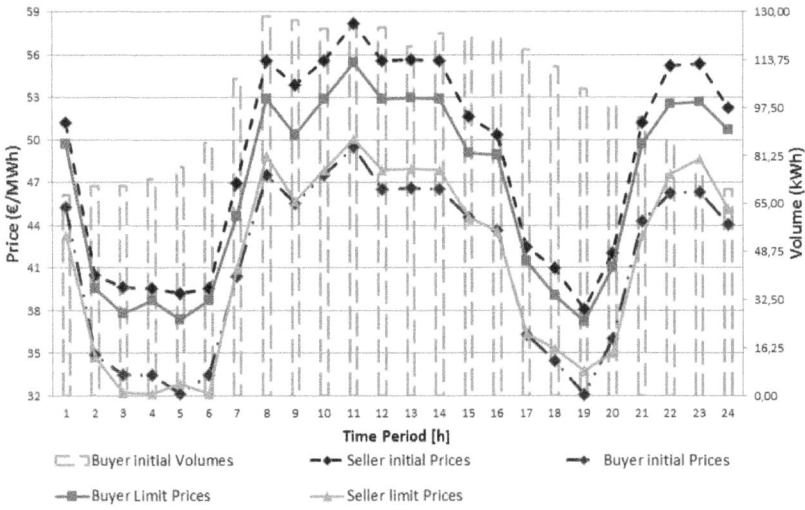

Fig. 1. Initial prices, initial volumes, and limits for price

At SCO Bank, it was previously agreed that there must not be any reduction in computer usage to keep normal bank operation. John Adams starts addressing the problem and notices that the peak consumption occurs normally between 8am and 4pm. The peak hour is usually at 8am, where 180 computers, 8 printers, 180 lamps, 8 HVAC systems, 3 lifts, 2 kitchens and 2 televisions are in use. Accordingly, John Adams suggests the following three response solutions:

- a shifting load response;
- a curtailment load response of 5%;
- a curtailment of 5% together with a shifting response.

In practice, the consumption curtailment will conduct roughly to the following energy usage: a reduction of around 20% of electric lamp usage, and a minimum of 4 printers, 4 HVAC systems, 2 lifts, 1 kitchen and 1 television in normal operation.

Next, Tom Britton (playing the role of a customer) contacts David Colburn, representing N2K Power (a retailer company), in order to negotiate a 24-rate tariff. Figure 1 shows the load profile of the customer agent, and the initial offers and price limits for the two agents. Some values were selected by looking up to real trading prices associated with pool markets in an attempt to approximate the case study to the real-world. In particular, market reference prices were obtained by analysing the Iberian Electricity Market.[2] The minimum seller prices (i.e., the limits) were then set to these reference prices. Also, some energy quantities were based on consumer load profiles provided by the New York State Electric & Gas.[3]

---

[2] www.mibel.com
[3] www.nyseg.com

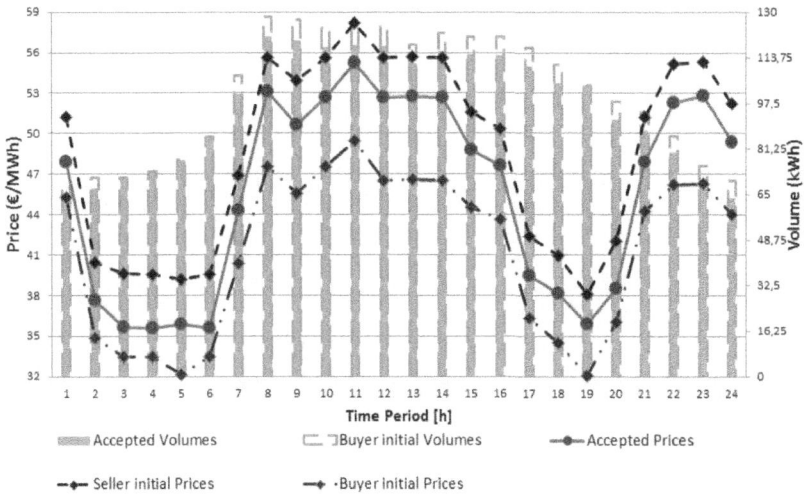

Fig. 2. Variation of customer volumes and energy prices

Negotiation involves an iterative exchange of offers and counter-offers. We consider the following:

- priorities are set indirectly for the prices and volumes of the energy (higher values mean greater importance);
- preferences are specified by using the multiplicative model;
- before starting the negotiation, the customer submits the initial load profile;
- after receiving the customer's load profile, the retailer submits the first proposal;
- the agents are allowed to propose only strictly monotonically—the customer's offers increase monotonically and the retailer's offers decrease monotonically;
- the acceptability of a proposal is determined by a negotiation threshold—an agent $a_i \in \mathcal{A}$ accepts a proposal $p_{j \to i}^{t-1}$, submitted by $a_j \in \mathcal{A}$ at $t-1$, when the difference between the benefit provided by the proposal $p_{i \to j}^t$ that a_i is ready to send in the next time period t is lower than or equal to the negotiation threshold;
- the agents are allowed to exchange only a maximum number of proposals, denoted by max_p.

Figures 2 and 3 and Table 1 summarize the results obtained. During the course of negotiation, the customer agent adjusts the load profile using the load response strategies formalized in section 3, in response to the prices submitted by the retailer agent. Also, the customer defines new values for the prices of the energy using (6). The retailer agent adjusts the prices of the energy by using the "Price Management" strategy formalized in section 3. As mentioned earlier, this agent accepts the load profile proposed by the customer.

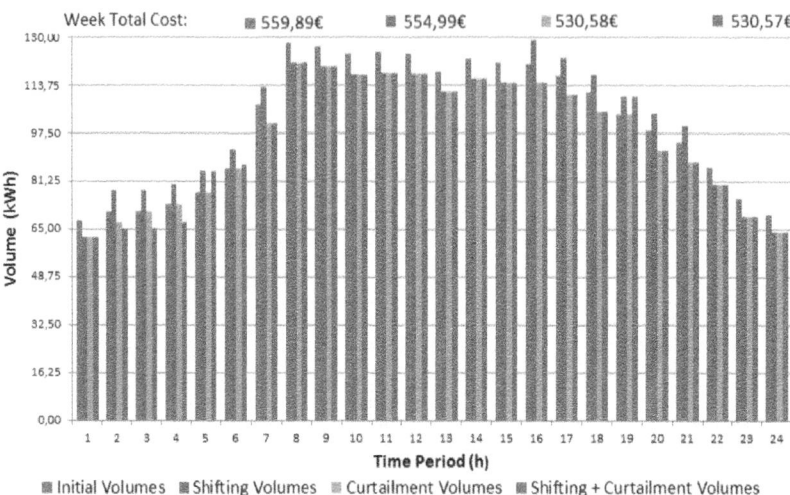

Fig. 3. Variation of volumes for the three proposed solutions

Figure 2 shows the variation of customer volumes and energy prices, considering the first proposal submitted and the final proposal accepted by both agents. Figure 3 summarizes the results of the three response solutions suggested by John Adams. Table 1 shows the cost values of the received and ready to send proposals of the customer agent. Taking into account the goal of reducing 5% of the electricity costs, defined initially by the CEO of the SCO Bank, John Adams dismisses the "shifting solution", since it does not fulfill this goal (see Fig. 3). Also, by analysing the results of the "curtailment+shifting solution" shown in Fig. 3, this agent concludes that it makes little or no sense to increase consumption in hours 5 and 19 (e.g., by turning on 1 HVAC system).

John Adams meet next with David Owen to carefully analyze the results and both agree that the "curtailment solution" seems to be the best one. In the worst case (peak hours), this solution results in turning off 4 printers, 40 lamps, 4 HVAC systems and 1 television. Technically speaking, turning off 40 lamps may be substituted by other actions, such as closing 1 lift or even 1 kitchen.

Table 1. Cost of received and ready to send proposals of the customer

Cost (€)	1st Round	2nd Round	3rd Round
Received proposal	596,00	545,00	530,58
Ready to send proposal	480,00	526,00	540,00

From the analysis of the results, it is important to mention that the customer agent reduces energy usage at times of high prices, notably from 8am to 6pm, in strict accordance with a fully automated demand response. Also, the cost of the energy has proven to be minimal for the distribution of volumes in the final proposal. Negotiation ended when the customer agent accepted the third proposal sent by the retailer agent.

5 Conclusion

This paper has described research work that uses the potential of agent-based technology to develop a computational tool to support bilateral contracting in electricity markets with demand response. From the perspective of end-use customers, it has investigated how different load response strategies affect the energy and monetary outcomes of consumers applying demand response during bilateral contracting. Specifically, it has studied the influence of both the curtailment and the shifting load response strategies on electricity prices and consumption using agent-based modeling and simulation techniques. To this end, it has presented a case study on forward bilateral contracts and customer load response strategies: a customer agent and a retailer agent have negotiated a 24h-rate tariff.

Although preliminary, the simulation results support the belief that the simulation tool can help the parties to make decisions during the negotiation of bilateral contracts in competitive electricity markets with demand response. Furthermore, the results support the belief that commercial customers adopting a curtailment response strategy can gain considerable benefits. In the future, we intend to perform a number of inter-related experiments to empirically evaluate different key load response strategies.

References

1. Kirschen, D., Strbac, G.: Fundamentals of Power System Economics. Wiley, Chichester (2004)
2. Benefits of Demand Response in Electricity Markets and Recommendations for Achieving them. Report to the United States Congress, US Department of Energy (February 2006)
3. Pechoucek, M., Marik, V.: Industrial Deployment of Multi-agent Technologies: Review and Selected Case Studies. Autonomous Agents and Multi-Agent Systems 17, 397–431 (2008)
4. Lopes, F., Mamede, N., Novais, A.Q., Coelho, H.: Negotiation in a Multi-agent Supply Chain System. In: Third Int. Workshop of the IFIP WG 5.7 Special Interest Group on Advanced Techniques in Production Planning & Control, pp. 153–168. Firenze University Press (2002)
5. Lopes, F., Mamede, N., Novais, A.Q., Coelho, H.: Negotiation Strategies for Autonomous Computational Agents. In: ECAI 16, pp. 38–42. IOS Press (2004)
6. Lopes, F., Coelho, H.: Strategic and Tactical Behaviour in Automated Negotiation. International Journal of Artificial Intelligence 4(S10), 35–63 (2010)

7. Lopes, F., Coelho, H.: Concession Strategies for Negotiating Bilateral Contracts in Multi-agent Electricity Markets. In: DEXA 2012 and IATEM 2012 Workshop, pp. 321–325. IEEE Computer Society Press (2012)
8. Lopes, F., ILco, C., Sousa, J.: Bilateral Negotiation in Energy Markets: Strategies for Promoting Demand Response. In: International Conference on the European Energy Market (EEM 2013), pp. 1–6. IEEE Computer Society Press (2013)
9. Lopes, F., Algarvio, H., ILco, C., Sousa, J.: Agent-Based Simulation of Retail Electricity Markets: Bilateral Contracting with Demand Response. In: DEXA 2013 and IATEM 2013 Workshop, pp. 194–198. IEEE Computer Society Press (2013)
10. Lopes, F., Algarvio, H., Sousa, J.: Bilateral Contracting in Multi-agent Energy Markets with Demand Response. In: Corchado, J.M., et al. (eds.) PAAMS 2014. CCIS, vol. 430, pp. 285–296. Springer, Heidelberg (2014)
11. Lopes, F., Coelho, H. (eds.): Negotiation and Argumentation in MUlti-agent Systems. Bentham Science, The Netherlands (2014)
12. Osborne, M., Rubinstein, A.: Bargaining and Markets. Academic Press, London (1990)
13. Raiffa, H.: The Art and Science of Negotiation. Harvard University Press, Cambridge (1982)
14. Keeney, R.: Value-Focused Thinking: A Path to Creative Decision Making. Harvard University Press, Cambridge (1992)
15. Pruitt, D., Kim, S.: Social Conflict: Escalation, Stalemate, and Settlement. McGraw Hill, New York (2004)

An Inductive Approach to Reconceptualizing and Theorizing about Digital Services

Mary Tate[1] and Elfi Furtmueller[2]

[1] Victoria University of Wellington, School of Information Management, 23 Lambton Quay, Pipitea Campus, P.O. Box 600, Wellington 6140, New Zealand
Mary.Tate@vuw.ac.nz
[2] University of Innsbruck, Semantic Technology Institute,
Technikerstraße 21a, 6020 Innsbruck, Austria
Elfi.Furtmueller@amc.or.at

Abstract. We posit that academic understandings of services and service quality have reached a point in their life-cycles when the use of "umbrella constructs" is no longer productive for researchers. We pose a theoretical argument for resolving the confusion of terminology and definitions of digital services, by inductively developing a taxonomy of digital service types, using techniques such as metaphor analysis that are relevant to multiple disciplines.

Keywords: Theory development, digital services, e-service quality, conceptualization, inductive methodology, taxonomy.

1 Introduction

It has been suggested that research constructs have a natural life-cycle, which progresses from broad "umbrella" constructs, through challenges by the "validity police", to clarification via taxonomy development, before being born again [1]. We argue that existing conceptualizations of service quality have been in the "umbrella construct" phase and are ready to move on to taxonomy development and eventual rebirth. There are two classical approaches towards building a taxonomy, either the conceptual/deductive approach [Starting with conceptual or theoretical foundations] or empirical/inductive [Deriving classification from objects] [2]. We suggest a grounded, inductive approach is required to refresh this research area. In the rest of this paper, we describe methodologies for the study of digital services, and present a future research agenda for breathing new life into digital services research.

2 Alternative Methodologies for Digital Services Research

Developing a grounded understanding of the way people think about digital services requires innovative research techniques that can span multi-disciplines. Various methods suggest themselves.

2.1 Metaphor Analysis

In organizational research metaphors can suggest a way of thinking, and guide our taken for granted ideas about organizations [3]. In software engineering the use of metaphor informs understanding of interface designs [4]. Existing pervasive metaphors of service delivery are inappropriate for digital services. For example, "service delivery as theatre" views the resource systems of the organization as the hidden "backstage" where actors prepare and rehearse performances. In contrast, many digital self-service offerings grant customers access to organizational systems and competencies "below the line of visibility", which is in danger of disappearing altogether as customers interact directly with the digital resource systems of the organization [5, 6]

Techniques exist in the social sciences for using metaphor as a research tool. Schmidt [7] offers an approach for eliciting and analysing metaphors in interview transcripts (or other texts, such as marketing collateral). Investigations following this path could begin to grasp that co-created and crowd-sourced services (e.g. travel recommendation sites) are inherently participative. These services could be conceptualised as a family, a conversation, or an ecosystem. Other digital services might be examined using a "personal assistant" metaphor.

2.2 Repertory Grid Technique

Structured qualitative techniques such as repertory grid technique can be used to elicit understanding of cognition about information systems phenomena [8]. Repertory grid technique is based on personal construct theory, where individuals use "personal constructs" to interpret events [9]. However, there are considerable degrees of communality between people's construct systems. Eliciting these similarities can form the basis for a classification system. Personal constructs are posited to be bi-polar in nature, forming the basis for repertory grid analysis. For instance, people may organize mobile phone apps into "useful" or "a waste of time". Further analysis can reveal the research participant's interpretations of the similarities and differences between them [8].

2.3 Grounded and "Soft" Literature Analysis Techniques

When the corpus of existing archival research literature is so large, heterogeneous and incommensurate, sense-making is extremely challenging. However, there are a number of methodological approaches which offer potential for progress in this endeavour. Various "literature as qualitative data" techniques (for example, [10-13]) exist that can be used to harmonize heterogeneous literature from multi-disciplines and to identify under-researched areas.

3 Implications and New Research Agenda

3.1 Better Digital Service Quality Measures and Instrumentation

The traditional conceptualization of service quality is almost always based on a comparative, "expectation disconfirmation" definition of quality, the discrepancy between consumers' perceptions of services and their expectations [14]. Face-to-face services are much more variable than many digital services, with the variability attributed primarily to the merchant. The idea that the quality of service received could be determined primarily by the customer themselves is not captured. However, studies of face-to-face services marketing in the hotel sector, for example, suggests that over time the gap between future expectations and past experience tends to close [15]. This is attributed to the cognitive dissonance arising from continually expecting something that is unlikely to be delivered [15]. Digital services are much more consistent; the expectation-perception gap for an experienced user is marginal. Further, the service is co-created. The quality of service a customer receives may be upgraded by improving their own contribution. There is a learning curve to achieve optimal effectiveness and the quality of service is affected by the user's mastery of fundamentals and self-efficacy. People reduce cognitive effort by developing habitual behaviours for digital services that they use frequently [16]. Their perceptions of quality may be determined by their familiarity with the service, rather than any conscious reasoning.

Improving the quality of community-based and crowd-sourced services depends on the network effect; the service normally improves in proportion to the number of contributors (e.g. review and recommendation services). In this case, the service is likely to be improved by encouraging community membership, engagement and participation. Understanding quality perceptions in bundled and customer compliant services raises additional complexities. The notion of a gap between expectations and perceptions makes little sense for a customer who has agreed in advance to comply with a set of terms and conditions [17]. The exact scope of quality evaluation in the case of bundled services (for example, data and communication services) may be difficult to determine. Individual services within the bundle may not be perceived by users as the "best of breed", yet customers may still prefer one service bundle over another.

3.2 Better Understanding of Value Creation for Stakeholders

Service value creation is frequently conceptualized as a value-chain or life-cycle. For example, the ITIL service quality management methodology includes strategy, design, transition (from design to operation), operation and continuous improvement. From a customer perspective, deriving value from the consumption of services is also modelled as a life-cycle [18], from with initial contact (e.g., via a shopping website) through actual service delivery (e.g., online payment and receiving the product) and finally service problem recovery (in the event of a service failure). While a complete analysis of value drivers and value creation is dependent on understanding of the idiosyncratic properties of different digital service types some observations can be made.

Services that are bundled, or form part of a service menu, or co-created; community mediated; crowd-sourced; or hybrid may have different life-cycles and value drivers. As mobile hand-held devices approach desktops in sales, to say nothing of the expanding universe of smart phones, all of these forms constitute rich opportunities for formulating brand new research questions. The increasing use of automations places a great deal of emphasis upon the strategic design of a range of compelling service value propositions that occurs *before* initial customer contact, when the bundle of services, or the service menu is developed (for example, a voice response system or online booking system). Once this is implemented, every stage of service consumption from initial contact through delivery and recovery, may be fully automated and will typically be very consistent. Other researchers have found that differentiation in services can be achieved through the creation of a "service inventory"[19], which is a bundle of information and pre-performed process steps that reduce the work required to respond appropriately to a customer request. The inventory can act as a "smorgasbord" where a full range of digital and self-service options along with their prices may be presented to the customer, who then selects the service level they require. In this context, the notions of service "delivery" and "failure" change, as a lower-than-usual service level may in advance have been selected by the customer. Many digital services utilise a "freemium" model, where basic services are provided free of charge (e.g. Skype VOPI, drop-box and assorted file sharing services). The notion of responsibility for service recovery is questionable when the service provided is free. A related model, which also depends heavily on automation and digitization, is the "customer compliance" business model (CCBM). It is essentially a "take it or leave it" approach aimed at cutting costs while still delivering compelling service offerings [17]. In return for compliance with company systems — such as following a company's automated procedure for ordering via its Web site or interacting with voice recognition software during a phone call — customers are rewarded with low prices and good service. This form of service aims to prevent failure by strictly controlling the nature of the interactions.

Other types of services such as co-created, community mediated, and crowd-sourced will likely continue having different value-drivers. For example, participants in consumer review sites may simultaneously be receiving a service and offering service to other community members. Some services may be so highly dynamic and adaptive that it very difficult to define the nature of the service itself as it regularly changes. For example, a bundle of location-based services on a mobile device may vary depending on the device, the user's preferences, the available services, and the proximity of friends, merchants, or other service users. The process of designing and managing these services may be adaptive and fine-grained, not standardized as the services are continually interacting with their environments. Overall, different types of digital services will likely have a unique mix of different value propositions, value drivers, and quality determinants. At the same time, on the customer side the notions of "delivery" and "recovery" are quickly evolving as the customer has an increasingly large role in determining their own service level by picking from a myriad of choices, followed by "compliant" self-service.

4   Recommendation and Proposed Approach

To understand the main characteristics of different types of digital services from a human perspective, we propose the following research program:

1. Resolve the confusion of terminology and definitions by creating a taxonomy of digital service types based on grounded, inductive qualitative techniques such as metaphor analysis and repertory grid technique that bridge multi-disciplines.
2. Extend this to improved theorization, quality measures and instrumentation. Research questions might include:
   a. Developing new models of the value creation and value drivers (from a user perspective) for new digital services types, such as bundled, hybrid, automated, adaptive, community-based and crowd-sourced services.
   b. Developing new measures and operationalization for service quality, beyond the expectation disconfirmation model. For example, measurement of the "quality" of the user of the service, the community of users, or the bundling of services are uncharted territory.

5   Conclusion

Services and service quality research needs to move into a new phase, beyond "umbrella concepts", and informed by research techniques that span multi-disciplines. This clearly requires a methodological agenda aimed at cross-disciplinary collaboration, communication, sharing and understanding of each other's viewpoints about the meaning of services. There is an urgent need for a taxonomy of digital services, based on people's everyday cognitions about digital service types that can drive new lines of enquiry about the nature, characteristics, life-cycle, and quality drivers for each type.

References

1. Hirsch, P., Levin, D.: Umbrella Advocates Versus Validity Police: A Life-Cycle Model. Organization Science 10(2), 199–212 (1999)
2. Bailey, K.D.: Typologies and taxonomies: an introduction to classification techniques. Sage, Thousand Oaks (1994)
3. Lakoff, G., Johnson, M.: Metaphors We Live By. The Chicago University Press, Chicago (1980)
4. Barr, P., Biddle, R., Noble, J.: A Taxonomy of User-Interface Metaphors. In: SIGCHI-NZ Symposium on Computer-Human Interaction, Hamilton (2002)
5. Tate, M., Evermann, J.: Descendents of ServQual in Online Services Research: The End of the Line? In: Americas Conference in Information Systems (AMCIS), San Francisco (2009)
6. Tate, M., Evermann, J.: The End of ServQual in Online Services Research: Where to from here? e-Service Journal 7(1), 60–85 (2010)

7. Schmidt, R.: Systematic Metaphor Analysis as a Method of Qualitative Research. The Qualitative Report 10(2), 358–394 (2005)
8. Tan, F., Hunter, G.: The Repertory Grid Technique: A Method for the Study of Cognition in Information Systems. MIS Quarterly 26(1), 39–57 (2002)
9. Kelly, G.A.: The Psychology of Personal Constructs. W.W. Norton & Company Inc., New York (1955)
10. Sylvester, A., Tate, M.: Beyond the "Mythical Centre": An Affirmative Post-Modern View of SERVQUAL Research in Information Systems. In: European Conference in Information Systems (ECIS), Galway, Ireland (2008)
11. Sylvester, A., Tate, M., Johnstone, D.: Re-presenting the literature review: A Rich Picture of Service Quality Research in Information Systems. In: Pacific Asia Conference in Information Systems (PACIS), Auckland, New Zealand (2007)
12. Sylvester, A., Tate, M., Johnstone, D.: Beyond synthesis: Re-presenting heterogeneous research literature. Behaviour and Information Technology, (0, iPrint), 1–17 (2011)
13. Wolfswinkel, J., Furtmueller, E., Wilderom, C.: Using Grounded Theory as a Method for Rigorously Reviewing Literature. European Journal of Information Systems 22, 45–55 (2013)
14. Parasuraman, A., Zeithaml, V., Berry, L.: SERVQUAL: A Multi-Item Scale for Measuring Consumer Perceptions of Service Quality. Journal of Retailing 64, 12–40 (1988)
15. Boulding, W., et al.: A Dynamic Process Model of Service Quality: From Expectations to Behavioral Intentions. Journal of Marketing Research 30(1), 7–27 (1993)
16. Gefen, D.: TAM or just plain habit: A look at experienced online shoppers. Journal of End User Computing 15(3), 1–13 (2003)
17. Kasabov, E.: The Compliant Customer. Sloan Management Review 51(3), 18–19 (2010)
18. Nasr, N., Eshghi, A., Ganguli, S.: Service Quality in Hybrid Services: A Consumer Value Chain Framework. Journal of Services Research 12(1), 115–130 (2012)
19. Chopra, S., Lariviere, M.: Managing Service Inventory to Improve Performance. Sloan Management Review 47(1), 56–63 (2005)

How to Create an E-Advertising Adaptation Strategy: The AEADS Approach

Alaa A. Qaffas and Alexandra I. Cristea

Department of Computer Science
The University of Warwick
Coventry, CV4 7AL, UK
{aqaffas,acristea}@dcs.warwick.ac.uk

Abstract. During recent years, the internet and online marketing have experienced a continuous growth. Web-based advertisement is used to target users easily, without place or time limitation. Personalization is an ingenious way to potentially increase the effectiveness and efficiency of web-based advertisements. In this paper, a model for creating personalisation specification for businesses (*adaptation strategies*), based on *adaptation rules*, is introduced. The paper also implements a version of this model and presents its evaluation.

Keywords: E-advertising, E-commerce, Personalisation, Adaptive Advertising, Adaptation Strategy, Authoring System.

1 Introduction

The growth in online advertisement has been rapid; this is demonstrated, for instance, in the case of 2012, when revenues from internet advertising in the United States became higher than that of cable television, recording the value of $36.57 billion, an increase of 15.2% from the previous year [1]. Traditional e-advertisements involve the use of methods like banners [2], which are used on the web pages through the graphic advertising display, to attract the attention of a wide market. Recently, advertisements have become more aggressive, by using methods such as pop-up ads, swimming across the screen ads and playing music ads [3], which push users to use pop-up blocking software.

As a more gentle alternative, personalization can be used to enhance customer services or the e-commerce sales. It is a form of direct marketing to the customers, as it enables the enterprise web pages to be tailored for specifically targeting individual customers [4]. It can be used to increase customer satisfaction and encourage repeat visits. Adaptation is the process of changing in order to fit a given situation or purpose. Whilst personalization is considered useful in many areas, the process of creating personalized experiences in any domain, and thus also in e-advertising, is complex [5].

Hence, the main questions this research purposes to address are:

1. *How can we support the creation of adaptive advertising by website owners?*; and more specifically:
    A. *What type of tools do website owners need to be able to efficiently add adaptive adverts in a lightweight manner (as an add-on) to their website?*
    B. *What kind of support do website owners need to be able to use these tools?*

This paper provides solutions to the above questions by recommending a series of tools that can be used in formulating adaptive advertising strategies. It also performs an in-depth analysis of an implementation of an essential adaptive advertising tool component, the *adaptation strategy tool*, by having it used by genuine businesses in order to conduct a realistic appraisal.

The next sections discuss related research, adaptation strategy implementation and evaluation. Finally, a conclusion and future work pointers are provided.

2 Background and Related Research

Personalisation has first been applied in the fields of distance learning and web-based educational systems. In this field, many models and frameworks for adaptation have been introduced in the past, e.g., XAHM [6], WebML [7], LAOS [8], AHAM [9], Dexter [10]. Most frameworks advocated the 'separation of concerns' [11] principle, which encourages creation of sub-models aimed at the main components of adaptive delivery and authoring. As a result, separate tools for creating adaptation have been used by most authoring systems for adaptive hypermedia [8]. Ways of modelling adaptation specification have been proposed before; for instance [12] identified three major adaptation layers and the different roles that they play in a typical adaptive model. Together, these three layers form the layered adaptation granulation (LAG). This paper specifically focuses on the *adaptation model for e-advertising*, illustrated by the tool created as a proof of concept, and evaluated with businesses.

This specific area is quite new, with pioneering systems such as MyAds [13], AdSense [14], or AdROSA [2].

However, a generalization of these systems into a model or framework, ready to be applied to any website, by any business, has not yet been proposed. This very challenging problem is tackled by the umbrella research. Here we focus on illustrating a part of it, *a simplified way of specifying adaptation to generate adaptive e-adverts*. The content of the adverts and its meta-data is considered to have been authored elsewhere [15]. The tools need to be simple, as advertising owners are less likely to be able or have the time to use complex adaptation models, and complex personalisation.

3 Authoring Adaptive E-Advertising

The overall Authoring model of Adaptive E-Adverts, as informed by prior research and implementations, especially in the area of personalised e-learning, includes:

1. *Domain model*, to be used by businesses to organise, label and categorise advertisements. The model, described elsewhere [15], is not further detailed here.
2. *Adaptation model*, which should enable business owners to adapt the advertisements they have organised after creating the domain model their customers' needs, is instantiated via an implementation, as described below.

The adaptation model is a crucial component of personalisation, and also traditionally the most difficult one to implement and use [16]. For our e-advertising purposes, we have opted for a straightforward rule-based model, describing *adaptation rules*. Moreover, we have identified two types of relevant rules (based on [5]): *general rules* and *behaviour rules*. General rules include typical rules, e.g., based on age, gender, device type and bandwidth (illustrated in Fig 1a). Behaviour rules link to user actions; e.g., after (1,2,3,4) clicks then (1,2,3,4) items from subgroups are displayed; if this advertisement appears to the current user (1,2,3,4) times and is not clicked, then let it disappear for (1,2,3,4) visits, etc. (illustrated in Fig. 1b). In addition, the client can select one rule or combine multiple rules for an item. Furthermore, the client can change and delete the rules of an item. The *Adaptation Strategy tool* is the second tool of the AEADS authoring package for adaptive e-adverts delivery, and illustrates the adaptation model proposed, as well as the simple approach to authoring of relatively complex adaptation rules that we target. The tool is aimed at proof of concept, and can be extended, based on the same adaptation model, to a different (or extended) set of desired general and behaviour rules, depending on the business's needs.

Fig. 1a) General Rules   **Fig. 1b)** Behaviour Rules

4   Case Study

4.1   Hypotheses

The following hypotheses have been defined to evaluate the adaptation approach, as described above and instantiated by the adaptation strategy tool:

H1: The tool is important for business.
H2: The tool is easy to use.
H3: This tool makes advertising work easier.
H4: A new staff can understand and use this tool with minimal training.

H5: *This tool is saving time.*
H6: *General Rules are useful and easy to use (e.g., age, gender, etc.).*
H7: *Behaviour Rules are useful and easy to use.*
H8: *Applying rules on items or advertisements is useful and easy to use.*
H9: *Combining multiple rules on items or advertisements is useful and easy to use.*
H10: *Changing rules for items or advertisements is useful and easy to use.*
H11: *Deletion rules for items or advertisements is useful and easy to use.*

These hypotheses have been tested by surveying a set of selected business owners and analysing their answers, as further described below.

4.2 Case Study Setup

A questionnaire has been created for businesses to evaluate the tool based on the hypotheses above, in terms of functionality and ease of use.

Eleven business proprietors chosen from a wide range of industries were asked to use the adaptation strategy tool according to the following guidelines:

Initially, they were given a general overview of the system and were also introduced to the concept of adaptive advertising. Following this, each participant was asked to use the tool and evaluate it. The questionnaire was provided at this stage to facilitate the appraisal process and was composed of three sections. The first section related to demographic data. The second section incorporated a Likert scale [17] to allow participants to provide a comprehensive evaluation of the tool's functionality and utilities, as illustrated in Table 1 and also referenced in Figure 3. In this survey, the Likert scale provided five response options to participants and they were required to select from these when assessing the tool; number one on the scale represented not useful at all or very difficult to use while five represented very useful or very easy to use. The final section of the questionnaire contained a series of open-ended questions that were designed to elicit additional feedback on the tool from the business owners.

Table 1. Key Features and Functions

A	Whole Tool	H	If this advertisement appears to the current user (1,2,3,4) and is not clicked then let disappear it for (1,2,3,4) visits
B	Having a rule on age	I	Show this advertisement after advertisement (1,2,3,4) is clicked
C	Having a rule on gender	J	Applying rule on item
D	Having a rule on device type	K	Combining multiple rules on item
E	Having a rule on bandwidth	L	Changing rules for item
F	After (1,2,3,4) clicks then (1,2,3,4) items from its subgroups are displayed	M	Delete rules for item
G	After (1,2,3,4) clicks on this advertisement then (1,2,3,4) items in groups are displayed		

4.3 Results

Participants in this experiment were chosen from a variety of industries, namely media, transportation, consultation, retail, telecommunications, construction and web-based education services. From the total of the businesses involved, 46% were SMEs, 27% medium and 27% were large companies. Furthermore, 55% were based in Saudi Arabia while 45% were based in the UK. In such a way, a representative spread for the initial case study was achieved.

The participants used the Likert scale to evaluate the usefulness of the Adaptation Strategy tool's features and functions (Black column in Fig. 2). Data analysis was performed on the responses and the table was compiled. Based on the outcome, it is clear that all key features and functions (A-M, defined in Table 1) were rated highly by business owners. Every respondent allocated a Likert scale mark of 4 or 5 (*useful* or *very useful*). The mean values were between 4.18 and 4.90 and the standard deviation values were between .30 and .60. The tool is thus useful, as the mean values were all greater than 3. Out of the 13 features, the 'rule on device type' received the highest score, together with the rule 'apply rule on item' and 'combine rules on item'. On the lower end of the scale, the features which scored the lowest were 'if this advertisement appears to the current user (1,2,3,4) and is not clicked then it disappears for (1,2,3,4) visits' and 'modify rules for (the current) item'. The possible motive for this is that business owners may not see a strong reason for an advertisement to disappear (they may be wary of it) and they don't see a strong need to modify rules that have been created. So, they felt that these functions may not always be needed. However, both of these features still received a score of at least 4, which indicates that they were still regarded as useful.

In terms of ease of use, all features of the Adaptation Strategy tool were reported as being easy or very easy to use (with mean values between 4.36 and 4.90 and standard deviation values were between .30 and .52, as shown in Grey column in Fig. 2), a result which indicates that the tool as a whole is accessible and easy to use. .Subsequent data analysis showed that the 'whole tool' and the 'remove rules for item' elements were rated 5 by all participants. The lowest rated element was 'show this advertisement after advertisement (1,2,3,4) is clicked' but this feature still received a score of 4 or higher, which implies that this element is still easy to use. Overall, these research findings suggest that the Adaptation Strategy tool is easy to use.

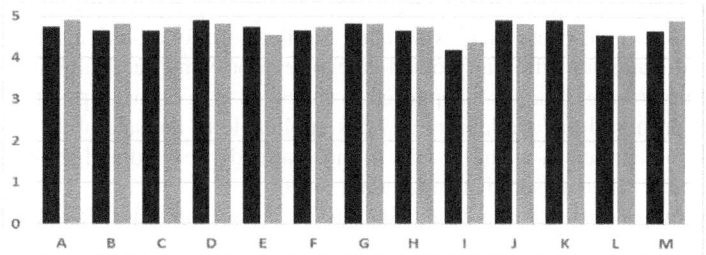

Fig. 2. Usefulness Ease of Use (Ox axis detailed in Table 1)

The final section of the questionnaire asked participants to provide *free feedback on the Adaptive Strategy tool* and was designed to obtain an appraisal of the tool as a whole and also to determine if there were any aspects of the tool that should be eliminated or developed further. This qualitative research approach is invaluable in the early design phase as any issues with accessibility, user interface or functionality can be rectified at an early stage in order to enhance the overall performance of the model. In terms of responses, several important points were made to suggest how to improve the tool and increase the likelihood of businesses incorporating it as part of their business model. Firstly, several participants requested that the application developers '*make it easy for business owners*'. This supports our initial assumption that business owners need extremely simple tools, to ever consider authoring adaptive adverts with it. In fact, this particular business owner further told the interviewee that business owners are typically very busy, and any complexity should be avoided, as they can only invest little time in learning such tools. Secondly, several participants mentioned that the design of the tool can be improved. Again, more insight would be required in order to determine which design elements need work, but further research could be conducted before a more user-friendly design is developed. We expect this to be dependent on the business and business owner, and that a smooth merger with their own website look and feel would possibly be the best approach. In other words, there is no universal solution, but each solution would need customised for a particular business.

Several participants made queries about the functionality and asked '*how will you know the device type?*'; this would be achieved by detecting the use of a mobile or non-mobile browser via website configuration. This query suggests that the developers may want to provide more in-depth operational information to clients, so that they are aware how the processes are implemented and how they are affected by the use of different devices. One participant stated that there was '*no reason to divide rules into two types*' while another asserted that they would like to be able to '*divide rules, based on products*'. This again shows a diversity in perspectives, as each business has unique requirements. However, it would possibly be useful to extend adaptation to implement a product-dependent rule as many companies would require a different set of rules based on product and their target demographic.

In fact, many participants stated that they would like to be able to apply their own customised rules using the system, or have a broader set of rules at their disposal. One participant requested a rule that would show another variation of the same product when a user clicked on it more than twice. This would prove effective in adaptive advertising, as many hesitant customers may be swayed by the provision of more options (even simple ones, such as colour). Furthermore, one participant requested a unique set of rules for different product categories; for example, different rules could be chosen in the sale of books as opposed to shoes. Also in terms of product type, one participant proposed the availability of rules applicable to the sale of services. These rules could be applied in a similar way to those already devised and show a range of related services when a user visits more than twice.

In addition, one participant would like the option to apply a different set of rules depending on who is accessing the website, the company or a customer. Another participant requested the addition of a colour rule, whereas a different business owner believes that a rule based on nationality could prove useful. In a similar context, another owner stated that a rule on education level or profession would also be well-received. The extensions above would facilitate a more advanced application of the adaptive advertising process, even potentially moving from the adaptation strategies to the adaptation language approach. This however would be more complex for business owners to apply, and thus benefits need carefully be evaluated against costs.

In terms of system features, three participants made suggestions on improving the range of services provided. One recommended the provision of a feature that would enable them to apply a specified set of rules to a group of specified products. This feature would streamline the implementation process, as many products would undoubtedly share a similar set of rules. This has been proposed before in adaptation language research [18], and that case-by-case it is implementable, but that a generic authoring method that is also easily usable would still have to be found. Another participant recommended that the system allows them to apply a selection of rules to an advertisement. A different business owner expressed the need for a strategy that would allow them to target their customers more effectively by narrowing in on demographics. This request might be inspired by the current way Facebook and other social networking sites are allowing businesses to create and semi-customise adverts, by selecting a number of demographic parameters, such as age group, nationality group, gender and knowledge. Addition of such rules is relatively straightforward, but it depends a lot on the type of data about their customers that they have access to. A different line of research undertaken under the same umbrella has proposed to extract such user-related information from social networks [5], or to have a different way of allowing business customers to provide the personal data that they are comfortable in sharing with the business. This is not further detailed in this paper, which is focusing on the authoring of the adaptation strategies, its first set of tools and their evaluation, but it will be part of the further research into the user modelling aspects of the overall research question. Finally, one user suggested that the system should incorporate a method that will highlight any item that has no designated rules applied. Again, this would improve the user interface and allow business owners to easily detect aspects that they haven't worked on yet, or products that have no allocated rules for. In adaptive hypermedia, adaptation engines usually have a default strategy for such objects (either 'show all' or, sometimes, 'hide all'). The respective default strategy in the business field is usually 'show all', with different variations thereof. For example, show all adverts present, by rolling through them at a given rate, depending also on the display size allocated in the browser. We expect this to be somewhat varied, depending on the business itself, and its standard ways of processing adverts. Adaptation has to sit in a lightweight manner on top of the existent webpages of the business, and using the default strategy, where no other information is present.

5 Conclusion

In summary, we believe that an Adaptive Strategy creation system would allow businesses to increase sales potential by facilitating the accurate targeting of advertisements based on a series of predefined demographic attributes and rules. This tool has been tried out by companies who wish to direct their advertising campaigns at specific consumer groups, as it could enable them to quickly and effectively assign a series of rules based on their target market. As discussed, the system, its features and usability have been evaluated, both theoretically and by established businesses, and the overall initial outcome has been positive. However, it is clear that there are aspects that require further development, and especially specific customisation for each business, as the feedback section provided a range of suggestions that could be used to enhance the overall functionality and usefulness of the tool.

References

1. InternetAdvertisingBureau. Internet Advertising Revenues Report 2012 full year results (2012)
2. Kazienko, P., Adamski, M.: AdROSA—Adaptive personalization of web advertising. Information Sciences 177(11), 2269–2295 (2007)
3. Brain, M.: How Web Advertising Works (2002), http://computer.howstuffworks.com/web-advertising.htm (accessed March 10, 2014)
4. Hogendoorn, R., Nu, L.: System Administration for Oracle E-Business Suite (Personal Edition): Lulu Enterprises Incorporated (2007)
5. Qaffas, A.A., Cristea, A.I., Shi, L.: Is Adaptation of E-Advertising the Way Forward? In: 2013 IEEE Conference on e-Learning, e-Management and e-Services (IC3e), Malaysia, pp. 117–124 (2013)
6. Cannataro, M., Pugliese, A.: XAHM: An XML-Based Adaptive Hypermedia Model and Its Implementation. In: Reich, S., Tzagarakis, M.M., De Bra, P.M.E. (eds.) OHS/SC/AH 2001. LNCS, vol. 2266, pp. 252–263. Springer, Heidelberg (2002)
7. Ceri, S., Fraternali, P., Bongio, A.: Web Modeling Language (WebML): a modeling language for designing Web sites. Computer Networks 33(1), 137–157 (2000)
8. Cristea, A.I., de Mooij, A.: LAOS: Layered WWW AHS authoring model and their corresponding algebraic operators. In: WWW 2003 (The Twelfth International World Wide Web Conference), Alternate Track on Education, Budapest, Hungary (2003)
9. De Bra, P., Houben, G.-J., Wu, H.: AHAM: a Dexter-based reference model for adaptive hypermedia. In: Proceedings of the Tenth ACM Conference on Hypertext and Hypermedia: Returning to Our Diverse Roots: Returning to Our Diverse Roots, pp. 147–156
10. Halasz, F., Schwartz, M., Grønbæk, K., Trigg, R.H.: The Dexter hypertext reference model. Communications of the ACM 37(2), 30–39 (1994)
11. Cristea, A., Stewart, C.: Authoring of Adaptive Hypermedia. In: Magoulas, G.D., Chen, S.Y. (eds.) Advances in Web-Based Education: Personalized Learning Environments, vol. 8, pp. 225–252. Information Science Publishing (IDEA group) (2006)
12. Cristea, A., Calvi, L.: The Three Layers of Adaptation Granularity. In: Brusilovsky, P., Corbett, A.T., de Rosis, F. (eds.) UM 2003. LNCS (LNAI), vol. 2702, pp. 4–14. Springer, Heidelberg (2003)
13. Di Ferdinando, A., Rosi, A., Lent, R., Manzalini, A., Zambonelli, F.: MyAds: A system for adaptive pervasive advertisements. Pervasive and Mobile Computing 5(5), 385–401 (2009)
14. GoogleAdSense, "Maximize revenue from your online content", http://www.google.com/adsense/ (accessed March 25, 2014).
15. Qaffas, A., Cristea, A.: How to create an E-Advertising Domain Model: the AEADS approach. In: The 2014 International Conference on e-Learning, e-Business, Enterprise Information Systems, and e-Government (EEE 2014), Las Vegas, United States (2014)
16. Brusilovsky, P.: Developing adaptive educational hypermedia systems: From design models to authoring tools. In: Authoring Tools for Advanced Technology Learning Environments, pp. 377–409. Springer (2003)
17. McIver, J., Carmines, E.G.: Unidimensional scaling, vol. 24. Sage (1981)
18. Stash, N., Cristea, A., De Bra, P.: Adaptation to learning styles in e-learning: Approach evaluation. In: Proceedings of World Conference on E-Learning in Corporate, Government, Government, Healthcare, and Higher Education Honolulu, Hawaii, pp. 284–291

Modelling User Behaviour in Online Q&A Communities for Customer Support

Erik Aumayr and Conor Hayes

Insight Centre for Data Analytics
National University of Ireland, Galway
{erik.aumayr,conor.hayes}@insight-centre.org

Abstract. With the increased popularity of Questions and Answers (Q&A) platforms, especially as a means to efficient customer support management, a lot of research has been carried out in order to study the user behaviour on Q&A sites. However, many research questions remain unanswered, as the underlying dynamics of replying in online communication platforms are not yet fully understood. One reason for this is that the interaction patterns in typical datasets with thousands of users and millions of posts are too complex to be broken down to the level of the individual users. In this paper, we present an agent-based model of online Q&A communities that is able to explain how these complex behaviour patterns evolve from the basic interactions of the individual agents. We evaluate our model on the SAP Community Network, and find that it closely reproduces Q&A behaviour of the real data.

1 Introduction

Online communities have become a standard way through which companies respond to and support a large customer base. The efficacy of online support communities relies on having members that are willing to assist other members with answers or advice. In a 2006 study[1], Nielsen has reported that in a typical community 9% of users contribute little and 1% of users account for most of the action. Several studies have been done to examine how to improve the online participation in communities. Arguello et al. investigated how user participation can be increased by ensuring that newcomers receive replies to their enquiries [1]. Sung et al. tried to detect expert users based on posting behaviour [2]. Others have tried to counter negative influences, e.g. by identifying malicious users [3]. The recent advent of reward systems, especially in online Q&A sites, introduced incentives to participation and a means of reputation ranking. However, reward systems can cause severe harm to a community in terms of trust and knowledge exchange if not deployed sensitively [4].

While observations from real world data allow for inferences about how user behaviour may be effected by different engagement strategies, these inferences can only be tested and compared in live contexts. Naturally, companies are wary

---
[1] http://www.webcitation.org/6Q8DLIE75

of alienating their customer base through various trial-and-error online experiments. In this paper we propose a simple agent-based model, calibrated and verified by real customer support data, that provides a means of evaluating the potential outcome of strategies designed to engage an online community. The simplicity of our model adheres to Axelrod's "keep-it-simple-stupid" (KISS) principle for agent modelling: the phenomena that emerge from simulations should be the result of multi-agent interactions and not because of complex individual behaviours [5]. An agent is an autonomous virtual entity that interacts with other agents according to a set of simple rules, imitating the behaviour of real people. We carefully evaluate our model to ensure that it accurately reproduces the behaviour we observe in a real online Q&A community.

2 Related Work: Agent-Based Models of Social Behaviour

The agent-based approach is well suited to modelling communities and social networks. Despite this, there has not been previous work on modelling the Q&A communities, which are at the cornerstone of many enterprise support platforms. In related work, other types of communities have been modelled. However, these models cannot be used to validly generate Q&A behaviour due to features that are unique to Q&A platforms, especially the two different classes of posts, i.e. questions and answers, and the mechanics of selecting a best answer.

Bernstein and O'Brien produced a domain agnostic model of the activity patterns of people [6]. The core part of their model is to define when agents become active, what role they choose to fulfil, and which of the available actions they choose to perform. This is similar to our work. The authors evaluate their model on a target dataset that was artificially created by another simulation. As such it is not clear how well it reproduces behaviour of the real world. For validating our Q&A model, we rely on a data-driven evaluation. Xu et al. created a model where agents create, review and update content in a collaborative knowledge processing environment such as Wikipedia [7]. Like this work, we initially used the notions of knowledge and quality in order to represent an agent's ability to contribute. After experimentation we summarised both concepts to the single measure of quality. This simplifies the model and also provides an easier basis for evaluation on a real world data set.

Gatti et al. developed a model of Micro-blogging community like Twitter [8] to examine how messages diffuse across the ego-centric network of a user. Agent behaviours were learnt from real data. In the experiments, however, the authors only showed limited aspects of how the model adhered to the real data. In this approach agent behaviour was dependent on the time of day. This concept could also prove useful for our model in future work. Mungovan et al.'s agent based study examined the factors that let a social network converge towards adapting one single social norm [9]. They found that a community converges faster towards a single norm when there are random interactions with unseen agents, and when agents are not fully rational in their behaviour. While not in the scope of this paper, this observation may help to further explain how users change their posting behaviour with respect to others. In summary, our model complements existing research by explaining emerging behaviour in online Q&A communities, while being validated on real data every step in the development.

3 Overview

A Q&A forum is a place where people ask for help or advice in the form of question posts, and other people try to provide support by replying with answer posts. Each question post starts a new forum thread, and all the corresponding answer posts are contained within that thread. We consider all replies to a question to be answers to that question. From all the answers that hold enough information to solve a given question, the question asker can choose one to be the best answer, which implies a reward of some sort in many Q&A platforms.

The Reference Data. The Q&A site that we use for our evaluation of the model is the SAP Community Network (http://scn.sap.com). In the SCN, SAP customers pose predominantly technical questions about SAP products, and other community members – customers and SAP employees – try to help them. We randomly selected twelve of the biggest SCN communities. Two for calibrating our model, and ten for evaluating it. For normalisation, we picked as many posts from each community as the smallest one contained. In order to capture the most active period of each community, we picked their most recent complete threads. In the end, each of the twelve communities contained about 20,000 posts, and covered more than two years of posting activity.

Methodology. Our approach can be summarised in three steps: observation, parameter fitting and validation. First, we examined the data in order to build a model that reproduces the Q&A behaviour from the SCN. We observed how many questions and answers are written by the users, and how many questions they solve with a best answer. Then, we designed the agents that represent real life users in our model, and created rules that enable the agents to act and interact like the users do in the data. Throughout this work, we refer to real people as users, in contrast to the agents that represent them in the model. In the parameter fitting stage, we calibrated the model according to the observed user behaviour, including the agent attributes and the interaction rules. Finally, we validated the calibrated model on the evaluation communities.

4 The Q&A Community Model

Our model aims at producing the same Q&A behaviour that we observe in the real data. Agents will join the modelled community at a rate that we observe from the reference data, and they become active by creating question or answer items in certain time intervals. We define time discretely as the total number of created question or answer items since the start of the simulation. In particular, an agent can create a question, submit an answer to another agent's question, receive an answer to their own question, or accept a received answer as best answer. The agents will differ from one another, as they are defined by a set of agent attributes: *expertise*, *activity* and *Q-A-ratio*, as shown in Figure 1. For example, some agents will post more frequently than others, based on their *activity* attribute. The question attribute *requirement* and the answer attribute *quality* determine which answers can solve a question by being of good quality.

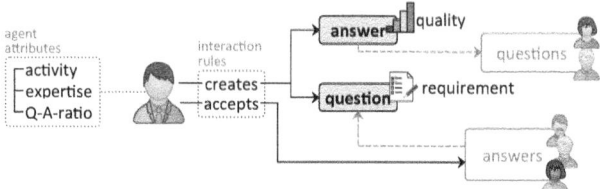

Fig. 1. Overview of the agent attributes and interaction rules between agents in our Q&A community model. An agent can create question posts for which they receive answers by others, and they can themselves create answer posts to the questions of others. Agents will also accept best answers if their quality exceeds the requirement of the posed question. Creating a post is equal to one time step.

4.1 Agent Attributes

We will show that there are three fundamental attributes that are sufficient to describe user behaviour in a Q&A platform: *expertise*, *activity* and question-answer ratio, or *Q-A-ratio*. The *expertise* describes the domain knowledge of an agent: agents with a lot of domain knowledge are more capable to solve questions than agents with little knowledge. The *activity* attribute captures how frequently an agent participates in the community, and the *Q-A-ratio* determines how likely it is that an agent seeks help in the form of a question rather than replying to questions of others. The three attributes are normalised between 0 and 1.

Expertise. The purpose of the agents' *expertise* attribute is to capture the users' capability to solve questions. When users write questions, they are seeking help. That means they have a certain *requirement* of information. On the other hand, when they write answers, they are providing help. And the information they provide has a certain *quality*. Based on the notion of information *requirement* and *quality*, we can now identify whether an answer is able to solve a question by providing at least as much quality of information as the asker requires.

Although we did not have access to any direct way of measuring expertise in online communities, we utilised the reward system of the reference data to estimate the user expertise. SCN's reward system provides the question asker with a way to select one of the received answers as best answer. We define the number of best answers scored by a user or agent i in relation to their total amount of answers as their individual expertise, as shown in Equation 1.

$$expertise_i = \frac{\#bestAnswers_i}{\#answers_i} \tag{1}$$

We acknowledge that the accuracy of this metric is limited, for example in cases where the asker does not select any best answer for some reason, or where there are more than one very good answer and the asker has to select one. However, these cases also occur in our model. In our experiments on the SCN data, we found that the users' best answer ratio is exponentially distributed. Very similar distributions we also found in different Q&A sites, such as Stack Overflow and Yahoo! Answers. Hence, we model the distribution of *expertise* as an exponential distribution as described in Equation 2.

$$expertise \sim e^{\left(-\frac{x}{0.2}\right)} \tag{2}$$

It is a variation of the natural exponential function that is based on the Euler constant e. Function 2 randomly distributes *expertise* among the agents, where $0 \leq x < 1$ is a uniform random number, generated by the simulation, and the parameter 0.2 creates the slope that best approximates the observed distribution. We obtained this parameter by fitting the *expertise* distribution of the agents to the observed distribution of the users' best answer ratio.

Activity. The *activity* attribute determines how frequently agents participate in the community by creating question and answer items. We measure the *activity* distribution directly from the reference data through the post count of the users, and we observe that it is also exponentially distributed. Moreover, our experiments revealed a strong correlation between the two attributes *expertise* and *activity*. According to our reference data, the domain experts are the most frequent posters. We assume that the more a user is active in their domain, the more they increase their expertise. We simplify this correlation by setting $activity_i = expertise_i$ for every agent i. Therefore, *activity* also follows the exponential distribution as described in Equation 2 for *expertise*. Finally, in every time step one agent whose *activity* attribute is above a random threshold will become active and create either a question or an answer.

Q-A-Ratio. The agent attribute *Q-A-ratio* determines whether an active agent is creating a question or an answer. Our experiments on the SCN data revealed that newcomers have a probability of $\frac{2}{3}$ to ask a question rather than replying to one. This ratio decreases the more users participate in the community. Our previous observation of a correlation between *activity* and *expertise* allows us to assume that there is a link between the user's expertise and their probability of writing a question. We define a linear dependency between *expertise* and *Q-A-ratio* in Equation 3 for each agent i, and find that it fits the SCN data well.

$$Q\text{-}A\text{-}ratio_i = \frac{2}{3} * (1 - expertise_i) \tag{3}$$

4.2 Agent Interaction Rules

The agents follow a number of basic rules in order to interact with each other by creating question and answer items, and by accepting best answers.

Creating Questions. Based to their *Q-A-ratio* attribute, an agent might decide to create a new question item. Similar to the agent attributes, also questions and answers have attributes. The attribute of the question is the asker's *requirement* of information, which is defined by their *expertise*, and therefore it is also exponentially distributed between 0 and 1. The information *requirement* sets a threshold that answers must meet in order to successfully solve a question.

Because of the observed interdependency between *Q-A-ratio* and *expertise*, novice agents create more questions than expert agents. These novice questions are easier to solve since their information *requirement* is low. However, expert agents occasionally create a question, which then can only be solved by another expert agent, based on their levels of expertise. We can observe a similar behaviour in the real data, where expert users might pose a controversial question which requires deep domain knowledge to be sufficiently answered.

Creating Answers. If active agents do not create a question, they will alternatively create an answer. Answers have a *quality* of information attribute, which is defined by the *expertise* of the answering agent. This is the counterpart to the question's information *requirement*. Only answers with at least as much information as the asker needs are able to solve the question, see Equation 4. However, agents of any *expertise* may reply to any question. We can observe the same behaviour in the SCN data, where users who cannot solve the question sometimes state that they are facing the same problem as the question-asker, perhaps also providing additional details of the problem.

$$A \text{ can solve } Q = \begin{cases} true & \text{if } quality_A \geq requirement_Q \\ false & otherwise \end{cases} \quad (4)$$

An answer always refers to an existing question, and the only restriction the agents have for answering questions is that they cannot answer their own questions. In our model, we assume that agents are able to formulate their problem completely in one question post, and do not need to reply to their own question with more information. This simplifies the model. The agents follow one out of two possible ways to choose which question to reply to. With a probability of $\frac{1}{3}$ an agent will reply to a question that they have replied to in the past. We saw this probability in the real data. Many users come back to a question they already replied to, often after they got more details about the posed problem.

The other $\frac{2}{3}$ of the time agents will choose to reply to a question from a pool of qualifying questions. Based on our observations, this pool contains only recent questions that have received very few answers and are not yet solved. The maximum age and maximum number of posts already received are randomly assigned in each time step, based on Equations 5 and 6 respectively. As we discussed before, the exponential function e describes best human behaviour, and the parameter 0.1 creates a slope of e that we fitted to our calibration data. The question age depends on a generated uniform random number $0 \leq x < 1$ and on t, which denotes the number of time steps that have passed. The purpose of t is to stretch the normalised exponential function over the whole range of passed time steps. The maximum age and maximum amount of answers reflect the users' observed tendency to reply to recent threads that have only very few answers, if any at all.

$$questionAge_{replyTo} \leq t * e^{\left(-\frac{x}{0.1}\right)} \quad (5) \qquad answerCount \leq -1 * \ln x \quad (6)$$

In our experiments we observed that the users' tendency for recency mainly affects the creation time of the question, and not the creation time of the last answer. We assume that users want to reply to questions that do not have any answers yet. The time of the most recent answer appears to be less relevant for them. That indicates that the community does usually not jump onto hot topics, as it might be the case in online platforms that are more focussed on general discussions and information sharing, such as reddit.com.

Accepting Answers. Agents who created questions will check whether one of their questions was solved, and they will accept one of the answers whose *quality* exceeds the *requirement* of their question, see Equation 4. Our experiments during the model calibration revealed that an answer is accepted with approximately 6% probability for each post that is created, and that the chance of a question to be resolved decreases over time. We implement the same behaviour into our model. In particular, questions can be solved based on the following criteria: first, they must have received at least one eligible answer, i.e. with a *quality* greater than or equal to the *requirement* of the question. Second, the question must not already have an accepted best answer. Third, it must be within a limit of time steps as defined by Equation 7, with x as a generated uniform random input and constant c.

$$questionAge_{markSolved} = c * e^{\left(-\frac{x}{0.1}\right)} \quad (7)$$

We find that a good approximation of the reference data is when the agents only consider selecting a best answer of questions that have been created in the last 1000 time steps. Hence, we set c to 1000 in our model. The parameter 0.1 fits the exponential function according to that observation to a mean of around 100 time steps. The average of around 100 time steps roughly translates to receiving the best answer within some hours up to a few days in the reference data, depending on the size of the community. Note that we cannot actually measure the time when an answer is accepted because we do not have that information in our data. We can only measure the time it takes for the best answer to arrive.

5 Evaluation

In order to evaluate our model, we implemented it in the freely available multi-agent modelling framework NetLogo [10]. The version of our NetLogo model that we describe in this work is available online[2]. For the evaluation, we observed the effects of the agent attributes and interaction rules on the shape of threads and the question solving behaviour. It is important to keep in mind that the plots in this section show the observed distributions from the data and the resulting output of the model. The internal parameters such as *expertise*, *activity* and *Q-A-ratio*, which cause the output, are not plotted.

To minimise bias and outliers, we averaged the results of ten runs of the simulation, and also of ten different communities from the SCN reference data that we described in Section 3. We compare the output of the model **f** with the reference data **y** by computing the average error δ as defined in Equation 8. It measures the average distance between each data point y_i and f_i, and normalises it over the maximum value of the reference data **y**. For each output, δ provides us with a direct feedback of how far off our model is from the reference data. A low average error indicates a good fit of the model.

$$\delta = \frac{1}{n} \sum_{i=1}^{n} \frac{|y_i - f_i|}{max(\mathbf{y})} \quad (8)$$

5.1 Validation of Agent Attributes

First, we look into the effects that are directly related to the agent attributes *expertise*, *activity* and *Q-A-ratio*, before we proceed to examine the interdependencies between the individual attributes. We set the model up to produce as many agents and posts as there are on average in the calibration data.

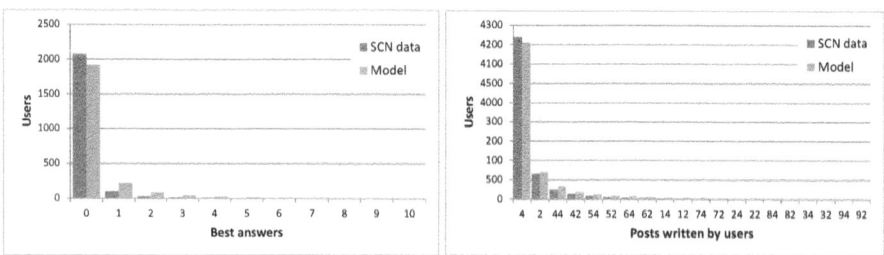

Fig. 2. Distribution of best answers per user as the result of the expertise attribute (left), and the total posts per user as the result of the activity attribute (right)

Expertise. In Section 4.1 we stated that *expertise* is exponentially distributed in online Q&A platforms. Figure 2 (left) shows the distribution over the SCN

---
[2] https://github.com/eaumayr/ABM-QA-community/tree/EC-Web2014

data and the distribution generated by our model. The majority of users fails to score a best answer, and only a very small number of users is able to solve more than two questions. The model simulates this exponential distribution of best answers per user well with $\delta = 0.010$.

Activity. Analogue to the expertise, we can show that the *activity* is exponentially distributed among the users. Our model simulates the distribution of posts per user very well, as we can see in Figure 2 (right). The average error δ for the number of posts per agent is 0.0064.

Q-A-Ratio. The *Q-A-ratio* determines how many posts an agent creates will be questions. Although the internal agent attribute Q-A-ratio is exponentially distributed according to Equations 2 and 3, it is remarkable that the observable distribution of the resulting question proportion per agent is so different. Especially noticeable are the peaks at 0, $\frac{1}{3}$, $\frac{1}{2}$, $\frac{2}{3}$ and 1, see Figure 3 (left). The reason for that is the interplay between the *Q-A-ratio* and the *activity*. Our model produces a very similar distribution with $\delta = 0.0503$.

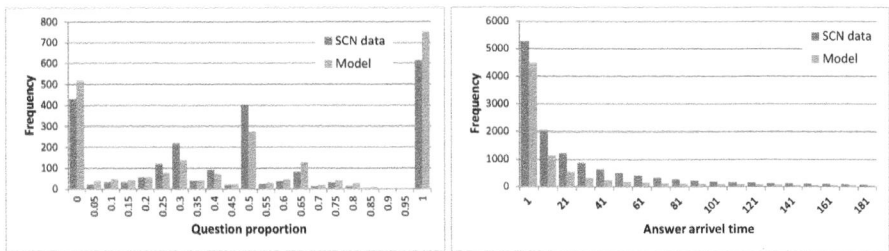

Fig. 3. Distribution of the proportion of written questions per user, which results from the agents' Q-A-ratio attribute (left). Number of discrete time steps it takes for a question to receive a reply (right).

Activity, Expertise and Q-A-Ratio Interdependency. In Figure 4, we plotted for every user (blue) and agent (red) the relation between the question proportion and post count, and the relation between best answer ratio and post count. The red plots are the results of the interdependencies between the agents' *activity*, *expertise* and *Q-A-ratio* attributes. The similarity to the trends that are exhibited in the SCN data plots proves that the model captures these interdependencies correctly. In both the real data and the simulation, the individuals post less questions the more active they are, and the most active users have a best answer rate of around 10%.

5.2 Validation of Agent Interaction Rules

We evaluate the question selection and solving rules in the following section.

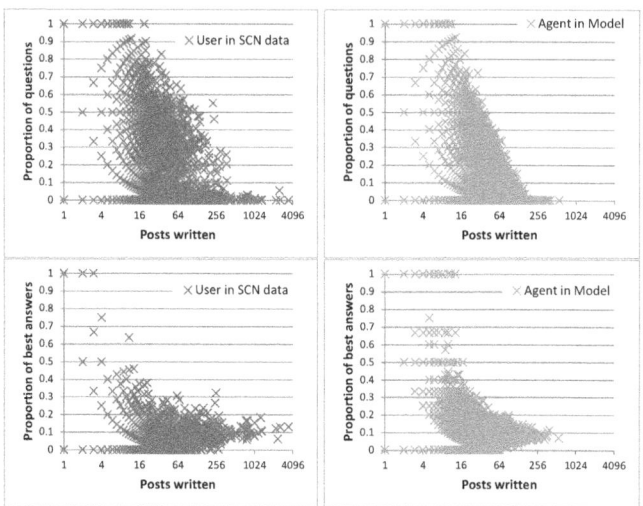

Fig. 4. Proportion of questions (top row) and best answers (bottom row). Every data point is a user (blue) or agent (red), with their post count along the x-axes.

Replying to a Question. Based on our observations from the SCN data, we defined the pool of eligible questions to reply to in Equations 5 and 6. The agent will pick an open question that is recent and has only very few answers, if any. Figure 3 (right) shows the number of posts it takes until a question receives a reply. Our model produces a very similar reply time behaviour, with $\delta = 0.0485$.

A common metric for online platforms is the average thread length or, alternatively for Q&A platforms, the number of answers per question. We can see in Figure 5 (left) that the model simulates the average number of answers per question accurately, with about half an answer less per question, and an average error of $\delta = 0.1378$. That is especially remarkable since the model does not contain any parameter that directly regulates the thread length.

Since the agents prefer to reply to questions with only few answers, short threads with two or three posts are predominant. We observe the same behaviour in the SCN community, as can be seen in Figure 5 (right). Our model simulates that behaviour with $\delta = 0.0871$. Although the number of short threads is lower in the SCN data, the number of questions that received no answer is well captured by the model. This is especially important for companies because they ultimately want to minimise the number of unanswered questions.

Solving a Question. Many Q&A platforms have the functionality of selecting one of the received answers as the best answer, which is often connected with a reward of some sort. We observed in the SCN data that only about 22% of the questions have a selected best answer. This low number of solved questions poses a twofold problem. Not only is a big part of the users not receiving their reward points, which might cause some frustration among the customers, but it also means that our measure of expertise is based on 22% of the data. That introduces

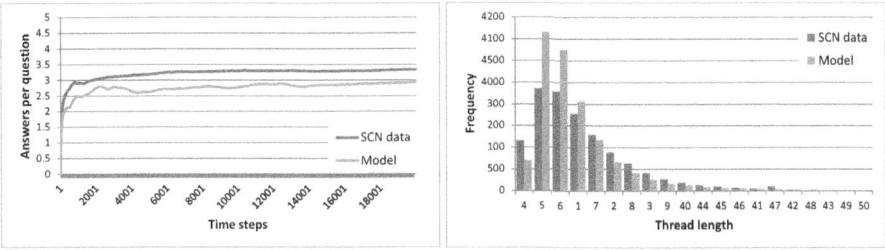

Fig. 5. Average number of answers per question over discrete time. One time step is equivalent to one created post (left). Distribution of thread lengths, where one-post threads are questions without replies (right).

bias because the actual number of solved questions per user is certainly higher. For example, instead of 10 to 15%, the most active users might actually solve between 20 and 50% of the questions they reply to. That would make them much more expert than the data suggests. Figure 6 (left) and an average error of $\delta = 0.0396$ prove that our model produces the same behaviour with 22% solved questions, and therefore also with the bias towards lower best-answer ratios.

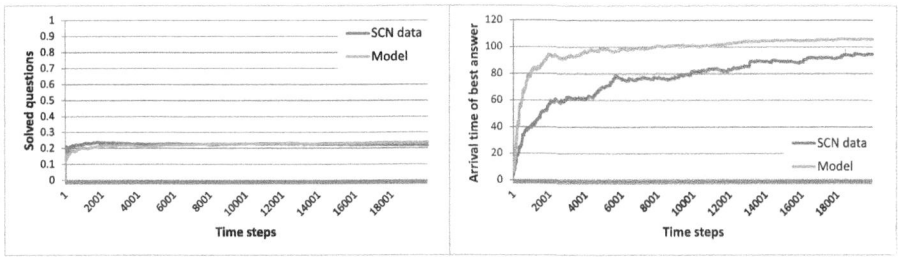

Fig. 6. Proportion of solved questions, i.e. questions that received an accepted best answer (left). Time until a question is solved by receiving a best answer. (right) In both plots, the x-axis shows the discrete time passed in terms of created posts.

In Figure 6 (right) we plot the discrete time until the average question receives a best answer. The best answer time increases slower in the SCN data than it does in our simulation, with an average error of 0.2272. However, the trend of the curve has been captured by the simulation, with a similar average solving time of around 100 time steps towards the end of the measured time period. A better fitting of the solving criterion in Equation 7 will reduce that difference.

6 Conclusions

In this work we present an agent-based model of an online Q&A community, and we show that the model accurately produces the interactions we observe from the reference data, the SAP Community Network. Although agent-based modelling is being used to study social interactions in many domains, it has not been used before for Q&A communities with their specific features such as the different classes of posts, i.e. questions and answers, and selecting best answers. Our decision for agent-based modelling was motivated by its power to explain the underlying dynamics from which the observed complex networks emerge.

The model provides us with a number of insights. First of all, we can show that the three agent attributes expertise, activity and Q-A-ratio, along with a set of simple rules, are sufficient to describe the question answering behaviour that we observe in the SAP Community Network. Furthermore, these internal attributes and rules exhibit exponential distributions that we fitted according to the reference data. A second finding is that some of the observed behaviours are not directly regulated by our model, yet still very accurately reproduced by it. An example for this is the average thread length. Finally, we note the good performance of the model although we only considered temporal factors rather than user generated content. This lets us assume that recency is far more important than content to capture question answering behaviour. In summary, we show that our model combines the two sides of explanatory power and predicting power by providing us with insights into the underlying user interactions, while also accurately matching Q&A behaviour of unseen data.

With this model, we created a basis on which we can study phenomena that we were not able to explain from examining the data, for example the effects of different types of users. In particular, our future work includes investigating what is the proportion of malicious users that a community can cope with until it fails to maintain a desired throughput of answered questions. Our ultimate goal is to develop an agent-based framework for providers of Q&A websites that enables the analysis of their platform in order to improve certain aspects, such as the ratio of solved questions, without having to perform risky trial-and-error experiments on the live community. Therefore, our next step will be to extend the current model and validate it on other Q&A platforms.

References

1. Arguello, J., Butler, B.S., Joyce, E., Kraut, R., Ling, K.S., Rosé, C., Wang, X.: Talk to me: foundations for successful individual-group interactions in online communities. In: Proceedings of the SIGCHI Conference on Human Factors in Computing Systems. pp. 959–968. ACM (2006)
2. Sung, J., Lee, J.G., Lee, U.: Booming up the long tails: Discovering potentially contributive users in community-based question answering services. In: Seventh International AAAI Conference on Weblogs and Social Media (2013)
3. Jnanamurthy, H., Singh, S.: Detection and filtering of collaborative malicious users in reputation system using quality repository approach. In: International Conference on Advances in Computing, Communications and Informatics (ICACCI), pp. 466–471. IEEE (2013)
4. Fahey, R., Vasconcelos, A.C., Ellis, D.: The impact of rewards within communities of practice: a study of the sap online global community. Knowledge Management Research & Practice 5(3), 186–198 (2007)
5. Axelrod, R.M.: The complexity of cooperation: Agent-based models of competition and collaboration. Princeton University Press (1997)

6. Bernstein, G., O'Brien, K.: Stochastic agent-based simulations of social networks. In: Proceedings of the 46th Annual Simulation Symposium, p. 5. Society for Computer Simulation International (2013)
7. Xu, J., Yilmaz, L., Zhang, J.: Agent simulation of collaborative knowledge processing in wikipedia. In: Proceedings of the 2008 Spring Simulation Multiconference, pp. 19–25. Society for Computer Simulation International (2008)
8. Gatti, M., Cavalin, P., Neto, S.B., Pinhanez, C., dos Santos, C., Gribel, D., Appel, A.P.: Large-scale multi-agent-based modeling and simulation of microblogging-based online social network. In: Alam, S.J., Van Dyke Parunak, H. (eds.) MABS 2013. LNCS (LNAI), vol. 8235, pp. 17–33. Springer, Heidelberg (2014)
9. Mungovan, D., Howley, E., Duggan, J.: The influence of random interactions and decision heuristics on norm evolution in social networks. Computational and Mathematical Organization Theory 17(2), 152–178 (2011)
10. Wilensky, U.: Netlogo (1999), http://ccl.northwestern.edu/netlogo/

Author Index

Algarvio, Hugo 153
Aumayr, Erik 179

Braunhofer, Matthias 77
Brewster, Christopher 46
Burke, Robin 101

Cantador, Iván 125
Castellanos, Angel 71
Chang, Chia-Hui 13
Chevalier, Edouard 64
Chuang, Hsiu-Min 13
Cigarrán, Juan 71
Cristea, Alexandra I. 171

Di Noia, Tommaso 89
Di Sciascio, Eugenio 89
Dudáš, Marek 34

Elahi, Mehdi 77, 113

Fernández-Tobías, Ignacio 125
Furtmueller, Elfi 165

García-Serrano, Ana 71
Gemmell, Jonathan 101
Godde, Adrian 1

Hagedorn, Bastian 1
Hayes, Conor 179

Jurain, François 64

Kao, Ting-Yao 13
Köpcke, Bastian 1

Korfiatis, Nikolaos 146
Krcmar, Helmut 26

Lopes, Fernando 153

Mertz, Matthias 146
Mirizzi, Roberto 89
Mobasher, Bamshad 101
Mynarz, Jindřich 34, 58

Ostuni, Vito Claudio 89

Peska, Ladislav 138
Pfaff, Matthias 26

Qaffas, Alaa A. 171

Rehberger, Martin 1
Ricci, Francesco 77, 113
Rubens, Neil 113

Servant, François-Paul 64
Solanki, Monika 46
Stahl, Florian 1
Svátek, Vojtěch 34

Tate, Mary 165

Vojtas, Peter 138
Vossen, Gottfried 1

Wollersheim, Jan 26

Zamazal, Ondřej 34
Zicari, Roberto V. 146

The manufacturer's authorised representative in the EU is Springer Nature Customer Service Centre GmbH, Europaplatz 3, 69115 Heidelberg, Germany. If you have any concerns regarding our products, please contact ProductSafety@springernature.com

Printed and bound by CPI Group (UK) Ltd, Croydon, CR0 4YY

23/03/2026

02076672-0016